PORTRAIT OF
AN ISLAND ON FIRE

Ariel Saramandi is a Mauritian writer. Her work has been published in *Granta*, *The White Review*, *LA Review of Books* and *Stinging Fly*, among other outlets.

'These overlapping essays form a coruscating portrait of a place and make for a searing indictment of our times. *Portrait of an Island on Fire* is written with a formidable intelligence and a precisely targeted rage, and comes from a place of passion and of deep love. Ariel Saramandi is a writer of Mauritius and for our whole twenty-first century world; these essays are cris de coeur, they are wake-up calls – they are essays everyone should read.'
— Lucy Caldwell, author of *These Days*

'Ariel Saramandi is a courageous and mesmerizing new voice, a chronicler of contemporary Mauritius whose writing refracts the influences of her Mauritian compatriots, Ananda Devi, Nathacha Appanah and Shenaz Patel in French, Lindsey Collen in English, in a voice which is wholly her own. *Portrait of an Island on Fire* unpicks the knots of Mauritius's entangled histories – of plantation slavery, of indentured labour, of colonization, of communalism and patriarchy – laying out the threads which make up her own history of ancestral oppression and structure her lived experience of privilege and pain; which form the fabric of contemporary capitalist Mauritius, and its particular intersections of race, class, gender and language – its politics – and its particular forms of the white supremacy, anti-Blackness and toxic masculinity acted out on the bodies of those without power the world over. Saramandi is laser-focused in her rage, joyful in both her refusal to look away, and in her insistence on what sustains her: writing, motherhood, her marriage, friendships, community – and the beauty of her island.'
— Natasha Soobramanien, co-author of *Diego Garcia*

'With an unflinching, searing clarity, Ariel Saramandi opens the festering wounds that have been sewn shut by silence in Mauritius since the time of colonialism and slavery. This legacy of racism sheds light on new forms of economic enslavement, the consequences of climate

warming, abortion rights, old and new misogyny, the utter irresponsibility of successive governments. This important book is both heartbreaking and a wake-up call.'
— Ananda Devi, author of *Eve Out of Her Ruins*

'*Portrait of an Island on Fire* is a fascinating look at Mauritius, a personal account of a homeland told with rage, rigour and love. Saramandi brilliantly, subtly teases out the threads of Mauritian history, politics and culture, honouring both the particularities of this unique place and showing the troubled connections – rapacious capitalism, racism, creeping authoritarianism, right-wing paranoia – that seem to stretch across the whole of our fragile planet. This is a beautifully written book of deep knowledge, righteous anger and fierce hope.'
— Lydia Kiesling, author of *Mobility*

Fitzcarraldo Editions

PORTRAIT OF
AN ISLAND ON FIRE

ARIEL SARAMANDI

CONTENTS

'I've got a cunt plastered over my mouth.'
— Virginie Despentes, *King Kong Theory*,
tr. Frank Wynne

MAURITIUS: A CHRONOLOGY

Around 10 million years ago: Mauritius was formed after a series of underwater volcanic eruptions. Volcanic activity continued until the near Holocene period. Mauritius is still considered an active volcanic region, even if the chances of an explosion in the near future are low.

The Late Middle Ages: Arab sailors crossed the Indian Ocean. They named Mauritius Dina Arobi, but didn't settle. Vasco da Gama, the Portuguese explorer, reportedly heard about Dina Arobi from a Gujarati pilot named Abdul Majid, who may also have shown da Gama how to travel to India. Portuguese colonists then devastated east Africa in the sixteenth century, but spared Mauritius from their activities.

1598–1710: The Dutch, interested in the Indian Ocean and the promises of the spice trade, crossed the perilous seas of the Cape of Good Hope and reached Vieux Grand Port on the south-east coast. The Dutch frequently used the island as a stopping point on their way to India, and settled in 1638. They called the island T'Eylandt Mauritius Van Nassau, after the Prince of Orange. Famously, in their time here, they killed off the dodo bird.

By the time they left in 1710, they'd massacred our ebony forests for trade; wiped out the lowland palm community; killed off the population of land tortoises and large birds; introduced rats and pigs to the island, which helped in the killing.

They enslaved people from around the Indian Ocean, mainly from Madagascar, Bengal, the Malabar coast and south-east Asia. Many enslaved Africans and Asians rebelled, despite facing almost certain torture and death.

The most famous rebellion involved Aaron of Ambon, Anna of Bengal, Ésperance of Bengal, Antoni of Malabar and Paul of Ceylon, who burned Fort Frederik Hendrik in 1695. The maroons who survived the island's colonization lived on in the mountains and valleys of the island well after the Dutch had left.

1715–1810: The French believed Mauritius was of strategic importance to their imperial ambitions. They called the island Isle de France and attempted to settle in the only way these Europeans knew how: through extraction of resources and chattel slavery. And slavery was cherished by the whites; it was upheld even after the French Revolution, in defiance of the First Republic.

There were a number of famous governors, but the enslaved men and women who built the country's infrastructure mostly go unnamed. They were taken mainly from Madagascar, but also from the south, west and east coasts of Africa, and some from India. Despite public torture and the decapitated heads affixed to poles, many enslaved people rebelled, marooned. Some of the most famous were Diamamouve and Madame Françoise. The latter was the leader of a maroon guerilla organization.

1810–1835: The British 'conquered' the island in 1810 and called it Mauritius. Though some French colonists left the island around this time, a good number of them stayed. They kept their language, their customs, their slavery. There was little improvement in the condition of enslaved people. Upon the abolition of slavery in 1835, colonists were paid a significant amount of money by the state as 'compensation', but the 66,000 or so enslaved people weren't granted anything, and had to work as meagrely paid apprentices in estates that they'd laboured in

16

all their lives. In the years following abolition they were pushed out of the plantations en masse, denied fair wages, their assets and land stolen from them.

At around the same period, the Colonial Office decided to expand sugar production and replace enslaved labour. There'd been a small population of South Indians in Mauritius from the time of Isle de France, people who'd come to work here as artisans and traders, but the Office required people in their hundreds of thousands. This is how the first indentured labourers from India arrived in Mauritius. The first great migration of Chinese immigrants to Mauritius came a while later.

1835–1968: About half a million Indian indentured labourers were brought to the island from 1835 to 1870. Sugar mills and their columns towered across all districts. Health and sanitation facilities were poor, and the island faced many epidemics. Slowly, despite crushing racial and class inequality, Mauritians of African, then of Indian descent began carving out a space for themselves in politics, trade unions and in media. That carving was often met with violence. Take Anjalay Coopen, thirty-two years old and pregnant, who was part of the 1943 workers' strike at the Belle Vue Harel sugar estate to demand better wages. After a few days of growing hostility, the owners of the estate asked police officers to intervene. The officers shot some of the labourers. Anjalay was killed, along with Marday Panapen, Kistnasamy Mooneesamy and Moonsamy Moonien, who was fourteen years old.

1968: Ebullience and bloodshed ripped through the island: there was talk of independence, and while this was negotiated, a months-long 'Bagarre Raciale' devastated the country, the capital in particular. The racial riots were arguably the most traumatic event of the twentieth century in Mauritius. They engendered a thorough cultural and ethnic remapping of the island, as Creoles left the capital en masse for towns in the Plaines Wilhems, abandoning their homes and entire livelihoods. A significant amount of those who fled would also leave Mauritius for Australia.

Still, on 12 March 1968, we gained our independence. In 1992 we became a Republic, with an Exclusive Economic Zone of 2.3 million km^2. Our islands comprise Mauritius, Rodrigues, Agaléga and St Brandon. The Chagossian Archipelago, before Independence, was under Mauritius' jurisdiction.

1968–1999: In 1967, the Independence Party – a coalition made up of Labour, the Independent Forward Bloc and Comité d'Action Musulman – won the majority of seats in the election. Once in power, though, the coalition effectively established an authoritarian state until 1976. The island was marked by multiple states of emergency and press censorship. By the late seventies there was hope for better days: economically, and despite international pessimism, Mauritius blossomed. The quality of life grew better with every decade; more and more Mauritians were able to study abroad and return to improve their island. A Marxist-socialist party was born in 1969, ushering in a new wave of trade unionism and activism. Anti-Black racism and discrimination were still rife, however, and the island took a markedly centre-right turn by the 1980s.

21 February 1999: Joseph Réginald Topize, known by his stage name, Kaya, died in police custody after being arrested for smoking marijuana during one of his

concerts. An autopsy report from Réunion stated that Kaya had been beaten to death.

Kaya was the island's most beloved artist, a pioneer of seggae music, and a campaigner for Black rights. After his murder there were protests across the country, and those protests were met with extreme violence. Berger Agathe, a singer of Rodriguan origin, was gunned down in public the day after Kaya's death. Sixty-two lead balls were extracted from Agathe's body during his autopsy.

1999–2014: Marxist-socialist hopes for the country waned in the 1980s; the nineties saw the rise and concretization of neoliberal monetary policies, of Offshore, the emergence of 'schemes' that allowed foreigners to buy luxury properties in Mauritius. The political climate changed, but never fundamentally: an almost comfortable sense of dynasty prevailed. Since Independence, Prime Ministership was conferred from Sir Seewoosagur Ramgoolam to Anerood Jugnauth; from Jugnauth to Ramgoolam's son, Navin; from Navin back to Aneerood Jugnauth and Paul Berenger; from Navin Ramgoolam back to Anerood Jugnauth; from Anerood Jugnauth to his son, Pravind.

By 2019, Pravind Jugnauth's broad vision for the economy was marked by infrastructure projects, an explosive vision for real estate through the 'smart cities' programme, incredibly strong ties with India – to the detriment of other nations – and a rise in Hindu nationalism. Despite growing concerns about corruption, Mauritians chose to give Jugnauth and the MSM a second mandate in 2019.

March 2020: The government imposed a nationwide lockdown during the first few months of the pandemic.

Small businesses shuttered, while conglomerates operating in tourism received considerable assistance. This time also saw a staggering increase in police brutality, particularly towards Creole men.

July–August 2020: The MV *Wakashio* wrecked off the reefs of Pointe d'Esny, and its oil spilled all around the south-east coast. The crisis could have been avoided, but no one in government resigned in its wake. Instead, the party in power attempted to stifle citizen-led clean-up operations and protests. A nationwide sense of outrage emboldened the population. Out of this anger emerged the figure of Bruneau Laurette, an activist turned politician, determined to radically change the island.

October–December 2020: A series of strange deaths made Mauritians fearful. The most talked-about murder was that of Soopramanien Kistnen, nicknamed Kaya, who was found tortured and burned to death in a sugarcane field. Kistnen was close to the party in power. The spectre of his murder would loom over the MSM's entire second mandate.

2020–2024: International concern, but also consensus, that the Mauritian government was rapidly autocratizing grew. A number of deeply troubling bills were passed in parliament, restricting freedom of speech and the powers of the Director of Public Prosecutions. The Speaker turned the House of Parliament into a grotesque carnival, ejecting and insulting members of the opposition. The political landscape beyond the MSM was fraught with conflict and unstable. The government promised ever greater increases in pensions and allowances, to quell rising discontent over the cost-of-living crisis. The

Mauritian rupee plunged.

We all knew that the 2024 general election woud be a watershed moment in our country's history.

¶ *I am back in the place I started.*

I'd seen my future as a straight line to progress, to getting out of here. A line that turned out to be a loop. I thought I had climbed the rungs of a driven and purposeful life. The best grades, one of the best universities, the best chance at a better life – though what that life would consist of I didn't know quite yet, only that I'd sacrificed so much to be on track for a semblance of personal and professional fulfilment. Ideally I would be studying and reading and perhaps even writing books in a place where I would be paid to do so, like a university. I wanted access to a decently stocked library. A city where I could walk around at night, alone. My dreams were banal, grandiose, formidably naïve.

I wonder if there are teenagers today who still believe in the pure attainability of their ambitions. Perhaps not in this world, this climate. I'd written step-by-step action plans in my diaries. I thought that I'd get somewhere by just following the plan, no matter the cost, the physical burnout. Those diaries are in the Mare Chicose landfill now, probably burnt given the repeated trash fires we've had over the years.

Still, sometimes dreams work out. Almost all of my close friends have left the country. I see them thrive, the joy and the pleasure they take in speaking freely across Europe and America, emboldened and safe in the mostly academic spaces they inhabit.

I left for university in England in 2012; I returned to Mauritius in 2016 with a BA and an MA in English Literature, unsure of what to do next. I started writing and publishing essays a year later. My work has not brought me any popularity. If this book is ever sold in shops back home, it'll ripen existing furore.

'How can you write this?' I am asked over and over again. 'Are you not ashamed?'

'You already know about this anyway,' is what I say now. They didn't have to read my essays to know about my life.

Mauritius is small, compact. Two degrees of separation between each of the island's 1,262,523 people. No one is allowed any privacy. Take the events in my essay 'An Education': my orthodontist knew all the details before I'd even written them down. Take a major row I had with my parents in 2021, an estrangement that lasted nine months: family acquaintances – who'd never spoken to me before besides saying hello – would ring me, asking me to 'stop with this', to 'listen', even 'obey'. '*Alors, toujours en bisbille avec la famille?*' asked a client of mine when I came over to appraise her house. She had, naturally, been informed of all the details. 'It's a terrible shame to see a family break apart like this,' said my husband's boss over coffee. He'd been informed of the situation by his secretary.

I had conformed to island-wide expectations: I was married with two children, I was mostly a stay-at-home mother trying to work odd jobs. But I didn't respect society's demands. I got angry in public: in schools, on the street, at dinner parties. I couldn't shut up. I opened my mouth wider and wider.

Housewife as wolf.

ALL MY LANGUAGES

I used to think that it could have gone either way. If choosing a language to write and think in was primarily a matter of exposure – so that, in the end, we picked the tongue in which we were comfortable, the language with which we were surrounded – then I would have chosen French. Or, at the very least, I would also have written in French.

I was born in 1992, brought up in English, French and Kreol. I spoke English with my English father; French and English with my mother; French with my aunt, who took care of me and my sister while my mother worked; French, Kreol and a smattering of Bhojpuri with the women and men who cared for me alongside my aunt; French and Kreol outside of our home.

All the leading newspapers and media outlets are in French, a postcolonial particularity. It stems from the British administration's decision not to impose English on the island's (mostly Francophone) residents when they colonized the country in 1810. As a child, I'd read the papers after watching cartoons early in the morning on national TV: *Babar*, *Petit Potam*, *Cat's Eye* and *Sailor Moon* were all either in French or French-dubbed. When I was around seven, our island was introduced to satellite television; to my knowledge no provider offered a mix of both English and French channels. My father made sure we alternated between English and French satellites every year, to balance out our tongues.

I spoke English at my international primary school. Later, when I joined a Catholic secondary school run by the Diocese, our textbook education was in English, but everyone spoke French. It was there that I learned the intricate ways in which language is linked to ethnicity in Mauritius.

The school was in the same town as the private French lycées, whose fees most of my classmates' families wouldn't have been able to afford. It was considered a better institution than the other public schools in the area. Within the school there was a separate building dedicated to prevocational education. The students attending these classes were often darker-skinned with unstraightened hair. They spoke Kreol outside of the classroom.

This was untenable to many of the schoolgirls I knew who would only speak French: Kreol was used sparingly, in jest, never spoken earnestly. These girls spent hours polishing their accents by watching French satellite television; lusted over the white boys of the lycée and the light-skinned boys at the school next door; straightened their hair, wore green contact lenses. When I was 15 I won a place at a prestigious state school, and the languages around me changed again: French was rarely heard, English, Kreol and Bhojpuri were dominant. Like the Catholic school, many of the girls were middle and lower-middle class; unlike my previous school, my classmates were now mostly Indo-Mauritian. The obsession with whiteness didn't change: some of the girls would buy bleaching creams advertised by Bollywood stars.

But I would hesitate to delineate a precise order of things. In Mauritius there's a tendency among people to equate light skin and wealth with languages of former European empires; darker skin and lower incomes with Kreol. People often assume I can't speak Kreol, for instance. When I do speak Kreol, people tend to react in three main ways: some will converse with me without commenting on my accent; some will giggle at my accent and try to place it (the main theory is that my time in England has forever altered my tongue – '*li anglez li!*'); some will look at me in a kind of awe, as if I were a woman of lofty heights seeking to be 'of the people'. It is the last reaction that hurts. There was a marked fourth way, too, more apparent when I was at secondary school: other children would ask me if I knew any Kreol swear words, as if, through the swears, through a performance of some crude idea of Kreol authenticity, I would show that I too belonged to this country.

And besides and beyond Kreol, locals across cultures generally assume that Indo-Mauritians prefer to speak English, whereas Creoles and Franco-Mauritians choose French. These linguistic schemata are blasted apart every day. None of them hold. A wealthy Indo-Mauritian child attending one of the lycées would probably speak French at home. And Kreol is spoken by over 90 per cent of us, across all spectrums of wealth and ethnicity.

I say 90 per cent, but the statistics are somewhat misleadingly presented. The 2022 census by Statistics Mauritius, for instance, seems to assume that Mauritians choose to speak in one language at home. '90% of people [are] reported to speak *only* Creole at home'; '5.1% speak Bhojpuri *only*'; '4.4% speak French *only*' (my italics). *Only, or*, instead of *and*.

A conversation with my friend Marek Ahnee, a researcher at the Ecole des hautes études en sciences sociales (EHESS) in Paris, complicates this assumption

29

of linguistic correlative order and single-language dominance. Both of us – and our families and friends in our Creole milieu – speak in a mix of French-English-Kreol every day without thinking about it. I've just said '*allume l'aircon s'il te plait mo pe mor*', for instance.

I've seen our parents and our friends questioned for their supposed 'allegiance' to French, when they speak and write in English and Kreol just as perfectly. Marek tells me that when Creoles speak French, it's often interpreted as French colonial mimicry. English, incongruously, is sometimes seen as a somewhat 'liberated' language. This whole line of thinking is another example of how colonial empires exist in relation to other colonial empires, and are experienced by social groups in different ways, ways which aren't necessarily grounded in historical fact. English is perhaps felt to be 'freer' since, as is oft repeated, 'the English abolished slavery' – but it should be mandatory to follow the phrase up with 'upon abolition in 1835 and until 1839, enslaved people were made to work as "apprentices" for seven and a half hours every day, without pay, "remunerated" in rations and land for cultivation, *for the same people that had enslaved them.* And, after 1839, the British government decided they would be properly free, but wouldn't give them any financial compensation.' Marek adds that French, which has been used (and is still used, in certain settings) as a tool of colonial power, is also a refuge for many Mauritian Creoles and marginalized Indo-Mauritian communities; it even serves as an instrument of social mobility for these people.

·

30

These supposedly neat equations between skin tone and language will hopefully go rancid in my lifetime. But the tough, complex systems of caste and white supremacy will take the efforts of a nation to dismantle. And besides race, there is money. A mother tongue, the product of an intersection of race and history and class. If it weren't for my father – his excellent position, his English nationality that I inherited, my private primary school, the English bookshops to which I travelled, the English books I amassed – I would probably be writing in French. Perhaps I wouldn't be a writer at all.

Mauritius in the mid-1990s: you could count the number of bookstores on one hand. They sold an excessive number of self-help books, as well as copies of classics in strange fonts, reprinted by local publishers with or without permission. The municipal libraries were (and still are) pathetically stocked. The British Council's library existed back then – it closed in 2016; English officials didn't think there'd be much interest in keeping it open – but I don't remember my parents taking me there. The Institut Français de Maurice's gorgeous mediatheque only opened in 2010. I don't know where their first library was, and definitely wasn't taken there. As for Kreol, the only book I had in Kreol was a poetry pamphlet. There were no Kreol books for children back then.

I had books in French: picture books of Disney movies, the *Martine* series, *Hector le Castor* and friends. These French books, bought in Mauritius, couldn't rival the number of books I had in English from abroad. There was a catalogue that my primary school sent out once or twice a year: I'd circle the ones I wanted most to read, the school would order them, and they'd arrive a few months later. My father also travelled several times a year, and there was often a book or magazine packed inside his suitcase for me when he returned. Once a year we'd all go to England. My parents would leave me alone in one of the bookshops in Canterbury and I'd emerge with ten to fifteen books. I depended on those bookshops well into my teenage years, when it seemed that people all over the world were able to buy books online except for me: Mauritius didn't exist in the 'choose your country' drop-down menu at most checkouts.

.

I was cushioned in English children's literature, and then PG classics like *Little Women*.

When I'd finished rereading my books, I'd search for others around the house. My father mostly read tomes on the World Wars and biographies of athletes. My mother, however, had a proper, literary, adult collection of novels.

I was 9 when I stumbled on the first volume of Henri Troyat's *Les Eygletière*. The volumes were furrowed under piles of *Cosmopolitan* and Anaïs Nin, stored away in a broken cream drawer in a spare bedroom. They weren't especially well hidden. As I started reading the novel – I didn't know there were two more books in the trilogy, and in any case, I never sought them out – I felt, acutely and for the first time, very young and stupid and scared. The Eygletière family live in Paris in the 1960s. Philippe, the patriarch, has married his second, much younger wife, Carole, whom he cheats on. Carole, in turn, begins to have an affair with Philippe's son Jean-Marc. Daniel, the youngest son, sets upon discovering himself in 'pure'

Africa (of course!).

I don't remember finishing the book, but I do remember putting it back in the exact place I found it and never telling my mother. I was cautious around her other books in French – and French literature in general – after that. I didn't want to relive the moral horror *Les Eygletière* had brought up for me. Given that I didn't have access to that many French books anyway, it wasn't difficult to read exclusively in English.

As I grew up, I turned to French literature again, but always with a certain apprehension. I prepared myself to be disquieted, thrilled. Some of the greatest reading experiences of my life have been in French: *Madame Bovary*, *L'Étranger*, *Vipère au Poing*, *Bonjour Tristesse*, Proust, Zola, Ernaux, Énard, NDiaye, Colette, Blanchot, Bachelard, Balzac, Levinas. Sometimes I wonder whether I hold the language as sacrosanct, the language of the sublime – my sublime – that I won't tamper with, won't attempt.

That may change. I think and dream in French. Over the past few years in Mauritius, it has become rare for me to talk in English for more than a few sentences at a time. My son is bilingual but chooses to speak mostly in French. Sometimes he will surprise me by repeating to me a sentence I've just said in the other language. Bookshops now are filled with French offerings, and though he knows and loves the classics – the animals of Eric Carle, Margaret Wise Brown's rabbits – it is the adventures of Timoté that he picks up again and again. He has books in Kreol, too, like the translations of *Tintin* by Shenaz Patel. He is more immersed in Kreol than I was at his age, borrows from all three languages to express himself. He sings and dances

33

to sega blasting from our phones, he says 'korek' when I ask him how he's feeling, uses 'manger' as both a noun and verb (after the Kreol word 'manze', food), and like most of us apologizes by saying 'sori' (Kreol for 'sorry'). He delights us with an abundance of gorgeous phrases such as 'j'ai flushé la toilette'. A fourth and fifth language may be budding, too: he sings along to old Hindi and Mauritian Bhojpuri songs in my mother-in-law's car; she explains the lyrics to him. My husband passes on fragments of his inherited Hindi: *ek, do, teen, chaar, paanch. Mera dil.* Perhaps, like me, he will hold a palm to his father's face and say 'ayo beta' when my husband does something a little silly. For now, he showers his dad with high praise: 't'es serieux papa' when my husband managed to get some apple juice in a village corner shop for him, *serieux* not in the French sense of 'serious' but in the Kreol use of *serye*, 'super'.

I wonder if he'll end up choosing one language over another. I hope he won't feel like he has to.

2021

AN EDUCATION

This is how it starts.

My brother's school asks me to be a guest teacher for their Day of Mauritian Literature. His lycée is part of the French system: private, proud, with only three or four such schools across the island. They are the institutions of choice for wealthy Mauritian parents and Francophone expatriates, seeking the best education the country has to offer. These students only learn about Mauritius through our country's literature; they are taught little to no Mauritian history. I feel part of an admirable, necessary initiative.

I won't be teaching my brother's class, but I will be teaching students of his age; they are nineteen years old, nine years younger than I am, and almost all of them are taller than me by a head. I see the students going into the classroom. A group greet each other near the class next door. They do not say hello, good morning, how are you. Instead they say 'Hey, my n–, my n–, my n–.' I can't tell whether the word ends in an –a or in an –er. In any case, it's an abomination in their mouths.

I can tell by their accents that they are white Mauritian, descendants of French colonizers, of which there are fewer than 10,000 living on an island of 1.2 million people. Mauritians can't refer to them as 'white people' to their faces, it is taken as an insult. We must call them 'Franco-Mauritians', 'Francos' for short.

'My n–! How are you my n–!' My hands shake. I walk in and forget what it is that I've prepared to say. I open my bag and fiddle with the books on the table, start with Nathacha Appanah's 2003 novel *Blue Bay Palace*. I talk about the protagonist, Maya: low-caste, she lives in the slums of Blue Bay and not in the luxe beachfront houses of Pointe d'Esny, where some of these students live and where there is very little talk of racial and class privilege. I hear some of the students cackle.

I hear 'Hey, my n–' over and over again in the class next door, everyone does. Their teacher must be very late. The teacher in my classroom is unconcerned; she shuffles some papers in front of her, marks them. My fingers can't find the extracts I want to read. I tell the students how Maya is used by her lover, Dave, a Brahmin who knows he'll never marry her but sleeps with her anyway. She finds out that Dave is married when she reads the newspaper: there's an announcement of his wedding to another rich Indo-Mauritian heir, an august union of two Indo-Mauritian sugar barons. Maya lies comatose in her bed for a few days before rising, monstrous, to seek her vengeance. She murders Dave's wife then plunges into the sea, lets her body be carried by the waves.

There's some nervous chuckling at 'Indo-Mauritian sugar baron'. The students think the term's an oxymoron. In my experience, Mauritians tend to believe that cane fields, mountains, the private sector mostly belong to the whites. It is often stated that 80 per cent of our economic production is tied to companies built on colonial sugar wealth; an approximate percentage, since essential documents that would allow historians to trace the history of white sugar capital are either private, lost or destroyed. I wonder if the students assume Indo-Mauritians are only to be found in politics and the civil service, not sugar, not the conglomerates that emerged from sugar.

I wonder just how much they know about Mauritian history. My brother, for one, isn't able to trace even the faintest outlines of its exoskeleton. The ancestors of most of these white students came from France, settled here, built the country on the muscle and blood of their slaves, then on the backs of indentured labour. They are known for what they stood against: the abolition of slavery in the eighteenth and nineteenth centuries, universal suffrage in the twentieth century and our independence in 1968. For my brother, this white history is the only one that matters. For him, the only person of interest in my mother's family is her Franco-Mauritian great-grandfather. Once, when he was about eight, before he learned such things were never said, he approached a white boy in his class with my mother's maiden name and said they must be cousins. The violence in my family home began a year or so later.

The chuckling does it. I stop what I'm doing and tell them I heard some of them using the n-word. They don't understand what I mean, so I must pronounce it for them. I tell them I've never used the word. I am light skinned with slightly wavy hair. I walk with privilege. The word does not belong to me. It belongs – if she so wishes to use it – to my mother, who is Creole and identifies as Black. It belongs to my grandfather, my grandmother, my aunts, my uncles, my cousins. It does not belong to the students in front of me.

I have only returned to Mauritius a little over a year ago, after four years away. The confident, pleasurable racism on full display is abrasive to me – only to me, it seems. Perhaps if I'd never left, perhaps if I'd returned years ago,

I'd have just rolled my eyes in distaste and continued with the talk I'd intended to give.

They scrunch their eyebrows, parsing out the terms I've used with the ones they know. In Mauritius one is 'Catholic' (Creole, Black), or 'Hindu' (Indian), or 'Muslim' (Indian). 'Chinese' and 'white' stand alone. This diction is new to them, alien in a country that melds ethnicity to religion, and these children see a Creole woman with Indian features, a product of our particular history, our own one-drop strictures, dissecting herself for their sake. An education.

I tell them n– is the ultimate insult. No, it is not the same as saying 'nasyon', it absolutely does not convey the same feeling of 'mo Nwar'. N– is an insult, in French or English. Their teacher, who is seated at the back of the class, asks casually for the name of the students who spoke the n– word. It is a banal matter for her. She doesn't seem particularly interested in what I've had to say, so far; she only asks the question for my benefit.

.

There is no secret to the way a dark-skinned child is born with a white surname. A white man has a non-white child and makes them legitimate, shows up to the birth registration office. Until the early 1920s at least, when such a birth happened in white families, they'd cut the offender out of the family tree. Some white families even legally modified their last names, adding extensions to better separate themselves from their black relatives. But my distant white cousins have kept the same name, though the family tree is cut jarringly in places. I'm not sure how my mother ended up with a copy of it, only know that neither my great-grandfather's Creole wife nor his Creole children exist in the sepulchral diagram, a black and white tree reaching from one page to the other like an outstretched hand. My great-grandfather's name, Gerard, is a neatly amputated phalanx.

When I am twelve, my sister and I go to a Catholic school once run by Irish nuns where our white father's unusual surname precedes us. In the first few weeks we're scrutinised, kept at a distance. We are asked why we aren't enrolled in the lycée.

The girls at school think it is incredible that my mother is not white. When they want to tease me, they call me milat, mulatto. They watch the boys in the school next door, assert feverous crushes for those with light skin, light eyes. They wear coloured contacts – green, because blue would be 'too much' – and bleach their skin. They watch the boys who go to the lycée on motorbikes with awe and giggle excitedly from a respectful distance. To speak to a white boy is not done.

We sunbathe on the concrete playground during recess, but not for too long. The girls don't want to darken their skin. The dream, they tell me, is a white boy. A white surname. There is nothing better.

My mother instructs me early on: 'Whatever you do, don't fall in love with a white boy here. His family will never accept you.'

I don't understand. My father is white. My sister appears white. She has green eyes and when she was young she had blonde hair. My father's body is unlike any that I've ever seen. His nipples are pink. Constellations in brown and red cover his whole body. I could trace his veins with a Pentel, so easy are they to follow.

I don't understand what my mother is trying to tell me, so I probe. She says: 'Never marry a Mauritian.' She says, 'White foreigners are different.' I can't parse the variances between white-foreign and white-Mauritian. They all look the same to me.

·

In the lycée I pay attention to the way the class is arranged. There are very few students of colour, they sit next to each other or they sit alone. After my explanation that the n-word is the ultimate insult, a discussion begins and the students have many opinions. A white boy in the front row says: 'It's fine to say n– as long as it's said well, right, like playfully?' Another girl says: 'It's just the way we say hello. No one told us it was wrong.' In silence I wonder if I am the first to do so.

At home, my brother calls my mother n–, kafre before he hits her. He didn't learn those words at home.

A girl intervenes. She is stunning, with straight hair and copper skin, and sits with Franco-Mauritians at the back of the class. I've seen her face on my brother's phone. He speaks of her with a certain reverence, the kind of reverence he only uses when reciting his Franco-Mauritian friends' names and surnames. Her name is Chloe. She's a cool girl.

Chloe says she's French but has lived here for a long time. She stumbles with her delivery; quickly, softly, she says her parents have African ancestry. Her eyes dart around the room. She says with more confidence that she has Creole friends and white friends, that she was taught never to use *ce mot* in her house. She's trying to take a stand and I appreciate it. A Franco boy speaks. He says, 'But n– is like saying "white", no?' I don't know how to respond. I pour a glass of water. The bottle shakes, my glass shakes, water spills onto my jumpsuit. I apologize and continue.

•

It is in Prisunic, the 'white' supermarket, that I learn how racism dictates our body language.

There, when the whites see each other, they instantly form a congregation. We walk around them. We do not say that they are in our way. We move aside when they walk in our direction. We are moved aside, through habit, in shops when a white customer walks through the door.

It is in church that I begin to learn how racism defines the places we occupy. The man we see nailed to a cross is supposed to be a symbol of absolute freedom; it is remarkable, then, that until my mother's time non-whites couldn't even choose their own pews.

The whites still favour the pews closest to the altar, even though the rule that banned people of colour from occupying those pews was abolished in the 1970s. All I know is that my grandmother once tried to secure a seat there. Mass was packed, it must have been Christmas or

Easter. Bodies congealing, squashed into benches, bodies standing at the back and to the sides, sticky in the summer heat. My grandmother was heavily pregnant. She made her way to the front, where there was still some space. The whites barred her entry, ordered her to stand or leave.

My mother tells me how we imbibe the strictures of racism until we cannot see the world in another way.

In the late 1980s, my mother and father start dating. They spend weekends together in the best hotels. Saturday afternoon, and my mother has laid out towels on the sand at a private beach, rubbed sun cream on her body. My father has left her to fetch cocktails from the bar. A Brown security guard approaches my mother, asks if she is Mauritian. She says yes. He tells her to leave. 'Why should I?' she says. 'It's reserved for guests of the hotel. I am a guest here.' He shakes his head in disbelief. 'There's a public beach just down there.' He sees persuasion will not work, starts to threaten her.

In late 2018, my mother decides to stock up on cushions. She visits a shop owned by a white interior decorator. The salesgirl is Creole. She tells my mother that she probably won't be able to find what she is looking for here, the prices are quite high.

My mother is well-educated. She left school at fifteen after her O-levels, top of her class. Her family couldn't afford to pay for her A-levels and, like most Mauritian women, she had to start working quickly to contribute to the household. Back then, one of the best jobs in the private sector for middle-class Creole men and women was at the local bank. She was superlatively qualified, but didn't get the job as a teller. They employed a white girl in her year with meagre grades. 'She's more presentable to our clients,' was the bank's reasoning.

When I used to work for a communications agency, I'd often visit the offices of the island's major sugar-estate-turned-conglomerates. The head management are mostly Franco-Mauritian. Demographics suggest that Human Resources must have gone out of its way to skew proportional ethnic representation in each of the companies. Take one of the biggest conglomerates, for instance. It has fifteen directors sitting on its board: eleven are Franco-Mauritian. One director is Creole, and two are non-Mauritian. Take the conglomerate's executive team, comprising fifty-two people: twenty-seven are Franco-Mauritian, fourteen are Indo-Mauritian, six are Creole, one is Sino-Mauritian, and four are not Mauritian.

The stories I heard then, hear now: Franco-Mauritian employees paid three times more than their non-white colleagues for the same job; quasi-meaningless jobs created just for whites to justify their higher salaries; white sons and daughters casually taking over senior leadership positions in their mid-twenties, because the company 'belongs' to their fathers and uncles and cousins, anyway.

.

In the lycée, I pick up Nathacha Appanah's 2007 novel *The Last Brother*. I explain that it's the story of a young boy, Raj, who lives in a hut in Mapou. After torrential rain sweeps away his home and kills his two brothers, his family moves across the country to live in Beau Bassin. His father finds a job at the local prison, where 1,600 or so Jewish immigrants were kept in appalling conditions from 1940 to 1945. Raj's father is an alcoholic. One night, he beats his wife and son to such a degree that Raj has to be treated in the prison hospital. There, Raj meets David, a sickly Jewish boy of about his age. The two become inseparable.

I tell the class that Appanah made sure that the novel wouldn't just be about abuse and violence; it would also examine the systemic oppression that generates such violence.

Some of the Franco children take out their phones and place them on their desks. They cradle their faces in their arms. They hide from me. They do not want to hear. There are two Franco girls who have not taken out their phones. They look at me and their eyes are glossy and wide, like they're afraid I am going to hurt them. One of the girls looks like she could be the daughter of one of the richest men of the island, she has his face. I had attended a guest lecture he gave at a local university a decade ago. He scanned the room, joked that he hoped no Jews were present. He said that, to him, Hitler was a model of leadership. No one in the class had disagreed or complained afterwards. I wonder what she hears at home.

.

A Franco-Mauritian who treats Mauritians of colour with respect is not called 'white'. Or they are 'white, but'.

I talk to my mother about her close Franco-Mauritian friend Anne, who leads her prayer group. One day, in private, Anne says: 'I want to apologize for all the hurt my ancestors did to you, and what the community still does today. I am so sorry.' It is the first and remains the only time my mother has heard this from the mouth of a white person. It is a miracle.

My mother says Anne is not white. 'I mean her skin is white, but she's not – she's Creole, she's –'.

A Franco-Mauritian who wants to make his allyship apparent will usually hark at his less-than-white origins, not knowing what else to do.

'You see my skin?' a white man fumbles. 'We are not white, exactly. We are more tanned. We have dark hair.' He marvels at the brown spots on his arms, the tan lines about his shoulders. He is just as pink as my father.

Not all of them are so maladroit. Some Franco-Mauritians who have emigrated, or who plan to emigrate, identify the mechanics of white supremacy and seek to remove themselves from the system as much as they can. 'We moved when my children started school at the lycée. All the racist tropes that I knew twenty, thirty years ago – I saw my children repeating the same words, insults. I was disgusted.' I tell them of what happened during the lycée's Day of Mauritian Literature and they are not surprised. 'It's gotten worse there, apparently. Remarkable that it could get any worse, in fact.' It was, after all, a school founded for the Franco-Mauritian elite in the 1950s; a place to get away from the British administration's plans to anglicize education; a private institution exempt from the gradual diversification of the student body in other prestigious schools across the country.

I look at Chloe, then at the Creole boy who sits alone on the opposite side of the room. I introduce my next subject as gently as I can. I tell them of one particular moment in Appanah's novel that embodies Jean-François Lyotard's concept of the sublime, a moment of such force and violence it overwhelms the mind, refuses cognition. It's when Raj and David meet a Creole man working in a colonial mansion, the governor's house.

'How did he,' I ask, 'a Creole mixed-race man in 1940s Mauritius, come to such a prominent position?'

'Maybe he worked hard,' one white student says.

I explain that this man could possibly be the illegitimate son of the governor: this would explain his position, his dress, his colour. I tell him that, though this governor is English, the practice of white men fathering children of colour – 'enfants naturels', they were (and are) called, 'bastard-born' – was common in Mauritius.

I tell them how much of Creole blood is the result of sexual violence: that this is probably not a happy story of a governor falling in love with his maid. How, 200 years ago, people of African and sometimes of Indian descent were considered property, bien meuble, to be used however white owners saw fit. That such violence is a legacy that we carry in our bodies.

A boy raises his hand to speak. He tells me he disagrees with this idea of violence as legacy. 'She was raped,' shoots Chloe in his direction. The boy struggles to find a rebuttal. He is worked up now, and I am unbearable to him.

I turn to Ananda Devi and her 2016 state-of-the-nation novel *Eve Out of Her Ruins*. I speak of poverty, abuse. I tell them how lucky they are to have such a wonderful school and pristine education, because most Mauritians don't have that luxury. The boy interrupts. He says he completely disagrees with me. He is French and has lived here for a while, believes I am too pessimistic in my outlook. He says racism exists, but if everyone works hard they'll get to the place they deserve in life. I understand immediately; I ask him if he is white. He tells me his mother is white but his father is darker than I am. 'Maybe you should talk to your father tonight, ask him about the racism he faced in France.' The boy is adamant that his father has suffered from no racism at all. I talk of microaggressions. He says his father is checked by the police in France 'as often as everyone else'. That he is a brilliant man, an entrepreneur. I say I have no doubt about that. He says I propound an ideology of the victim. I'd have recommended *Light in August* if he were older, but even then Faulkner would slip through his fingers. He has bleached himself into oblivion.

·

In the early 2000s I look in the mirror and cry. My hair is thick, voluminous in the humidity of our tropics. It weaves itself into knots at the back of my head, snaps brushes. Conditioner is of little use, only oil will do. I tie my hair using six, seven, eight elastic bands, not because they keep my hair in place but because the tight pain grounds me somehow. My nose is aquiline, too bold for me. My teeth are crooked and the girls at school say I have a man's jaw. My thighs are thicker than my mother's. In no way do I resemble the girls on glossy magazine covers,

Keira Knightley, Mischa Barton.

Mauritians are enamoured by my sister. They clasp her face in one hand and pronounce her the next Miss Mauritius. She is uncomfortable with the attention. She tells me how she has to fight to be taken seriously in the new school she's in, a half-white anomaly. We're suspended in a place of belonging and unbelonging.

I am eighteen, about to leave the island to study literature at Durham. The coolest friend I have tells me men will come after me in England, and they do. The spray-tanned models I grew up seeing on advertisements in Boots have established an ideal of beauty that I somewhat fit, with their temporary melanin, straight-ish hair. My own is now manageable with oil and the country's dry air. I appear, incredibly, as a dark-skinned white girl. The English are quick to reassure me that I look Spanish or Italian.

I am treated differently to my aunts, who immigrated to Europe in the 1980s to work as nurses. They are stunning, with their coiled hair, their features we call 'African' for lack of a country of origin. My aunts rarely speak of the initial years following emigration. 'I have a blank across many years, don't remember anything', one of them tells me mock-cheerfully. I know enough not to ask any more questions.

My cool friend warns me to be careful of white men in Mauritius, too. 'They won't speak of their desire in public. They marry white women. But alone in the elevator with you, they'll turn their heads to smell your neck, they'll say your skin has such a beautiful scent.'

'None of the mistresses are white,' my mother laughs, as if this is somehow a source of power. She is proud of her beauty. My father, after seeing her once at a party, knocked on every door in the neighbourhood – every door, it must have taken him the whole afternoon – until he found her, hair thick with oil, mango flesh in her hand. A vision.

.

The bell rings and the teacher has many thoughts about my lecture. She makes sure to point out that she has a PhD from France. 'I disagree with Appanah and Devi,' she says. 'They believe the cycle of violence has no end. Look at today, for instance, what happened with the n–situation. Isn't it a sign of progress that these kids use that word without a care for the past, that they don't care?' I ask her if she is Creole. She says no, she is Tamil. 'Worse than a Creole', she jokes, but stops chuckling when she looks at me. 'If there was a word that embodied the torture and enslavement of your Tamil ancestors, would you be okay with these kids using it?' She doesn't reply. In the staff room ten minutes later, she hands me coffee and says she knows the white children didn't react well to what I was saying, 'but you must understand, they have a lot of weight to bear.'

All communities are the same here. The consensus is that, as an educated person of good standing, you must not see race. It is the only acceptable position to take. Racism is a general practice. Time and time again I hear 'but look at the Chinese, the Hindus, the Muslims. They all have their own racist systems and methods. It's not just the whites.' Constant racial gaslighting.

She leaves for her next class, leaves me alone with the school's Franco-Mauritian history teacher. I tell her about today. I ask her if she noticed the segregation in the classrooms, in the playground. She says yes, very little has changed here. The maintenance staff have come out for cigarettes. I ask them and they agree, too. The history teacher tells me that there's everything to correct in the education system.

I don't attend any of the other sessions at the lycée on the Day of Mauritian Literature. I go home and make tea. My hands are still shaking and I can't find the teapot, the strainer. I've been invited to meet the French ambassador's wife at a cocktail party at midday. All the other artists and intellectuals of note who have participated in the Day of Mauritian Literature will be there. I tell myself I have to go.

They are all there, gathered in a room. I wait until everyone is inside and close the door. I place myself in the centre of the room, break protocol, speak before the headmaster, the ambassador's wife.

'I am honoured to be here,' I say, 'but I've spent two hours at the lycée listening to the most incredibly racist things. We're here to celebrate Mauritian literature after all, but what's the use if, minutes upon my arrival, I hear students greet each other by saying n–? I hate that I even have to pronounce it.'

The intellectuals and artists have formed a circle around me. They are of all ethnicities. They don't react. Some look amused, can't believe I am making a scene. I tell them of the teacher's reaction, how profoundly disturbing it was. My voice is louder now, keeping calm is impossible.

I tell them that my grandfather was called n– all his life, the son of a rich white landowner and his maid, forced to bear his own grandfather's name due to his father's whimsy. My mother too was – is – called n–. There is still no reaction. I tell them my brother suffers from racial discrimination in this very school. Silence. Later, a friend who was at the gathering tells me he overhead the person next to him saying, 'I can't believe we're hearing such violent opinions. I didn't come here for this.'

The headmaster thanks me for my thoughts. He says, 'Do you think, then, that we don't do enough?' I say no. Another teacher smirks and looks disdainful. He is tall, with a grapefruit-hued shirt that accentuates his pallor. 'I cannot believe what you are saying. I am French. I've taught here for five years; I've never seen or heard what you are describing.' I tell him what the history teacher and other members of staff have told me. The segregation in the playground. He shakes his head. I tell him and the headmaster that if I walked in the corridor and heard n–, said not in hushed tones but loudly, full of confidence, so clearly and with teachers present, then such greetings must be common. He shakes his head. I don't tell him – I am too embarrassed to tell him – that I had believed, until today, that this word was only ever muttered in secret.

The headmaster tries to regain control of the situation. Tells the audience that he, a white man, also knows what it is to suffer from discrimination. He comes from the Franco-Swiss border and for the longest time he wasn't considered properly French. He says language is a very important thing. He has taught in Houston and in Brazil. He says, 'If I tell a Black man he is stupid, then that's like telling him he's a n–.' He says n–. My friend, my only friend in this room guffaws, says he can't be serious. I tell the headmaster that this is scandalous.

·

That night I go to the clinic. The doctor who takes my blood pressure sees that I am in shock, tells me he went to the same school ten years ago and he's glad someone's finally called them out. He doesn't charge me.

The next day a shrill woman demands to speak to me on the phone. She is part of the administrative staff at the lycée. I hang up. In a series of ebullient messages she describes how she was made incredibly distraught by my behaviour. She believed me to be an elegant woman. She says I've disgraced myself.

You broke protocol, my mother mouths, rocking back and forth on the bed. The ambassador's wife. Oh my God. She thinks that I have brought white wrath upon my family, that now I will be castigated wherever I go.

Your brother, your brother, she repeats. If he finds out he'll explode. Couldn't you think of your brother before opening your mouth?

My parents are called into the school. The headmaster wants to know if what I said about my brother is true. 'He calls me negre' my mother says. 'And I forbid you to talk to him about it. It'll just make things worse.'

The headmaster is flustered, seeks reason in my father. 'You see, though I sympathize with the anger of your eldest, it seems to me that her actions constitute reverse racism.' My father nods. He wants to get it over with. My brother has his final exams this year.

'And the teachers and I agree, the word they use, n–, they learn it from American rappers.'

The headmaster never speaks of my outburst to my brother. The school's only too happy to keep the tirade a secret.

.

My brother hates himself. He is the darkest of all my mother's children, with wavy hair that curls in the water, flared nostrils.

It starts with the print of his knuckles, neatly indented on our fridge. Door handles are broken.

Clots of blue appear on my father's wrists, but it is my mother he cannot stand. The sight of her is too much for him. Pansies bloom on her arms and neck.

My brother is accepted into the circle of Franco-Mauritians by virtue of our white father and his wealth. He speaks with the Franco accent, uses withering, degrading terms for all ethnic groups, including his own. He spends his weekends at his white friends' houses as much as possible. His violence is always worse on Sunday evenings, when he comes back home. One Saturday, his friend whisks him around the lagoon in a speedboat. His friend steers the boat though he's underage, doesn't have a licence. He knows the national coastguard won't arrest him. He approaches Isle aux Cerfs, then doubles back. 'We can't go there,' his friend says. 'There are animals there,' pointing to all the non-white Mauritians who've come to enjoy the islet's famous beaches for the day. My brother comes home and recounts the incident with pride. Later, before bed, he turns to my mother and says 'You're ugly. You're fat. You're Black. *Tu me fais honte.*'

My mother goes to the clinic a few times. The doctors who treat her are sometimes white, they've known her for decades. 'It's the school,' they tell her, without her having to say a word. 'You won't believe the number of mothers who come here, like you. White and Black and Brown.'

One night, when I think he'll send my parents to the clinic, or worse, I call the police. They arrive at my family's house. The police chief doesn't understand how money hasn't made our problems go away. He is disgusted.

I get calls in the middle of the night from my father, asking if I can come home, impose an authority I don't have on my brother. For years, I try. 'You are not white,' I tell him.
'I am white. I am white. I am white.' He hurts himself. Smashes his head against the wall, rolls around screaming. Another trigger is when I speak Kreol. He screams until I stop.

I am the only one in my family who sees a psychologist. My mother will only talk to God. My psychologist says my family needs intensive, collective treatment. This doesn't happen. My brother agrees to see her alone. 'He is a very, very difficult case,' she tells me. 'He'll need a lot of work.' He only sees her three times. I tell her my parents dismissed the warning signs – violence, tantrums – as bad behaviour he'd eventually grow out of. 'He is a child,' she says, 'in excruciating pain.'

She attended the lycée two decades ago, one of the few students of colour. Her child is now a student there. 'Like today, the school was very segregated, students of colour to one side, white students grouped all together. I went to our high-school reunion a few years ago, and you'd have thought nothing had changed at all. We were in the same groups as before.'

.

My brother's ex-girlfriend's mother thinks that the region we live in should be for whites only. She doesn't greet her non-white colleagues at work.

The ex-girlfriend came to our house a few times. She seemed to genuinely like him. We liked her too, wondered if this was a sign of progress, or if the relationship was her one great act of defiance to her family, her form of teenage rebellion. 'It's not like she would ever have married him' was my mother's take on the matter.

I thought it was ludicrous to talk about marriage in high school, but I am told that white relationships are taken very seriously in the lycée. Franco-Mauritians tend to inter-marry, and courting begins early.

My sister dates a Franco-Mauritian man for a few

years, but it doesn't work out. She spends considerable time getting to know his friends and family, attending white-only weddings, white-only dinners. After they break up none of her Franco friends speak to her ever again. 'You won't be able to find a man to marry now' her ex-best friend sneers in a text message.

.

White supremacist documentaries on South Africa are making the rounds on Facebook. 'White genocide', Mauritians write, with teary, angry emoticons.

A white man I know quite literally rubs his hands in glee when he hears that white Mauritians in South Africa are returning to the island. There was a tradition of Franco-Mauritians emigrating, by choice, to South Africa in the late 1960s after Independence. Fears of the 'Hindu Peril' were written in the white-owned newspapers; fears that, even as a dominant minority, an elite, the Franco-Mauritians would be subsumed.

'They went and they were treated like kings,' he says. 'Now look at them. They've lost everything.'

No one speaks of apartheid.

We do not speak of racism in the press. We do not speak of it online. And we do not speak of it in public, ever.

And I am only just learning how to speak. A local woman in a bar clutched my face one night. We'd barely exchanged a word, but her husband was enthused with one of my friends, telling him all about his white expatriate lifestyle. The woman was Mauritian, of mixed Indian descent, proud to be his wife. 'You are Indian too, aren't you?' she said, holding my face, thumbs pressing down on my cheeks. 'You can't be Creole. Creoles, they have such vulgar traits. Ugly.' I felt slapped in the lungs.

'Let it go,' says my mother. 'Just let it go. You won't change anything. You can't change anything.'

•

After the Day of Mauritian Literature, I spend the next couple of months talking to twenty or so ex-students of the different lycées around the island.

'Once, a fight broke out between a student of colour and a Franco. The white girl ended it by saying "your ancestors were the slaves of my ancestors."'

'A boy told me he was shocked that I could speak French because, according to him, I looked like I could only speak Kreol. We were both in the same lycée. He justified himself by saying that I was Black. I am Indo-Mauritian. I thought it was all so stupid.'

'There were these virtual "white-only" areas in the playground.'

There are still other students of colour who have systematized the racist behaviour they have witnessed, won't even call it racism: 'It's normal that they only sit together. They're pretty much all related to each other.'

I try to contact a few teachers; some are interested, but all are too afraid to talk to me. From what the students say, racial discrimination's rife in the administration, too.

Franco-Mauritians are also terrified of speaking to me, but some do, under the promise that I never reveal their names and only write their stories down, not record them.

'They said n–? Out in the open? When I was at school, they'd say it in private, in the changing rooms, when it was only us. They'd say, "*sa pue le negre ici.*" It stinks of n– here.'

I learn of segregation in their own community. 'At the top you have the Big Whites, the sons and daughters of some of the people who own and manage the biggest private companies in the island, or those in equally wealthy positions. Our parents work for them.' The Big Whites have been Big since the sugar industry centralized its operations in 1867. 'The Big Whites set the rules. You can't cut your hair differently from them, for instance. They invent all these rules to exclude you. Swear words you can or can't say. Lots of rules like that. Things only got better once the expatriates started to arrive, when I was fifteen or so – the control the Big Whites had over the rest of us lessened, then.'

I remember an anecdote my brother told me, proudly, about the son of one of the 'Big Whites' at a nightclub. Some kid of colour accidentally spilled his drink on his shirt. The white boy's friends, including my brother, gang up and beat the coloured boy for having 'dared' to touch 'the son of –'.

A white, lower-middle-class girl explains that routinely, white people will demand that she recite her family tree, her many cousins and cousins removed, her many possible links to the community. 'This happened at school, and then at work. White isn't just skin colour,' she tells me. 'It's what you do on the weekends. It's hunting, fishing, social clubs you belong to. It's a postcode. A lifestyle.'

I've only been asked to conjure my family tree once. In the clinic after the events at the lycée, a Franco-Mauritian woman next to me asks me my name and surname, her eyebrows furrow at the ambiguity. She asks me if I have a maiden name. She is not satisfied. She proceeds to tell me of her family name, her maiden name, her children's names, where they are employed, who they are married to, where they live. It is imperative that she tells me all of this. She doesn't stop until she reaches the end of the line, her grandchildren.

.

Weeks after my outburst at the school, the local literati talk about me on social media. They don't mention me by name. The administration has carefully orchestrated a Facebook campaign to promote the Day of Mauritian Literature at their school. Different authors, poets, persons of local importance talk about how happy they were to contribute to the enrichment of our culture. On their private profiles, they discuss my 'performance'; that my 'act' should be considered as 'theatre'. I won't – and don't seek to – change their minds, wired to white supremacy. But I must write this down.

2018–19

AN EDUCATION: ÉCRIRE EN C(H)OEUR

'An Education' went viral.

It was the first time in recent memory that someone had written about Franco-Mauritian racism so extensively – and in the first person. But I was just one of many Mauritian writers who'd questioned white, patriarchal systems of power, analysing the ways such systems of power are exerted. In literature I think of Marie-Thérèse Humbert's *A l'autre bout de moi* and Alexandre Dumas's *Georges*; in history, the work of Vijaya Teelock, whose *Bitter Sugar* – an extraordinary book on slavery and sugar production in nineteenth-century Mauritius – proved so untenable to the Franco-Mauritian elite that bookshops were coerced into removing the tome from their shelves upon its publication in 1998; accounts by writers such as Abhimanyu Unnuth and Deepchand Beeharry on racism faced by indentured labourers; the work of journalists and writers over two centuries, from Evenor Hitié to Rémy Ollier and Père Filip Fanchette. In particular, Hitié's *Histoire de Maurice*, published in 1897, was a no-holds-barred account of Mauritian history and inter-ethnic relationships, and a scathing account of Franco-Mauritian racism. There were two volumes of his history, and copies of the second cannot be found: Franco-Mauritians, incensed, gathered all the copies they could and burned them.

This tradition of writing continues in other forms: Mauritians on YouTube and TikTok and other social media platforms, creating anti-racist content, writing, sounding back, with audiences surpassing those of an essay.

I interviewed quite a number of people for 'An Education' and several stories were cut. The original piece was about 9,000 words. The editors of that piece, which was published in *Granta,* felt that the testimonies included were sufficient, and they were right. I did feel, however, that I'd been entrusted with people's experiences, and those experiences should be housed in what I'd written, because they were so valuable. It had been difficult for most if not all of the interviewees to talk to me, and they'd agreed only under the guarantee that I'd never publish their names. Collecting the testimonies was liberating for my interviewees; those who I met in person seemed somewhat purged after giving me their accounts, their body language and expressions growing more animated as they engaged in a subject that was and is still taboo.

There were many stories of children of colour not being invited to birthday parties, under the pretext of the host's mother 'not knowing' them. Friendships culled the minute children entered the *grand lycée.* Non-white children (and their parents) treated differently, worse, than their white peers in class by their teachers. Non-white children routinely beaten almost every day at school, the administration fully aware of their ordeal but refusing to act, afraid of these white children's usually wealthy parents.

Another story that was cut: a Franco-Mauritian couple brought their six-year-old son to a psychologist, claiming that he had difficulty making friends. After spending time alone with the boy, the psychologist learned that the son did, indeed, have a friend – a best friend, even, an Indo-Mauritian boy who sat next to him and played with him at recess. The psychologist asked the boy why he didn't invite his friend over to play. '*Maman a dit, pas de marrons à la maison.*' The mother had made a rhyme so it'd stick.

And another: a teacher-therapist of colour who tutored a Franco-Mauritian boy in his house twice a week, an arrangement that went on for several months. One weekend, this teacher decided to go to the beach with her family in Pointe d'Esny. They set up their picnic baskets and blanket. A white man emerged from a bungalow nearby. He screamed at them to get off 'his' land, that they had no right to be there, the usual vitriol. It was the father of the student she'd been tutoring for over half the year. He didn't recognize her, or pretended not to. Just kept on screaming.

•

My pseudonym had given me some protection from online harassment abroad, but in this speck of a country no one had to work hard to learn my real name. The consensus was that I was either mentally ill or cruel beyond reckoning, to have humiliated my well-known family in this way. To have endangered my husband's position at work and my then-six-month-old son's chance at societal success.

The invitations that used to trickle in every few months disappeared – art exhibitions, book launches, literary festivals. I've been told that I was a scandalous figure, 'too angry', *hautement bizarre*, a disruptor of peace and good social conduct. Still, I was glad to find whole swathes of the population hadn't read my essay, didn't know about me at all. I'd have created more of a stir had I written in

French, and if the piece had been published in a local paper (which it never would have been, naturally).

After the piece was published, I received many a coruscating glance from notable Mauritian artists and intellectuals. My friends who'd shared the piece were also treated with disdain. I felt that some of the artists resented me because they too wanted to write about the racism they'd faced, but they'd so ingratiated themselves over the years to the Franco-Mauritian cultural elite that they were afraid of ostracism, of compromising their cocktail party invitations and French embassy soirées. Some of them depended on this elite for income and jobs. Others believed that staunchly defending the Franco-Mauritians was the best way to gain their favour and even friendship. Some, so ensconced in local structures of power, still maintained that I had stormed over nothing; that I'd imported the American revulsion for the n–word, even though the French equivalent in Mauritius was just as repulsive (and known by the students, who toyed with the n–word in English, taking such pleasure in getting away with saying n– in public).

Sometimes I try to understand what comes to their mind when they think about slavery. In their imaginations perhaps slavery resembles something like Millet's 1857 painting *The Gleaners*, with Black labourers replacing the peasants. I've seen online posts by some of the younger generation of Creole artists and would-be thinkers equating neoliberalism to slavery. Surely they know – they must know, they must have been told – that slavery was torture, torture in all its possible forms? That a fifty-five-hour workweek is just not comparable to physical torture, systemic rape and grotesque abuse, the dismantling of families, the physical and intellectual plundering of lands, intellects and cultures, physical and mental labour erased and replaced with a white name on a plaque? Did they listen when their mothers and grandmothers told them the stories? Did they eavesdrop on conversations not meant for children? I have been told, in confidence, in abrupt statements, of white historians who burned evidence of Franco-Mauritian torture experiments and other 'compromising' material. And even despite these historians' efforts to curate historical knowledge there is still an abundance of material on enslavement and resistance. Which is why it's so dispiriting to see non-whites agree when a white pseudo-historian attempts to 'contextualize' chattel slavery by performing a rollcall of slaveries throughout human history (Africans enslaved themselves! What about the serfs!), a disingenuous analogy made in bad faith, because there has been nothing like chattel slavery in human history, in kind or in magnitude.

Then there was the matter of my person – a light-skinned Creole woman who didn't necessarily 'look' Creole. If I looked more like my aunts, perhaps my essay would have been more acceptable, as in I'd have written a piece in a somehow more *authentic* voice. Perhaps there was the belief that I'd taken the place of an 'authentic' voice, as if spaces for anti-racist work were somehow limited. They wanted a token, and expected that poorer, darker-skinned Creoles should be doing anti-racist work and be rewarded for the attention. But I was honest about who I was and where I was coming from. And everyone in that room, at that non-alcoholic cocktail party, should have been enraged at what was so evident in every classroom, at recess, on the playground.

Still, the essay generated an effervescence of témoignages on the internet, mostly from young Mauritian students at university abroad and middle-aged Mauritians from the diaspora. Essays and blog posts were published, group conversations initiated, memes created. Stories of discrimination in white-owned bakeries and hotels, by staff (usually people of colour) and by the clientele (white, in places like Tamarin and Grand Bay). Stories of women of colour making sure to dress 'expensive' and ensuring that their children were well-behaved in these spaces, then giving up on respectability politics once they realized it wouldn't make a difference.

A constellation of stories. *This also happened to me.* And in that 'also', a new confidence, a new power. *This happened to us. You can't gaslight us anymore.*

I was uncomfortable when I learned that the essay was going to be published: the hurt of my family, the societal repercussions that would follow, the idea that I'd somehow mined trauma or taken part in the so-called 'trauma essay economy'. But I hadn't read anything that documented, named, interviewed, analysed the way racism operates on our island today, or in the last fifty years or so. And I didn't believe that an account like mine would be written. I tried to rationalize it in all the ways, convincing myself at one point of a utilitarian morality: I'd be hurting four people, but I'd be validating the experiences of thousands of others, and this essay would hopefully last longer than any of our lives, could be something people referred to later on. And this is what I hold on to, in the end: that the essay has done wake work, has catalysed other forms of wake work in its readers.

But let me be clear: my brother hasn't forgiven me.

I didn't ask for permission before writing this, and he wouldn't have given it. It doesn't matter that the violence I speak of happened when he was a child; it doesn't matter that this collection is written under a pseudonym. I will live with the hurt I have caused for the rest of my life. And it is excruciating.

2024

THE INHERITORS

It is a story told in every Creole home I know. It is often narrated during a long drive: a window rolls down and a hand gestures to stanzas upon stanzas of sugarcane, or bungalows on the coast, or valleys now privately owned. 'This used to be ours,' says a parent. 'They took it. We lost it.' There are several common narratives of the taking. The Creole child of a white man is forbidden from inheriting his property. An illiterate widow signs acres of land to corrupt notaries, who promise that her progeny will be taken care of. Families are chased out of their homes.

These are old stories, learned by rote and handed down like a relic, a warning: Look at all we had. Look: you could lose everything too.

With time and pain these stories often become nebulous – sometimes intentionally.

My mother's way of coping with her family history is near-absolute silence; she fears, perhaps, that poverty and stigma will return to plague her once it is spoken out loud. Details of her life are sparse and often excruciating. A lower middle-class upbringing. The shame of having bronze skin with a white surname. On my mother's side of the family, my great-grandfather was a wealthy white man who had many mistresses; one was a woman of African descent, his maid. They had several children together and eventually married. My great-grandmother loved her husband fastidiously. They brought up their children in the big house; my grandfather and his sisters carried the white name, though according to my mother it would have been a kindness if my great-grandfather had given them my great-grandmother's maiden name instead. My great-grandmother would hide in another part of the house when my great-grandfather's white friends drove up Montagne Longue to see him.

My mother took me to Montagne Longue only once, when I was around five years old. I remember that she was with her eldest brother, and that we were in the region to visit a friend. My uncle probably decided we should look at 'our' land again, though there was no former family home to visit, no graves. It was late afternoon, and we walked through golden, parched grass which reached up to my knees. The crest of the mountain surrounded us. My uncle pointed to the cascading hills below, covered in pineapple plantations. 'All of this was ours. Covered in pineapple like it was back in the day, but we also had vanilla and cane.'

These lavish tracts of land were now lost, but my mother wouldn't tell me exactly how. Over the years, and after putting many impertinent questions to family members, I've gathered fragments of a story of dispossession: an eccentric old man, with many eminent French friends, who was estranged from his kin and society once he'd decided that his Black son would carry his name; his land taken from him by his white family and business associates, while other parts of the land were lost to debt. There's a family tree that my uncle was able to recover: it was drawn by my great-grandfather's white family and their descendants. Some of the branches were drawn to look like fingers; at my great-grandfather's name there's an amputation, a cut to mark the place where whiteness ends.

The documents that would tell the story of our

inheritance are also lost, according to my mother. When my grandfather died my mother took care of the funeral and the household expenses; my grandmother thoroughly cleaned the house and disposed of old papers that she thought weren't of any value. My mother was too wrecked by grief to take much notice of what she was cleaning, but she suspects now that this is when the papers disappeared – parchments inscribed with plans and letters in her grandfather's hand that she remembers seeing as a child. The papers were sold or thrown away; possibly used as scrap paper to envelop gato pima sold by the road.

Until I heard of Danielle Tancrel's fight to reclaim her land I thought that the stories of Creole dispossession were mundane, irrevocable facts of life. I met her through Jean-Clément Cangy, a family friend whose work as a journalist, researcher and writer has produced invaluable material on Creole culture and history. Jean-Clément and Danielle wrote the book *Spoliation des terres et crime contre les droits fondamentaux* (Spoliation of land and crimes against fundamental human rights) in 2019, which provides an overview of cases of land dispossession as well as their historical context, tracing the changes in land ownership laws throughout the centuries.

Danielle is a very different woman to my mother. She has no interest in ossified memory.

She lives a few minutes away from the small village of St Julien, in the district of Flacq. Her house is surrounded by sugarcane fields. When I walk into her living room, I see her ancestry laid out in hundreds of papers classified into boxes. These documents sketch the initial story of her family.

'My grandfather and father worked for the sugar company. Their factory is just there,' Danielle says, pointing to thick smoke rising about three miles away. The company is one of the largest sugar producers in Mauritius.

My father was a mechanic. He was also a handyman for the white management, he organized their grand dinners in their bungalows. One day, while he was working, one of the white men asked his name. Upon learning it he was shocked and said, "The Tancrels have plenty of land right here!" My father then spoke to his boss. His boss said, "I can't help you. You have to seek help from higher up." When my father came home that night and told us what he'd heard, we had no idea what to do next. My brother went to the archives to find out if all this was true sometime in 2006. He found our family name on page 666 of the civil status records for 1795–1815. I told him it was the devil's number. Maybe that's why my family suffered so much. My grandfather was raised only by his mother. He never talked about his childhood. He was illiterate. My family was very poor. My mother would cook the vine leaves that grew in the garden for us to eat almost every day. I visited the archives too, and soon grew obsessed. I wanted to know the truth about my family. I spent all my weekends there, my holidays from work. I photocopied every document with the Tancrel name on it,

she says, handing me another pile of documents to look at. We go through them one by one, interpreting the thin cursive, deciphering eighteenth-century French. After an hour she brings out cookies and juice for me. She takes silent note of my penchant for the chocolate ones and serves me some more.

I marvel at the fact that she's been able to trace her family back through eight generations:

> It was really difficult. When I asked for my great-grandfather's birth certificate at the Civil Status Office they said they didn't have it. My childhood friend worked at the National Archives. She rang them up and pestered them. They eventually gave it to me. In another office, they tried to prevent me from accessing notarial documents. When they understood that I was just looking for my ancestors, they let me in. The staff told me that they'd caught lawyers and notaries ripping up papers here before.

Danielle was able to trace a deed granting eighty-six arpents (the equivalent of approximately one acre) to Antoine Tancrel, her direct ancestor, in 1783. She examined the map detailing the area: the land, covered in virgin forest and in cane, is claimed by the sugar company. She wasn't sure what she could do.

But then came the Truth and Justice Commission of Mauritius. Launched in 2009, it was the first truth commission in the world to independently investigate the legacy of slavery and indenture. In a six-volume report, it offered a revisionist account of the island's history, detailed the racism and economic oppression faced by descendants of slaves and proposed recommendations for reparations. The volumes are strewn with hundreds of stories of lost land; the second volume is entirely devoted to land reform and cases of dispossession. One tale in particular is legion: 'the sugar company stole it.'

The Kreol word for sugar company is tablisman. It is derived from the French *établissement agricole,* or agricultural establishment. French colonists were granted acres of land to grow variegated crops in the eighteenth century; after the British took over Mauritius in 1810 land was used almost exclusively to grow sugarcane, and sugar companies emerged in their hundreds. A typical establishment would consist of a colonial home; buildings used to house enslaved men and women, then later freedmen and indentured labourers; a sugar factory not too far away; a chapel, and then a Hindu temple, all surrounded by fields of cane. With time, these sugar companies consolidated and turned into conglomerates in the twentieth and twenty-first century. They now dominate the private sector.

Four hundred or so official claims were made to the Commission. Danielle was among the first to present her case. The Commission advised her to contact a land surveyor, who studied her dossier and drew up a report in July 2011. The surveyor's report described how the land isn't found in the company's title deeds, their sugar estate records or in their mortgage files. The surveyor stated that the land is covered in sugarcane and is occupied by the company 'in utter bad faith'. The Commission then summoned the company's Chief Executive Officer in September 2011. He couldn't produce any evidence supporting the company's claim to the land, except to say that it had been under 'continuous and uninterrupted occupation' by them since 1938. The Commission told Danielle that she should go to court with her case, as it was clear that she'd been dispossessed.

The first time I spoke to the CEO in 2011, he told me that he would not negotiate with my family, and he awaited the report of the Commission. Then he died a year after the

Commission gave its verdict. The following year, I thought I would try again. I gathered up my strength and rang one of the company directors. He answered in a harsh voice. I said, "Please don't intimidate me. It's taken all my courage to talk to you." I explained my case to him and sent the files. He said, "I'd like to know what the Court of Justice thinks of this." I then sent the company a formal legal notice asking them for my land back. They said the claim was "baseless and unjustified". They can pay the best lawyers and keep deferring the case until my money runs out. And I have no money to continue the legal fight.

In the days that follow our meeting I send Danielle several emails. The Truth and Justice Commission outlines her case in the report, and when I read through it, I find a possible error. Their verdict states that 'it seems to be a typical case of dispossession by sugar estates, of land belonging to a French colon, who had children with a woman slave.' The Commission suggests that the dispossession happened around 1850, but slavery was abolished in 1835. Their timeline of events doesn't make sense.

'My grandfather was illiterate. That's how our land was stolen,' Danielle says in an email to me. She sees her family's poverty and illiteracy as the cause, not the consequence, of the dispossession. It doesn't make much sense to me, that somewhere along the way her family became poor and then lost all the land they owned. The land would have kept them rich. If they'd had serious debts, they would have started selling their land in order to recover some financial stability. There wouldn't have been large parcels of land left – certainly not one of eighty-six arpents so close to the family estate.

I want to understand what happened. I ask too many questions. She tells me that she feels embarrassed, that I am being intrusive, that she can't go through the pain of the investigation again. She is exhausted. I apologize, feel stupid and clumsy. In my attempts to elucidate the mystery of her dispossession I've barged through her life. Her personal history is also a public case of great historical and legal importance; public, and still so raw, so sensitive. She graciously sends me more information, though, and examines my hypotheses on her stolen land even as she believes that we should be concentrating more on the case as it stands at present: no matter how her land was stolen, she has proof that it was indeed stolen, and that's all she needs in court.

I attempt to trace her ancestry myself and establish my own timeline. I visit the National Archives. On my way there, I drive past districts, towns and villages that have been almost entirely rebranded by sugar conglomerates, which are mostly white-owned and white-run. 'The government only manages 10 per cent of the country's land, and the private sector owns the rest. Ten families cultivating cane on about 100,000 arpents', writes Jean-Claude de l'Estrac in his 2020 book *Terres: Possession et dépossession*. Ten white families, and whites make up less than 1 per cent of the population.

These freshly rebranded areas are often part of 'smart city' schemes: I pass by Mon Trésor and Moka, with their new floral logos. Sugar is worth next to nothing now, and all that land has to be monetized differently. The most lucrative way seems to be real estate.

Some of these cities hope to draw upper-middle-class

Mauritians away from their dying locales and into new urban areas, which promise cutting-edge infrastructure and sustainable, nature-centric lifestyles. There are lots of shopping facilities, too: my drive to the archives takes me past Bagatelle Mall of Mauritius, the country's premier shopping mall built with a colonial aesthetic. The chimney of an old sugar mill stands in its centre, an on-the-nose metaphor for our island's history.

The National Archives building lies in the industrial zone of Coromandel, a town at the edge of the capital of Port Louis. The building is decrepit. Four years ago I went through 300-year-old documents kept in a cardboard box. The papers were speckled with dead moths. Cellophane had been used to stick pieces of paper together, and the adhesive had corroded them like acid. This time around my work is easier. Many people come here to trace their ancestry, and so the staff have laminated and photocopied essential, in-demand material. I can't access the notarial records, though: they are out of bounds, and I'd need an affidavit from a family member to consult them.

I wonder just how much more I'd be able to uncover if our archives hadn't been pillaged. In the 1820s, about a decade after the British took over the island, the chief archivist took seventeen suitcases filled with documents and registers to London and they've not been seen since. And this is just one instance of colonial looting; anecdotally, there are a great many stories of documents disappearing pre- and post-independence. It is extraordinary to contemplate the mass of historical documents found in England, France and also America, when they should be here. So the truth of Danielle's dispossession could be found on the island, in the inaccessible private archives owned by individuals or sugar estates. Or it could be found in archives abroad. Or it could have been destroyed.

I go through civil status and district registers, scrutinizing records bearing Antoine Tancrel's coarse, heavy signature. I use the family tree Danielle gave me and add more branches, defining each branch as best as I can. At home I go through numerous online genealogies and ancestry testing sites, cross-checking the data. I talk to historians, show them what I've collected, gather their opinions. White histories here are so detailed, their ascendancies so easily traceable, but at some point in the Tancrel line there comes a gap. A gap to mark the place where whiteness ends. A gap that explains how the descendants of one of the island's wealthiest white families grew up in poverty in Mauritius. In the end, I don't know if the timeline I establish for the family is a close historical approximation or fiction. I wonder if it is brash audacity to construct a narrative out of fragments.

.

A carpenter in Brittany hears that there's a fortune to be made in one of France's colonies. He is nineteen years old and unmarried, thinks there's everything to gain, joins packs of men from the region who are eager to leave their dismal country and their current prospects behind. After months prowling the African coast his ship docks in Mauritius in 1748. He looks at the indigo mountains, the flurry of foliage, the thriving town of Port Louis and its grandiose, Brittany-inspired colonial mansions, the port that bears the beloved emperor's name.

Antoine Tancrel is given 312 arpents of land by the French administration upon arrival, along with plenty of enslaved people, the lot of the average colonist. And he is happy with his lot, had never dreamed of owning so much land before, swathes of forest by a river, framed by rugged hills in the distance, a place named Camp de Masque in the district of Flacq. He won't even have to work the land himself. He thinks he can make a home here, ascend, establish a legacy. He sets out to make a name for himself, and it starts with the basics – learning to read and write, finding a wife. He secures property in the capital, involves himself in trade, ensconces himself in society. His days as a carpenter are over.

He gets married, eventually, to a Mauritian girl of French descent named Marguerite Talec. He's thirty-seven and she's fifteen. She becomes pregnant at sixteen; they name their firstborn Louis. They name their second son Benjamin, a name which traditionally denotes the youngest member of the family; perhaps they believe that after five years of trying he will be their last. Eight children follow over the course of three decades, ending with Baptiste, born to Marguerite at the age of forty-six. Their children marry into slaveholding families of good repute.

By 1827 Antoine is dead and Louis is married with twelve children. The Tancrel family own land the size of Central Park. Their estate is actively managed by Louis, Benjamin and Baptiste and some of their brothers-in-law. Sugar is the colony's new king, and the brothers have their slaves build two factories to produce it. But not everything prospers in the tropics; Louis buries his wife in 1830, then witnesses the deaths of many of his children in close succession.

Perhaps Louis envies the Michel family, who live in the same district. They would have seen each other at balls and at church. The Michels are white, prosperous and have copious children – children who survive. The names of the Michel progeniture are meticulously registered at the civil status office; such good record keeping is a sign of education, wealth, a secure social position. There are so many Michels around that Louis can barely keep track. But he knows, of course, about the scandalous, eccentric Michel: the man had children with an enslaved woman; he freed those children, gave them his surname! Unforgiveable. Bastard children with bastardized names, like Angel and Ortencia.

Still, Louis hopes that his surviving children will marry well; that his youngest son, especially, will consolidate the Tancrel reputation. But Jules has no interest in the old ways of living and loving. Almost all the marriages he has attended were made for money, connections, preserving whiteness – and decent matches aren't easy to find. He doesn't want to be like his sister Héloïse who married her distant cousin, a man thirty years older than her and a widower en plus. Jules doesn't want to marry any of his cousins. He was fifteen when slavery was abolished in Mauritius and feels like he could be the harbinger of a new generation. He's in his early twenties now and he's furiously in love with Ortencia Michel.

Louis can't fathom where they met: she wouldn't have been invited to any of the balls; she would have been at the very back of the church at mass. He is livid at their relationship, then desperate. Why won't he just keep her as a mistress, set her up in a lavishly furnished house in Port Louis, keep his love at an agreeable distance from the family estate? Why must he marry her? He tells Jules that as his son he has the weight of his ancestors and all their achievements on his shoulders. That the Tancrel line won't survive for much longer if Jules doesn't marry into another white family. That he will destroy his family, in fact.

Jules and Ortencia get married anyway, buoyed by the freedom of a new age, brave enough to withstand the estrangement that their marriage produces within Jules's family. His in-laws love him, thankfully. They live in Trou d'Eau Douce, a village by the sea. Jules grows close to Ortencia's brother, Angel; when Ortencia becomes pregnant, the couple decide to name their child after Angel if the baby's born a boy.

Louis doesn't live to see his only grandchild. He dies a few months before Angeli is born. Though his marriage may quite literally have killed his father, Jules hopes that the other Tancrels will come to accept him and his new family. His sister Josephine still loves him, for one.

In time, Jules and Josephine become the only remaining heirs of their father. They all move to Trou d'Eau Douce, well away from the hills and forests, away from the Tancrel family estate in Camp de Masque. They still hear rumours, though: it is whispered that the sons and grandsons of Benjamin and Baptiste are deeply unhappy with Jules. Rumours that Jules's extended family is finding the best way to punish him.

The white Tancrel rage is brewing. Their sugar estates are struggling. In the boom of the mid-1820s they thought they'd be rich forever; now, forty years later, they are on their knees, hit by fickle market prices and multiple financial crises. Crops are battered by cyclones, people die of malaria. The number of sugar estates is declining every year. Some of the whites, ever-growing in reputation and prosperity, seem to ride the flux of the economy and band together. They buy factories that can't keep up. The Unité and Mon Reve estates are sold. The white descendants of Louis Tancrel feel the need to regain control. The need to feel good.

Jules and Josephine head to Port Louis, obtain a legal attestation claiming that they are sole heirs of Louis Tancrel. They cling to this document and its copies, believe that this will protect them and what they own: their share of the land in Camp de Masque and around the district of Flacq, the properties in Louis's name in the capital.

But the law won't save them. In the night, Jules and Josephine hear horses and the laughter of men. The laughter sharpens as it clusters around their home, a wooden mansion in the Brittany style. The men take pleasure as they torch the place. They beat Angeli when he tries to fight them. In their joy they throw Josephine to the ground as she tries to reason with her cousins and uncles, and she dies from the blow. The Tancrel's Creole neighbours alert the police, but the Englishmen at the station say they won't interfere.

Jules, Ortencia and Angeli escape from the ruins of their home and move in with Ortencia's brother and his family. In time, as Angeli grows up, he falls in love with Angel's daughter Eugenie. He works as a blacksmith, like many free men of colour, but struggles to feed his family.

80

Angeli's son, Wilfrid, turns to the sea. He doesn't have to take his boat far out into the lagoon to catch fish, and he believes other fishermen when they say that the produce in this region is the best in the country, that maybe it's because of the blend of freshwater and saltwater. From these men he hears scraps of the goings on about town, hears the news of white men working for sugar estates and helming large businesses in the capital, recognizes some of the surnames as those of his cousins. He learns that the Tancrel's ancestral property in Camp de Masque is falling into ruin, but there are so many other homes elsewhere, closer to the capital, to society. In any case, there's no going back there, he thinks. He doesn't want any of it. He's tired of his father's stories, of French-style mansions and clothes imported from Europe, tired of the tales of how we lived and what we had. His father's all worn now, his body beaten like the metal he hammers, all he has is the comfort of memory. He barely even registers Wilfrid's presence at home, and so Wilfrid moves away.

Wilfrid doesn't tell his wife anything about the weight of the history that he bears. There's no time for such talk, anyway. Life is difficult. Wilfrid's health is failing him. When he dies she's left to take care of their only son, Benjamin. She doesn't know that Angeli is still alive, figures that even if he isn't dead he wouldn't be able to take care of his grandson, a child with eyes the colour of the lagoon.

Benjamin grows up. He hears that there are jobs at the sugar company in Flacq, thinks his prospects are better there than in Trou d'Eau Douce. He's little more than a child but his body is strong. He'll work at the factory for the rest of his life.

The biggest event in his career is the day that the Indo-Mauritian owners ordered him and the other factory workers to hold fast against 200 or so planters and labourers, who'd come armed with sticks. They'd set fire to plantations, they were rioting, irate at the price at which the factory bought their sugar. The management opened fire, killing four men.

Every day he walks across acres of sugarcane without knowing that they are his inheritance. The ruins of the Tancrel estate are there somewhere; bedrooms are now grown through with sugarcane. Part of the estate was never sold to the sprawling factory, but it grew its crops on the land anyway, in the way it usually happens: stems of cane shoot up on and around the neglected estate, encroach upon the land; the managers of the company know but do nothing about it. He walks, knowing nothing. His son would have died without that knowledge, too, if it hadn't been for a white manager who asked him for his name.

.

Around the time Danielle was born, the factory had over 21,300 arpents in their control. This is excluding land that they have no ownership over, but which they claim is theirs anyway. They reap the profits of the value of that land and the cane grown on it, too.

'One drop of black blood is enough,' Danielle tells me. I am at her house once again, going through her documents one last time. I nod as she speaks, looking at her hands, whiter than mine. Her eyes are the colour of river water. She shows me pictures of her family. 'Every sibling turned out different,' she says. I reply that the same variations are found in my family, too. Creoles are primarily descended from enslaved and free Africans and Malagasy people. Rosabelle Boswell wrote in *Le Malaise Créole: Ethnic Identity in Mauritius* (2006) that Creoles have experienced 'both fragmentation and hybridization, such that three hundred years later, Creoles are a people of mixed African, Indian, Chinese and European heritage.' We identify and are identified as Creole, and represent about 30 per cent of the Mauritian population.

I think about who we are and where we've come from. Upon the abolition of slavery in 1835, the 66,613 enslaved people on the island were made to work as apprentices. Nine thousand or so of them purchased their freedom by 1839, and many bought small plots of land: some had deeds of sale, some had verbal contracts. Most chose to settle as far away as possible from the estates in which they'd been tortured and held captive. Assiduous, unrelenting racism ensured that enslaved people and their descendants had to fight to remain self-sufficient, fight to be employed, fight to keep ownership of their land. Many ended up leaving the island for better lives elsewhere.

I think about the kinds of machinations involved to prevent Danielle from claiming her land. The confidence of the sugar companies, who know they can just pay lawyers to defer the case until Danielle's money runs out for good. The eighty-six arpents that she claims are worth millions, but I suspect this is still just a sliver of what she is owed.

After many false starts by the government over the last decade, parliament passed a bill late in August 2020 which would establish a Land Division of the Supreme Court. This Division promised to facilitate 'the just, expeditious and accessible resolution to land disputes', in their own words, but four years later nothing had been done. The Truth and Justice Commission's recommendations have hardly been implemented either.

'If I win I can lift my family out of poverty,' Danielle says. 'Sometimes I imagine how different the country would have looked if Creoles hadn't had their land stolen. If they'd been able to prosper in business. If they hadn't needed to emigrate en masse for a better life.'

When I leave her house I visit the St Julien cemetery. Danielle has been able to identify a few Tancrel tombs, all of them from before the gap, before the mixed marriage. She's searched for Jules Tancrel's tomb for years and hasn't found him yet.

Some men employed by the parish sit on tombstones and smoke. They tell me that all the eighteenth-century graves are at the periphery of the cemetery, by the edge of a ravine. Some have fallen off the edge into the forest below.

I spend hours trying to decipher names and dates on black slabs, some covered by moss, others smashed into pieces. Few are legible. A young gravedigger tries to help me by brushing some slabs. He rubs others with soil, hoping that the earth will transform random dents into legible identities. I only find one of Antoine Tancrel's grandchildren here, Héloïse, buried with her husband. Her vault is one of the largest in the parish. A branch has pierced through the stone; it adorns the marble plaque bearing her name. As I walk back to the entrance I see white smoke churn from the mastodonic sugar factory nearby. Briefly, I wish that I could summon the dead to speak the truth from the ground.

2020–21

The Government of Mauritius does not fully meet the minimum standards for the elimination of trafficking but is making significant efforts to do so... However, the government did not demonstrate overall increasing efforts compared with the previous reporting period, even considering the impact of the Covid-19 pandemic, if any, on its anti-trafficking capacity. The Office of the Director of Public Prosecution (DPP) did not prosecute any suspected traffickers under the 2009 anti-trafficking law, nor did courts convict any traffickers. Police did not report initiating investigation into cases of potential labor trafficking for the second consecutive year. The government provided minimal services to identified victims and did not officially identify any labor trafficking victims for the third consecutive year. Protection services available to adult trafficking victims remained inadequate, and the government continued to lack victim-centered approaches in the provision of assistance. Authorities continued to compel some adult foreign victims to participate in criminal proceedings using threats of deportation and arrest. Police regularly investigated potential trafficking cases as other crimes with lower burdens of proof, and prosecutors routinely pursued lesser offenses with lesser penalties in cases initially investigated as trafficking. Courts continued to provide lenient sentences to first-time offenders of many crimes, including trafficking; this approach weakened deterrence and did not adequately address the nature of the crime. Therefore Mauritius was downgraded to Tier 2 Watch List.
— *2023 Trafficking in Persons Report: Mauritius, US Department of State*

Before *Boulevard Magazine* originally published this essay in 2018, it was rejected by an editor who asked me to 'reconsider the "we"'. Reconsider implicating all Mauritians. I didn't know how to do that. Bangladeshi immigrants bake our bread, build our homes – whether they're social housing or luxury villas. They clean our malls and offices, make our clothes.

·

We call them 'Bangladesh' or 'Bangla', similar to the Mauritian Kreol word for 'them', 'bann-la'. No one remembers their names, no one wants to learn them. They are referred to as *those people* from *that place*, a mass of around 27,000 workers occupying a tiny island of around 1.2 million people, aliens in a country where two degrees of separation is a real phenomenon.

We call them 'workers', never 'immigrants'. We can't cope with the idea of them staying here post-contract, post-use. 'Workers' comes as a necessary prefix when we talk about them, as if to heighten their temporary nature: *get sa bann travayer bangla la.* Look at these Bangladeshi workers sitting by iron fences, women in sarees, men in jeans and long-sleeved shirts, eating, resting by the highway. Behind the fence is the multi-storeyed textile factory where they work and sleep. Clothing lines stream from end to end of each floor. The factory is an uncanny symbol for the lives of these people: a place where the division between work and home doesn't exist, where the vivacity and complexity of a human life is reduced to a number in an entity's accounting books. Legal diction, in fact, doesn't even describe Bangladeshi workers as 'immigrants'. Naturalization is incredibly rare here; so picky are we about who gets to come into the country and for how long, we've devised a permit system that acts like a giant sieve, a wealth-filter. We proudly present this new form of immigration as one of the pinnacles of our multitudinous investment promotion schemes.

There are three classes of permit bestowed to foreign workers. The first class is an 'occupation permit', designed for investors, 'professionals' and their employers. A 'professional', here, is defined as a person earning a basic minimum monthly salary of 30,000 Mauritian rupees. The occupation permit for professionals is valid for up to a decade. If you've held an occupation permit for more than three years, and you fulfil the necessary monetary conditions – for a 'professional', that means your monthly salary must have been at least 150,000 rupees during your three years here – then you're eligible to apply for a 'permanent residence permit', which gives you the right to work and live here for two decades. The application fee starts at $300.

Most Bangladeshis here won't ever get the chance to apply for a permanent residence permit. They're not the right kind of professionals. They have a 'work permit' that they obtain through their employer, which won't let them apply for any kind of residency after their time's up – Mauritius has made sure of that. There's one way they *could* stay, of course: as commonwealth members, they could apply for Mauritian citizenship if they have lived in the country for over five years. They are generally given four-year contracts, maximum; if these are renewed, they have to swear an affidavit stating that they will not apply for Mauritian citizenship. This law concerns those employed at the 'managerial, supervisory and technical levels', which englobes most if not all the types of jobs that the Bangladeshis do.

Unlike the occupation permit or the permanent residence permit, where the documents address the reader as a *person*, where the website information is enticing – 'Work in a Global Carrefour and Reside in Heaven' – the work permit is a different document altogether, found in another government department. It is not addressed to a single person, to a professional; it is destined for those who are recruited en masse: bann-la. This is a new kind of labour, where one must exist in an economic diction devoid of any sentimentality – 'labour', 'human capital', 'productivity', 'economies of scale'.

.

They exist alongside us though at a distance, quietly exiting buses at around eight o'clock every evening, walking in file, tiffins clanging along as they make their way to their lodgings. On weekends or on their off-days, I see them walking around the volcanic crater of Trou aux Cerfs, taking photos of each other and of themselves, organizing picnics.

Newspapers often report on their putrid living and working conditions. It's almost a weekly occurrence now, to read of how Bangladeshi workers haven't been paid in such-and-such company for months on end, how they haven't received their promised end-of-year bonus, how the boss told them they had to be 'nice' in order to be paid, how they were left without any food due to 'low productivity'. Though there are companies that organize proper housing for these workers, many are made to live in places without basic sanitary facilities, sometimes deprived of water and/or electricity.

It's a small miracle that these news reports ever come out in the first place – deportation is swift, common business. Clause (b) of the Deportation Act of 1968 says that any 'undesirable person' may be dealt this fate: 'undesirable' is a vague enough term, describing a Bangladeshi who talks to journalists, union members, one who dares strike, dares stay after their contract is up.

Newspapers have taught us that the Bangladeshis auction themselves for jobs. A machine operator earns about MUR 3,000 maximum in Bangladesh; here, with hundreds upon hundreds of overtime hours, they can earn about MUR 12–14,000. The way it works is usually as follows: a Mauritian company contacts a local recruitment agent; the latter contacts his colleagues in Bangladesh. The job advertised in Bangladesh gets a thousand applicants; the Bangladeshi who pays the highest amount wins the post, with fees sometimes going up to MUR 400,000 to obtain a four-year contract in the country. In true neoliberal style, companies can pay a fee 'per head' or 'in bulk'; these companies also have a 'quota' to respect concerning the number of workers they can bring in.

There are all sorts of ways in which the Bangladeshi worker is exploited even before he sets foot in this so-called Eden. Under Mauritian law, the travel and airplane costs should be borne by the local company who employs the Bangladeshis. By giving MUR 400,000 to the recruitment agent, however, the worker-to-be has essentially paid his transit himself. There's also the fact that some of these agents work illegally, and some companies actively seek their services: they are cheaper, and whatever flimsy rights the Bangladeshis hoped for concerning their health and safety is blasted away. There's also quota trafficking: if a factory has a quota of say 200 workers, and employs 150, it rents out the extra 50 to other factories.

The promise of better wages sometimes disappears on their first day of work. Their contracts are withheld from them, as are their identifying documents – a 'normal procedure', apparently. Duped into coming here, they often have to work second or even third jobs to send enough money back home.

•

Most Bangladeshis are employed in the textile industry and in construction, though not all of them live in factory-dormitories. Many have also found work in industries including food processing, hospitality, education, healthcare, you name it. They rent houses in local neighbourhoods. A few of them speak a little Kreol; conversations are made easier if you know a little Hindi. Mauritians are deeply uncomfortable talking to Bangladeshis, though they'll often assert that they've never met such hard-working people in their lives. I've heard meagre positive stories, of slivers of friendship or at least courteous interaction between employees and management.

On social media, some Mauritians worry that the Bangladeshis may turn violent: if Mauritian bosses are as horrible to them, as is claimed, then what would stop them from exacting some sort of terrorist-inspired reprisals? This argument made the rounds on Facebook after Akayed Ullah attempted to detonate a pipe bomb in New York in December 2017. The rise of Hindu nationalism in recent years has sparked similar paranoias, marginalizing Bangladeshis even further.

Manic xenophobia: the sight of Bangladeshis is so unbearable, I think, because when we look at the always-anonymous 'Other', we see ourselves. This distance that we enforce is so deeply, absurdly ironic for a country built by slaves and indentured labourers. There were no indigenous people to massacre on this island; Dutch, French and English colonists imported their free labour from around Africa and East Asia. Later, when slavery was abolished in 1835, the English colonists decided to bring in shiploads of wretchedly paid Indians (how cost-efficient!) to mitigate the costs of abolition. As a people, we know what it is to be defined in cost ratios and balance sheets, to be assigned some arbitrary notion of worth ascribed to our 'productivity'. Yet when it comes to raising our own worth – 'standard of living', 'high income country' – we don't hesitate to treat others the way our own ancestors were treated, as long as we don't have to look. The way they work isn't so different from the way we did 100, 200 years ago. We don't want to be reminded of what the heavily exploited body looks like. We've mythologized our ancestors to the point where they're no longer thought of as human: our indentured labourer grandfathers, our slave grandmothers, were a kind of homo deus. Their pulsing, bloodied muscles built this nation. They are not, they cannot be like these meek yet lithe men and women, eating plain rice with a little vegetable curry from their tiffins. They can't be these young adults spread-eagled under the frangipani trees of the Caudan waterfront, enjoying the view of the harbour, unable to buy anything from the waterfront's shopping centres but having a good time nonetheless. These can't be the people picnicking on our floral roundabouts, their little garden away from slick machines.

We Mauritians are clean, now. We buy our clothes in glossy malls. We work in so-called 'cyber cities'. We live in 'smart cities'. We are a 'technology hub'. We are Africa's success story. We are not –

.

'Them' is 'Bangladesh'. No one questions this; it's an equation built into us when we talk about the 'workers'. Built into me. In 2017 I rang Veena Dholah, a social and political activist who is a member of the Private Sector Employees Union, affiliated to the General Workers Federation, and a member of Rezistans ek Alternativ, an eco-socialist political party. I wanted to know more about the work they were doing with the Bangladeshis, and confirm some rumours that have been going around but have no paper-based evidence.

'I know you are writing an article on Bangladeshis. But would you be interested in hearing about other communities, too?' In the Rezistans ek Alternativ office, Veena introduced me to Olivier.

When I met Olivier he was one of the 8,379 Malagasy workers living here. Then, as now, hardly anyone I knew had met or spoken of Malagasy workers in Mauritius. We only knew 'Bangladesh'. There were some newspaper stories on a Malagasy drug trade network and on

Malagasy sex workers, but that was about it. Madagascar is the place where many of our ancestors came from, the ones forced into slavery, but few of us know about the forced labour of Malagasy workers here today.

Olivier risked everything by meeting us: like the Bangladeshis, if he was caught talking to a union member he'd be deported back to one of the poorest countries in the world. And even union members aren't safe: trade unionists like Fayzal Ally Beegun, who represent immigrant workers, have over the years repeatedly been threatened for their work.

In Antananarivo, Olivier signed a contract stating that he'd work in Mauritius as a security guard. He arrived here and his contract was taken away from him. He lived in a dormitory attached to the factory. In a space that was around 10 x 12 metres, he slept, bathed and cooked with six other men. They slept on bunk beds, about a metre in length. They tied brightly coloured pieces of fabric to each post, a flimsy wall, a semblance of privacy. Olivier showed me photos of protruding metal, unfinished fittings; his accommodation violated every single article in the Occupational Safety and Health Regulations Act. His living conditions, apparently, were still better than what some Malagasy workers had to put up with. I was told of a building where the workers had to live on the third floor of a factory, without access to clean water. They washed themselves in a river nearby. In 2019 I read a news report of a Bangladeshi worker living in makeshift cardboard boxes. 'In this space – see there – that's where we throw our trash. Right next to our beds. The smell is awful.' He spoke a little Kreol and French.

He didn't have to put up with the smell for long, though. Olivier worked twenty-two to twenty-four-hour 'shifts'.

> As a security-guard, I start at 6 a.m., I finish at 6 a.m. the next day. Then, when I try to sleep – even for one hour – the bosses come for me. They don't knock on the door, they hit it, smash it, open it. Scream at you. You can't sleep. They tell me to get up, I have to unload all the products in the trucks. If it's not products, it's other jobs around the factory.

He showed me photos of his feet. You couldn't even see his ankles, although he was very thin: purple veins webbed around two masses of swollen flesh, two stumps. He received no medical care.

> They punish you if you say you are too ill to work. I've had to work even though I could barely stand with fever. No doctors, nothing. To come here today, I said I had to go to the hospital. They've deducted my pay.

His salary was paid at the boss' whim, an amount from which there were unexplained, haphazard 'deductions'. No payslip. Olivier couldn't open a bank account, so he transferred the money back home by Western Union. I met him on 21 December 2017: he knew that he wouldn't receive a holiday break or a bonus. He worked non-stop for almost nothing.

> They say, "We've given you bread today, so we'll cut the bread out of your salary." A loaf of bread costs MUR 8. They'll cut MUR 50. Sometimes, they'll invent things. They'll say, "There was a tap running in your dormitory. That's MUR 14,000. Do you have 14,000? How are you

going to repay this?"

His experience is largely representative of the immigrant workers who come here – be they Malagasy, Bangladeshi, Chinese, Indian and even Nepali. These men and women are not allowed to have a partner, fall pregnant, have children. No family planning services. Pregnant women are deported. In 2018 two Bangladeshi workers were given a three-month prison sentence on the charge of 'procuring miscarriage'.

Olivier believes that the Malagasy community is treated worse than others:

> In our factory, they segregate the communities so that we don't talk to each other. There are Mauritian, Bangladeshi and Malagasy workers here. They don't want Mauritians telling the others about trade unions, or who to contact, what to do, what are our rights. They don't want us knowing how much the Bangladeshis are paid, how much the Mauritians are paid. We earn a lot less than all of them. They move us around a lot, they have factories all over the place. They pit communities against each other, too. One time, the boss told us that a Malagasy man had stolen a phone from a Bangladeshi. We said, "If what you are saying is true, then you should have no problem seeing who did it on CCTV. There are cameras everywhere." The boss got very upset. He said we talk too much.

He was constantly surveilled, tracked:

> You are harassed every day. They watch everything you do. It's like blackmail. You can't open your mouth: they tell you, "We'll send you back – but if you want to go back, you'll

have to pay your own ticket." They'll throw us out and we will have nowhere to go. The Mauritian boss, he says, "I can hit you; I can do whatever I want – I am protected here. You are not."

Veena read Article 6 of our Constitution. '"Protection from Slavery and Forced Labour: No person shall be held in slavery or servitude. No person shall be required to perform forced labour." As you can see, clearly, we have some kind of neo-slavery operation going on. And this, in a country issued from the horrors of slavery, of indentured labourers.' She shook her head. 'There's the "International Convention on the Protection of the Rights of All Migrant Workers and Members of Their Families." Mauritius didn't sign the treaty.'

•

I return to this essay in 2024. It's been seven years since I met Olivier. He might have returned to Madagascar. His employer wouldn't have been able to extend his four-year contract, though if he was blatantly violating the law in his treatment of his employees, anything could have happened – he could still be working here, imprisoned and tortured, no papers, no contract.

He could have been one of the thousands of workers who contracted Covid-19 in the dormitories; immigrant workers weren't sent to dedicated quarantine centres, forced instead to remain within their lodgings.

Perhaps his employer went bust. A number of factories in Mauritius shut down after the pandemic. Maybe he's found another job. I've seen calls for African and

Malagasy immigrant workers on Facebook. I see more African workers in petrol stations, supermarkets, even garden centres. Eugene, from Ghana, used to help me buy my plants; after we'd met a few times he'd tell me quietly how he hated the island, that the racism here was intolerable. One day I came to the centre and Eugene had disappeared.

He could have escaped. Over 2,224 workers are missing. Their photos are brandished by construction sites and dormitories. Some news reports say these men and women are still working here, that some have married Mauritians.

Mauritius' population is declining and the country's a construction zone. Major infrastructure projects in both the private and public sector seem eagerly concocted to facilitate the jump from 'developing' to 'developed' nation. The government's quest to terraform the island has left bodies in its wake. A lavish stadium was built to host the 2019 Indian Ocean Island Games; three workers died during its construction. On 9 September 2022 a man hanged himself from the ceiling fan of his dormitory; he was employed by Larsen & Toubro, the Indian multinational company with ties to the Indian military. Larsen & Toubro have been contracted to build the island's tramway system, a $550 million project financed by a grant from the government of India. The number of dead and grievously injured grows almost month by month.

Then there are the cases that aren't covered by Mauritian media. A Bangladeshi newspaper reported the story of a Bangladeshi woman who said she'd been raped several times by the owner of a major local textile company in Mauritius. The owner has sued the paper for defamation.

Even outside the hell within which they work, immigrant workers face ever more discrimination. It took no time for the opposition to brandish the 2019 election as 'stolen'. There were the supposed voting ballots found in sugarcane fields, which led to court cases and electoral recounts (but no change in power); there were the 6813 citizens who turned up to voting centres and were unable to exercise their rights, due to 'errors in registration'; relative unknowns in each district suddenly propelled to power, armed with a hitherto-unknown popularity. It didn't matter to the opposition that the working class had solid reasons to vote for the MSM, the party currently in power: they were promised a worthy pension, better working conditions, a better minimum wage, subsidies on basic goods and cooking gas. For the opposition – particularly the Labour Party – the election was stolen. They brandished photos of Bangladeshi workers with sun-printed shirts, posing in MSM election meetings. Soon social media was alight with rumours: it was the workers' fault. It didn't matter that, of the 24,000 or so Bangladeshi workers here at the time, only forty-five of them were allowed to vote under Mauritian law. In the run-up to the 2024 elections it seems that the party's discourse hasn't changed: in a meeting, the head of the Labour Party claimed that 'when a person doesn't vote, the Bangladeshi votes in his place. He doesn't know it, but the Bangladeshi has voted for the MSM.'

Thousands of immigrant workers have been and will be contracted to build this new island, but, like cement, they're only seen in terms of their use-value, as material, blamed for our social problems, to be ejected from the paradise we claim to be as soon as possible.

2017; 2024

SNAPSHOTS OF AN ISLAND
ON THE FRONT LINE

These are the years of summer, the years of heat.

I read the reports, the models that show how rising sea levels will efface coastlines and cities around the world. Miami, Cairo, Mumbai, Jakarta, London. The simulations that show rising temperatures, changing rain patterns. Mauritius is too small for these models, and so our fate is hazily mapped out. Journal articles describe future conditions in 'Sub-Saharan Africa'.

¶ *Le Morne*
My husband and I married in September 2018. We planned our wedding a year in advance. We didn't even think about the sea, its surges, its rhythms. It was a feat of stupidity, for two people who grew up on an island surrounded by the Indian Ocean.

Two days after our wedding we watched the butter-hued moon rise above the water. A hiss as the waves drew back from the coast then thrashed against the shore, gaining ground by the minute. If we'd chosen to get married forty-eight hours later we wouldn't have had a venue.

We were married on a stretch of basalt rock leading out to sea, an elevated slice of shore covered in sand, garnered with thatched huts, wooden tables and a structure that served as our secular altar. Now they were all soused in brine. We walked along a stretch of coast owned by a hotel group, examining the damage. The sea stripped the plump beach of sand, laying bare the fat canvas bags underneath; the waves exposed the roots of coconut trees, gnarled, purple-black like gum disease.

I hadn't realized then that this place had been so eroded. The hotel's manicured efforts made me believe the beach was natural, unaltered: not a carefully constructed simulacra of the beach as it was fifty years ago. A beach perpetually injected with fillers. The waves raked the sand and threw it up elsewhere. We picked up the corpses of iridescent sea snakes, viscid sea cucumbers, threw them back into the ocean.

My friend was stricken by all these little deaths splayed on the shore. She'd marvelled at the island's beauty when she first arrived, waded into the bathtub warmth of the sea, picked up a bleached fragment of coral and asked me what it was. In the three weeks she spent with me I felt like I was her tourist guide of disaster, of death in the making. Before the wedding we'd gone on a brief submarine tour of a Northern lagoon. We saw an octopus picking at the cabbage coral, red lionfish undulating in the sand, peppery bouletang and palette surgeonfish hovering by the carcass of a ship. The captain apologized for the lack of fauna we'd see today: we were still in winter and fish hadn't migrated back to the lagoon yet, but also, and more importantly, there wasn't much of a home for them to come back to. Instead of expanses of coral there were small mounds; the wreck of the ship provided the largest habitat.

Mauritius lost between 2 and 56 per cent of its living coral cover across the lagoons from 2001–2016. Seventy-five per cent of these animals have turned to white bone in the heat.

¶ *Curepipe*

March 2019, Antoine's birthday. A few dishes lay unwashed in the sink; no water to clean them. I could already picture little insects all over them the next morning.

In the bathroom I opened the tap and hoped for water but there was nothing. The pump shrieked, the shower-head barely trickled. Even if there was water, we were too high up in the building to get any of it. We'd taken our precautions, bathing at my in-laws', but I wanted to scrub the sweat from my body again.

So we cut some more birthday cake, ate it on the balcony while watching the fires.

It was the season of cuts. We were allowed water for eight hours a day, four if supply was particularly dire. Water at sunrise and sunset, to cook, to bathe. In my town there were places where no water had flown from taps in three days. Fires marked those places now, spots of orange light in the distance.

Curepipe is the coldest, wettest region in the island. Our apartment block wasn't built with air-conditioning units in mind. Over the past few years summer nights have involved fans, windows hinged as wide as they can go. In summer we slept naked, sweating through the bedsheet. Sometimes I'd open the bathroom door and slide onto the tiles, relatively cool on my skin. Lychee trees grow here now, unthinkable a decade ago. I've eaten Curepipean lychees as plump and sweet as those grown on the coast.

We watched videos of the riots on our phones. Restless young men burned tires, threw bricks and pieces of wood on the road. Armed police came and hosed down the mess. 'Oh *now* there's water!' said a man being filmed. 'But when we want water to drink, we don't get any!'

Most protesters took care to appear collected, respectful, dignified in front of the cameras. 'We're not bad people. We are honest, we're just fighting for our right to water. We have children. Do they think that because we live in social housing, we aren't human?'

They said that the water tankers brought mud water from the river. 'I washed myself with it, started itching all over. Hives all over my skin. I can't use the water to cook, it's infested with creatures. We had to go to the supermarket and buy bottles of water, it was a blow to our budget. My children, they are going to school without having showered.' Toilets wouldn't flush, their contents fermenting.

The fires were lit in mostly working-class neighbourhoods populated by Creoles. Politicians rushed in, hoping to calm protesters, reassuring them that things would be different when they came to power.

In a different suburb, Curepipeans filmed water the colour of diarrhoea pouring from chrome taps into chrome sinks. 'We ring the authorities, we ring, we ring, no one answers. Or they make promises. And nothing happens.' The authorities said there was no water because they were replacing centennial pipes; it's reported that over half of our water supply is lost through our piping system. 'What happened to the electoral promise of water 24/7?' everyone asks.

We wait for the bursts of torrential rain between periods of drought. Reservoirs hold considerably less water than in previous years. The rains that come, later and later each season, are too sporadic and in the wrong places to be a benediction. Rainfall has decreased by 8 per cent every year since the 1950s. A few summers ago someone once stole a 9,000-litre reservoir tank from a cemetery.

And when water comes it arrives with Old Testament fury.

I was fifteen when torrential rains killed four people in 2008. We were warned of potential heavy rain but told that schools were open. In Curepipe, I watched from our classroom as rain submerged the grounds; watched as our paper boats coursed through the water, then were pelted into pulp by the force of the rain. When the government told us to go back home it was already too late. Throughout the town water rose to our knees, our thighs. I waited for a long time before my mother's driver was able to collect me from school; I was lucky. Some of my friends took their chances and waded to the bus station. They saw excrement running past their legs. A girl in the north of the island crossed a bridge engulfed by a river; it was the only way she could get home. She was swept away.

¶ *Moka*
A standstill, on my way to work. Our island is a case study in terrible urban planning: you'll be stuck in a traffic jam no matter which road you take, so I choose the most scenic route, always. Sugarcane fields to my left and right, in-

digo mountains in the distance, a jagged crescent circling the green. The sun only rose an hour ago. An elderly woman was in the back seat of the car in front of me. She stuck her arm out of the window, blocking the sun's migraine light from her face. She kept her arm like that for twenty minutes, until we reached a bend in the road and the sun was behind her. The man in the truck behind me poured water on his hands, on his face. I blocked the sun and its heat as best as I could with the car's visor and air-conditioning. A hive sprouted on my cheek, exposed to the light nonetheless.

In the car mirror I saw that plaques of discoloured skin on my neck had crept up to the edges of my face. 'Eczema,' my dermatologist said a month later, pointing to my cheek. 'Champignons,' tapping my neck and chest. Fungus, sprouting with the sun, the heat. My mother would scrub at my neck with particular vigour when I was a child, convinced I wasn't showering properly, that I'd neglected the washcloth. I was given two creams and though my skin remains uneven, the patches stopped spreading.

¶ *Tamarin-Black River*
The human body shuts down once the wet-bulb temperature exceeds 35°C in over 90 per cent humidity. These temperatures aren't unfamiliar to us.

When the power grid in Black River blows people sleep on the floor. Living on the west coast – or any of our coasts – without air conditioning now is impossible. The wealthy shower multiple times a day, as much as their water tanks allow.

My fitness instructor has lived in Tamarin since she was a child. 'I've never seen anything like it, and I've lived here for forty years. The soil used to be so parched that it was cracked all over. The wind would stir up dust, like in Westerns. And now we're seeing torrential rain that could pull the houses on the mountain down.' I told her of the videos of water pouring off the mountain, good water cascading straight into the sea since Tamarin has no reservoirs. 'The salt pans were all flooded,' she replied, looking out of the window.

I read of dogs furiously digging holes in the ground to escape the 35-degree heat. Children fainting during assembly early in the morning.

¶ *Cottage*
'I was sitting in my kitchen, cleaning beans. I saw this great ball of fire, in the window. My eyes were blinded with light, I dropped my knife, and everything burst. Windows, wires. The ball wrecked the electric lines. It went from house to house.' The man in the video who is being interviewed tries to draw the ball with his hands. It's like a ballet movement, or a clichéd description of a voluptuous woman. There are shots of a flooded nursery, Mickey Mouse cribs rippling in filth. Another woman says she has nothing left. She cries as she recounts her misfortunes, which have come to her in quick succession. 'My husband died fifteen days ago. If the neighbours hadn't come to rescue me I would have died in my house when the rain came in. I don't even have fifteen cents. I just bought a bed and now it's ruined. And I have to wait for my pension next month. I don't know how I'm going to live. I don't know.'

¶ *Trou aux Biches*

December 2019. I opened the wooden shutters of the bungalow to the sight of rain pouring down like thick white hair. The northern part of the island was at a standstill, schools closed, traffic snailing down the motorway. We swam in the lagoon, torrential rain beating on our skulls, thunder overhead. Peak holiday season, and tourists, disgusted by the weather, caught early flights back home. This was not the sunny island that had been promised.

I could smell salt, but also the fruit trees that adorned the multicoloured houses on the beach; the rain must have pummelled their fruit into scent. The trees' roots were apparent, grabbing onto the sandy grass. The crescent beach was thinning almost by the week. The owner of the bungalow we were staying in told us that he didn't give this coast another ten years before the sea lapped at his walls.

The United Nations Development Programme said our beaches have shrunk by as much as 20 metres in the last few decades, that the loss of tourism could cost us over $100 million per year by 2060, if nothing is done to save our coastline.

December 2022. Our November rains are expected in mid-January. Our reservoirs are 3 per cent full. It's the worst drought since the early 2000s.

There's nothing to do but swim. We listen to the radio for jellyfish warnings: 'explosion' is the word of choice experts use to describe the creatures who've smothered every coastline. Manifestations of a sick ocean, they spawned due to warmer temperatures, overfishing, changing weather patterns.

Today the sky is postcard-perfect, the sea devoid of jellyfish, the beach packed with tourists.

I think of the carbon emissions of each plane that lands here. The emissions of each of our 106 hotels. Air conditioning units struggling to cool rooms in peak season. Tourists pouring themselves a bath, cleansing themselves of their twelve-hour flight. Ignorant that the rest of us have to live on only four to eight hours of water flowing through our taps most days in high summer. Tourists, their sunscreen-coated bodies plunging into the lagoon, leaving a film on the water, poisoning corals. Tourists, delighting in our bathwater lagoon, *look it's so crystal-clear you can see the bottom*, a dead zone framed in buoys, cleansed of most of its creatures.

¶ *Port Louis*
January 2021: I worked here over a decade ago. I must negotiate the capital's streets differently now, my body adjusting to this new heat. My shoes abrade my feet and my shirt is stuck to my back. I slick the sweat running from my forehead back into my ponytail. When I arrive at the National Library my feet feel like they're sloshing in their own blood.

To get to the city centre I use an underpass, which now closes at the merest sign of torrential rain. You can't walk through here without remembering the flash floods on 30 March 2013; Port Louis was flooded within minutes, water tumbled down the mountains that flank the city, sparing only the tops of palm trees. Eleven people died, six in this tunnel. They couldn't leave fast enough, the rails and tiled staircase were too slippery for their hands and feet once the water poured in.

January 2024: The underpass is flooded. Roads across the capital are submerged, cars crash into each other as they are carried downstream. Passengers trapped in a car film the taupe waves rolling in from Bell Village; in horror, they capture the moment a bloated body rushes past them.

People all over the country wonder why the infrastructure around Port Louis hasn't been modified to cope with torrential rainfall; why, after ten years in power and countless grandiose infrastructure projects, the government has effectively left the nation's capital to rot.

¶ *Chitrakoot*
The island sometimes turns to sepia at sunset, and in the jaundice light I like to think that I can predict the intensity of the thunderstorms to come. Schools are regularly closed, houses are flooded, people say they're too scared to sleep. 'We have to elevate our beds on bricks. I don't know what to do anymore,' people say on the radio. 'I've lost everything, again.' Our water drainage and waste-water management systems are a mess, though serious work has begun over the past couple of years to fix them. Still, progress is slow. 'When will we have drains? When we're dead!' say men and women across the island. Videos of people removing water from their shops with buckets, throwing the water back into the road that's become a river.

Torrents pummel the vulnerable hillside village of Cottage almost every year. 'When the big rain falls you hear a sound, like the house is cracking from beneath the earth, and then water rushes in,' a man said on the news. 'I know that we can't live here anymore, but I don't have a choice.' An image of another man, naked from the chest up, pressed against a large gate by a river of mud. Beyond the gate there's a floating coagulation of detritus.

¶ *Sebastopol*
The occasional aberration forms in the air. Freak tornadoes uproot electric poles, whip wires into a maelstrom, rip tin roofs from homes, and once shattered an entire village. I saved one photo of a kitchen post-devastation on my laptop: upturned plastic chairs, burst pipes, glass fragments. A singular bitter gourd on the ground, pale green on the red floor, like an omen. There's a common phrase used here to refer to difficult times, the times when we were poor. Letan margoz. Bitter gourd times. I've heard this phrase often in the last few years: during the height of the Covid-19 pandemic and after, now, in the heat of the cost-of-living crisis.

¶ *Bambous-Black River Gorges*
There were only four Mauritius kestrels in 1974; they are endemic to Mauritius, and were, at the time, the most endangered bird of prey in the world. Colonialism had quite a lot to do with their decline, practically from the moment the Dutch set foot here in the early eighteenth century: the colonists shrivelled our forests, brought rats on their boats. Three hundred or so years later – after the French and English colonial administrations had their

go, pillaging the environment; after they'd driven species to extinction; after Mauritius claimed its independence and multiple economic booms and further, consequential ecological devastation – the kestrels were left with almost no homes. By 2009, however, they'd flourished to around 600 individuals, thanks to the work of the Mauritian Wildlife Foundation and other organizations. They are beautiful animals, though I've never seen one in the wild before. Their fluffy white breasts are spotted with brown, as if they'd been dotted over with a thick brush. We have 1 per cent of our natural forests left and they live there, up in the Bambous mountains and in the Black River Gorges National Park.

Recent data, however, indicates that their numbers have started to plummet again to something like 200–300 individuals, and climate change is partly responsible for their decline. Changing rainfall patterns are hurting their breeding and feeding habits. 'Geckos are the kestrel's prime food source. When it rains, geckos hide, and the bird's visibility is reduced. If the rain only occurs for a few hours, it would still be manageable. But when you have continuous days of high rainfall, it means parents aren't able to find food for their young,' explains Dr Vikash Tatayah, the Conservation Director of the Mauritian Wildlife Foundation.

Similarly, laying eggs is directly related to rainfall patterns in July and September. If there's a lot of rain in August, the kestrels lay later on – but, in biology, the earlier you nest, the better you fare. On top of this, the rainfall in December correlates to the number of birds who will fledge. A very wet end-of-year is bad news. Then the birds have to face the cyclone season, from January to March; the chance of a kestrel surviving its first birthday depends on the number of cyclones hitting the island in this period. Even if the kestrel survives, if a female hasn't been well-fed as a chick, she'll be able to lay less eggs as an adult.

¶ *Round Island*
There is nothing remotely positive about the Meteorological Office's predictions on cyclone formation in our region. Though there is 'no convincing signal in an increase in the number of storms', 'there is an increasing trend in the number of storms reaching tropical cyclone strength... The anticipated rapid or even explosive intensification of tropical storms has asserted itself,' writes the Ministry of Environment in July 2023.

Off the northern coast of Mauritius there's a place no humans are allowed to visit, except those working for the Foundation. A dome-like mound of rock, a sanctuary for endemic and supra-rare animals across most phyla. An islet that has never been contaminated by rodents, an act of exceptional grace. The islet's called Round Island, the bird the Round Island petrel, a species that breeds here for three to four years before travelling the world. This petrel is a hybrid animal, birthed from three different species (Trindade, Kermadec, Herald) – 'and possibly a fourth species, too,' adds Tatayah – which makes it unique in the world.

They are also vulnerable. Seabird populations across the world are in decline, the second most threatened group of birds after parrots. Changing sea temperatures are fatal; among other things, they alter the migratory patterns of fish.

If fish are difficult to find and aren't plentiful – if the food source shifts an extra 200 km, say, and an adult petrel therefore has to fly 800 km for food – the journey takes longer, and will affect the chick's growth. Several feeding spells like this and the chicks will die or fledge when they're still underdeveloped. Its chances of surviving before returning to breed on Round Island as an adult are severely compromised, and we have stats to prove it. We've charted the flight patterns of ringed chicks and adults in El Niño years. Birds who hatched in an El Niño year did not survive, or didn't survive into adulthood.

Cyclones, again, exacerbate the problem. 'When cyclone Dina hit the island in 2002, it killed all of the chicks and 71 per cent of the eggs. We've seen that weaker cyclones pose less of a problem, but if cyclones get more intense, the birds are at great risk.'

¶ *In Government*
There isn't a single member of the government or the opposition who denies the existence of climate change. Successive Prime Ministers have pleaded to the supposed first world, urging them to reduce their emissions for all our sakes. And yet.

Mauritius' power lies in the sea, the 2.3 million square kilometres under our jurisdiction. We 'co-manage' an additional 396,000 square kilometres with the Republic of Seychelles. The government describes our seas as an 'untapped reservoir.' 'A major pillar for economic development.'

(Sometimes I think about the people employed to

write about our environment in this way. Mauritians raised on, raised by, the lagoon, longing for family picnics on the beach on the weekends like the rest of us. Fibre mats, a stereo, a ravanne, djembe, biryani, roast chicken sandwiches. Adults shielding their eyes underneath filao trees, looking on at their children and grandchildren playing in the sea.)

On 7 December 2021 our government passed the Offshore Petroleum Bill. It had been introduced to parliament in October and had been stamped with a 'certificate of urgency'. A new Department – helmed entirely by the Prime Minister's Office – was appointed to act as the regulatory body for petroleum activities in our waters. It will issue permits, negotiate agreements, facilitate the conduct of petroleum activities. The Bill aims to be so comprehensive in the Department's scope that there's a clause stating it will 'do such other things as may be necessary for the proper conduct of petroleum activities'. Vague diction to enable less-than-transparent activities.

There's no suggestion of an independent body, of audited actions. All the money from our petroleum activities will be stored in a 'fund' under the control of the Ministry of Finance. The Department is also protected from all liabilities, civil or criminal, that could be incurred 'in respect of any act done or omitted in good faith'. If an officer of the Department 'disclose[s] any matter which came to his knowledge' while working, they risk a fine of MUR 100,000 and imprisonment with a two-year maximum sentence.

Rumours have abounded that there was petrol in our seas since I was a child. When the Bill was read out to parliament the Prime Minister confirmed that four sites have been identified by CGG Services SAS, a French multinational geoscience technology services company. Two of the sites may be the Saya de Malha Bank and an area to the north of Agaléga. Saya de Malha supports the world's largest seagrass meadow, and is one of the ocean's biggest carbon sinks.

¶ *In My Body*
I read books written mostly by white men in supremely rich countries on how to think about climate disaster. Some concepts I understand in my body: global warming as a hyperobject, heat like honey glistening all over my skin, so viscous that showering won't remove the stickiness.

I read books that trace the contours of my lifeline. The statistics that predict our future, that suggest the manner of our deaths, the stages and degrees at which our bodies will gradually shut down.

'Recently, researchers estimated that by 2050 as many as 150 million people in the developing world will be at risk of protein deficiency as the result of nutrient collapse,' writes David Wallace-Wells in *The Uninhabitable Earth*. '138 million could suffer from a deficiency of zinc, essential to healthy pregnancies; and 1.4 billion could face a dramatic decline in dietary iron – pointing to a possible epidemic of anaemia.' I'm already borderline anaemic, like many women in my country and their mothers. In the Ministry of Health's Health Statistics Report 2021, 38 per cent of all Mauritian women who received antenatal care in public hospitals were reported as anaemic.

'Sudden rainfall shocks – both deluges and their opposite, droughts – can devastate agricultural communities economically, but also produce what scientists call, with understatement, "nutritional deficiencies" in foetuses and infants,' writes Wallace-Wells.

> Between a quarter and a half of all those exposed to extreme weather events will experience them as an ongoing negative shock to their mental health... Climate affects both the onset and the severity of depression... Heat waves bring waves of other things, too: mood disorders, anxiety disorders, dementia... Heat death is among the cruellest punishments to a human body... First comes "heat exhaustion"... profuse sweating, nausea, headache... Water won't help, your core temperature rising as your body sends blood outward to the skin, hoping desperately to cool it down. The skin often reddens; internal organs begin to fail.

Consultants believe we'll cross the 1.5 degree mark here in 2030. In the summer of 2024, our temperatures were already 2 to 3 degrees higher than average.

¶ *Endnote*
I've come back to this essay at the end of January 2025. Our summer rains, which historically have arrived in early November, still haven't fallen. Our country's economy is now so weak that if the government were offered an opportunity to mine our underwater petrol reserves, it would probably take it. In America, a felon, a man accused of sexual assault, has become President once again. He has promised to take drilling and fracking to new heights. In the days before and after he took his oath, Los Angeles burned. Here, our reservoirs are

117

near-empty. Our cyclones are named from a predefined list validated for our area. Member countries contribute to the list, such as Mozambique, Réunion and Zimbabwe. I propose that we review the system: we make a list of individual politicians and CEOs of companies who have done the most harm, name our ecological catastrophes after them. Hurricane Trump. The Darren Woods Fire. The Wael Sawan Flood.

2017; 2025

THERE IS TOO MUCH FEMINISM

I.

I had muted Arun for months on end. We weren't close, but I knew him pretty well – we'd hung out a few times over the past decade or so, attended the same sporadic cultural events. Arun liked to write. His gift was irony. And his social media platform of choice, like that of most Mauritians, was Facebook. He'd have diatribes at the ready on everything from poverty to politicians, crafted in his signature tone, a perpetual smirk. The smirk would give way, in the last line or so, to genuine feeling. The technique made him seem like a generally good dude, caught in the Mauritian system like everyone else but with the intelligence to write about it. He amassed quite the following. In 2016, he started writing these generic posts on feminism, the kind that elicited LMAOs and general approval sans sincere twist. He irritated me but I wasn't worried about him. I thought Mauritian men were mostly like that: retrograde, patriarchal, no matter how different they claimed to be from their fathers. I thought that progress was coming whether they liked it or not and that soon, in a decade or so, they'd be embarrassed by their puerile rancour. I had hope in our generation – well educated and directional, ravenous in ambition, ravenous for the world. I knew about the alt-right, but thought the word stood for 'white supremacist' and little else. Ninety-nine per cent of our population isn't white. I hadn't even entertained the notion that this European-American export had found a following here. I'd muted Arun and the chronology of his radicalization.

Early in 2019 I'd shared two pieces on the ties between domestic abuse and the alt-right on Facebook. 'What is toxic masculinity?' he commented publicly. 'Is simply being a man who stands up for his opinions considered toxic?... Is it reasonable to impliedly dismiss the fact that a substantial amount of women are radicalising, too?' He carried on, effervescent, using diction I'd never heard before: 'Cultural Marxism', 'Regressive Leftists', 'Red Pill'. He assured me he'd read feminist theory, cited Katherine K. Young's *Sanctifying Misandry: Goddess Ideology and the Fall of Man*. I had no idea who he was talking about; after some research I discovered that Young is a marginalized, poorly reviewed academic. Arun could only have heard of her in the undergrowth of the internet, probably in a forum. Her work on misandry is convenient for men like him: they can say that they've read feminist theory, through her; that they aren't making 'groundless claims'. He retaliated when I blocked him, posted screenshots of our conversations, said he had thought I was 'open to dialogue' and that he would talk to me about toxic masculinity when we next saw each other. It seemed natural to him that he should impose his presence on me, ask for free emotional and intellectual labour, take up my time under the guise of 'debate'. His friends quickly provided him with support: 'What of toxic femininity?', 'holy crap that mindset reached Mauritius', 'that reads like foreplay'.

On 8 March 2019, International Women's Day, a piece in a supposedly prestigious local paper made the rounds on social media. 'Overcoming Feminist Ideology for Equality' contained all the necessary references to Jordan Peterson and Camille Paglia. The piece's highlights included: 'Feminist ideology is responsible for having turned the whole women's rights movement into a joke'; '[Feminism] is also responsible for the widespread and yet twisted view that throughout history, women have been oppressed by a "male-dominated patriarchy"'; 'All heterosexual women have to choose between career and family-building at some point in their lives, and that is the PREDOMINANT reason for which [sic] we do not see a proportional gender distribution in politics, or in most other traditionally male-dominated professions, for that matter ... a disadvantage imposed on women by NATURE, not by some loosely defined "male-dominated patriarchy".' Arun praised the article and its author, Kavi. They had attended the same 'star' school, Royal College Curepipe, one of the most famous in the country; though there was an age gap, I wondered if they knew each other.

Arun was undoubtedly proud, too, of his own contribution to International Women's Day: a post titled 'Gender Equali–cunt', in which he said, 'Don't forget, it's women who have the monopoly on equality narratives. Men don't suffer and women can do no wrong. All men are shit, all women are great. Remember this well. It's a new social rule.' His friends were jubilant. The editor-in-chief of another local paper openly endorsed his post: 'For once I totally agree with you! You've spoken the truth.'

Kavi's article was shared on the Shame Them Facebook group, a safe, anonymous space for Mauritian women to speak of their abuse and receive support. The very act of sharing one's experiences is radical here; it is radical to speak of being groped and violated on public transport, in doctor's offices, on the street, at work. Alt-right vitriol quickly followed: 'Triggered! The feminist starter pack: weirdo, man hater, fact hater, victim card premium level'; 'all the intersectional bullcrap'; '[not] one iota of proof ...

to support their arguments... the author had the decency to write his opinion in a national newspaper... there is too much feminism.' That last comment was supposedly by a woman; a quick look at her profile suggests that it's fake; she's only friends with the alt-right, has no history on the site.

II.
If a Mauritian writer's words are to have any validity whatsoever, they must be published abroad. When Ananda Devi and Nathacha Appanah write about violence they are taken seriously, though not much is ever done at policy level.

Devi and Appanah left the island decades ago. All the girls I knew in school wanted to leave the island and its rapacious violence behind, too.

I grew up hearing stories of men murdering their female partners with crossbows and other implements, dismembering the women in their lives with grinder machines, raping their grandmothers mothers daughters stepdaughters infants, tossing female bodies into forests. I saw school friends married off at fifteen to men twice their age. Saw bruises on the bodies of the women who cared for me. Women with nerves so frayed they'd break whatever it was they were holding – glasses, plates, cups would just fall out of their shaking hands, even when they were well away from their husbands. I know what it's like to feel unsafe walking on the street in the late afternoon, or walking alone at any time of day. I know trans women and queer women who've sought asylum in Europe, since it's still illegal for them to be themselves here. I know what it's like to live in a country where abortion is illegal.

Mauritian girls are told that the best way – the most prestigious way – of leaving the country and its violence behind is by becoming a laureate, a scholarship winner. The government would pay for a laureate's education abroad, under the condition that they returned to serve their country. As a teenager the scholarship was desirable, even for wealthier students, like me, who could pay their own way (though it didn't mean that competing was ethical): it meant getting access to the best universities, who probably wouldn't accept me otherwise, since international students had it harder. I already had no chance of getting to Oxford or Cambridge, apparently, because my School Certificate exams weren't perfect by four points.

The first step to the scholarship was to get faultless or near-faultless grades at fifteen, in the School Certificate exams. That allowed me to gain a place at the government-run 'star schools', where I'd supposedly receive a better education. Quickly, I understood that the main point of these schools was to meet the girls I'd be competing against for the scholarship. Even the classrooms were organized by prestige: the two main scholarship categories were in Economics and Science, and so the 'Economics-side' and 'Science-side' classrooms were next to each other, on the top floor, taught – reportedly – by the better teachers. As far as I can remember, I was the only student in both classes who was of Creole descent, but because of my profusion of privileges – my famous, wealthy British father, my light skin, straight-ish hair – I was treated well by my classmates. There were more Creole students downstairs, in the classrooms that taught literature and arts; they too were competing for the scholarship, they too had excellent grades, but the teachers treated them (and the subjects they chose) as inferior.

The teachers weren't considerably better than in my previous school; I was wasting six hours of my life every day, and making up for it after hours, in tuition classes. Tuition was Step Two: socializing with my classmates at the star school informed me of who the best tuition teachers were, and I sought them out. There were two or three illustrious tutors for every subject in the whole country; you'd secure your place months in advance and you'd endure their teaching methods. Sometimes, you'd take deep breaths before stepping inside their homes.

'He helps me, of course. So it's a trade-off. He gives me books, he pays more attention while correcting my papers…. He tells me that he'll tutor me.' I read Ananda Devi's *Eve Out of Her Ruins* too late, after I'd finished school. It was the first time that I had seen, in print, what I thought would forever be condemned to whispers. Girls across the island were, and still are, at the mercy of predatory teachers. Sexual harassment and abuse by teachers didn't just happen to girls living in precarious circumstances, though it happened to them at a greater rate. I remember there was an accountancy tutor so depraved that my friends would blanch in the hours leading up to the end of the school day. He'd hit, he'd caress, he'd married a former student or two.

I'd still take the violent, copybook-throwing, spittle-splattering men over the tutor I had every Thursday afternoon for that unique subject we all had to sit, Cambridge International Examinations' 'General Paper' – a test of English fluency, reasoning, general knowledge. The tutor

124

was highly esteemed, a bastion of the English language in Mauritius, chair of associations, committees, boards, prizes. He held his lessons in his house. He liked it when girls came in and kissed him on both cheeks, which my friends and I refused to do. We'd work silently in the main room before being called into his private office for a good ten to twenty minutes, individually, so he could check and correct our work. We'd sit alone in this office, at a knee's distance from him. His hands could easily rest on our legs. If our pens fell to the floor we were warned by other girls never to bend down and pick them up; he wouldn't move to create space. Once, as part of his weekly exercises, he asked me to write a sentence using the word 'thin'. I handed him my copybook. He waxed poetic on how I, for instance, wasn't thin. I was slender.

Something must have happened the day I came back home and told my mother I wasn't going there anymore, but I can't remember what. I've blanked it out. 'You'll lose your chance for the scholarship,' my mother menaced, her throat tight, her jaws clenched. This wasn't the first time I'd disappointed her; she'd already tried to force me into tuition with the sadistic accountancy tutor. Perhaps she believed that I'd be safe with both men, that my father's surname and our family wealth would offer protection. All over the country parents glossed over the miseries of their daughters for the sake of their becoming one in twenty-one laureates. There was no choice. This is how they earned their future.

'There was the nothing of my father's eye, which alcohol had turned oily. The nothing that was my mother's mouth and eyelids, both of them stapled shut.... [My mother has] deliberately insulated herself so as not to

125

feel or regret life,' says Eve. My mother can't stand *Eve Out of Her Ruins*. 'Too violent,' she says of Devi's work in general, indigeste, violence that won't be excreted away. When I asked her if she thought Eve was a realistic portrayal of Mauritius, she said yes, but the novel describes violence where Mauritians expect violence: as occurring to (mostly) working-class Creole people living in poverty. We guessed that the book would have caused an uproar here if Eve was a middle-class Indo-Mauritian girl from a town like Vacoas.

My mother's eyes were always open. She was the paranoid watchwoman of my body. She screamed when I left the house at fourteen wearing a top with the subtlest décolleté. 'Someone will reach out and grab you like this! Do you want that to happen?' She grabbed my breast and hurt me. It had happened to her; when she was around my age, a man on a bike cornered her into a bamboo hedge. Eleven years later, when I told her of sexual harassment at work, she told me how she was thrust into a car by a former boss; her chances of promotion were dependent on what she'd be able to do for him. These stories are routine.

Perhaps she saw my suffering as a series of little hurts. Endurable. She thought she was protecting me from greater pain.

For years, I slept about five hours per night. My eyesight grew worse, dropping to minus seven. A hard lump in my neck grew bigger; my mother said it was stress, and the stress would be worth it once I was abroad. My back curved, hurt from the hours I spent sitting in chairs. I felt dizzy most days. But I wasn't hospitalized, like some of the other girls. I was driven to tuition, I didn't have to take the bus. I had it so much easier.

III.

Before I moved to my star school in Vacoas in 2008, I attended a Diocese-run girl's school in Curepipe. Antoine was a student in the Diocese-run boy's school across the road. It was larger, with more facilities and better teachers.

The boys would loiter around after hours. We couldn't really interact with them – hanging out automatically conferred bad reputations, and besides most of our parents would beat us if they knew. But because both schools were run by the Diocese, the older boys were often summoned to help in the organization of our school's events. This is how I met Antoine, seventeen years ago, at a fair he'd helped organize.

In the few, illicit minutes we met every afternoon – he was always in and out of detention, and I had thirty minutes before I was driven to tuition – he'd tell me stories of rebellion, of a wildness that couldn't be restrained. Smoking in the toilets. Jumping off walls, escaping. A teacher who was blind; a teacher who was perpetually drunk; a teacher who never went home. His friends, selling dried chayote leaves, claiming it was marijuana. Selling pornographic CDs inside copies of *La Vie Catholique*, the Church's weekly magazine.

My own stories sounded so intolerably bland in comparison. There was no possibility of adventure, of unleashing. Girls were surveilled. And even when they slipped under the watch of their parents and teachers, the stories they told afterwards felt wrong, no matter the triumphant tone in which they were described. Sex with a European tourist at twelve years old, in a hotel, did not sound glamorous to me; sex with older men in bars seemed grimy (the fingers!). But I pretended to be just as awed as the others, not horrified, because I'd already been told that I looked like the Virgin Mary and didn't want to seem even more uncool. It was bad enough that I didn't have my period until I was fifteen.

When I moved to my new star school, Antoine and I couldn't meet in secret anymore. My school was in other district, with difficult bus routes. My mother relented to our relationship occasionally, when she was in the mood, so sometimes we met for a few hours on a designated Saturday. My mother was terrified that Antoine would affect my grades, my chances of getting out of the country.

Antoine went to a tuition teacher after school once a week, occasionally. His teachers, though somewhat better than mine, were still shit: he had a 'laureate-maker' as a school teacher who told him, outright, that if he hoped to pass his exam he'd need to pay him for tuition after class.

He valued his freedom, roaming the streets, taking buses to other towns, drinking with friends, sometimes even with girls. I knew some of the girls he hung around with, who announced with bravado that they'd 'given up' on school. But the establishment had given up on them a long time ago.

Antoine didn't go to a star school after his School Certificate exams. He didn't have the grades, didn't want to go anyway. He said the 'culture' there was too different, which was to say: all the boys there were like me and my friends, studying until they almost broke from the pressure. Also: irrespective of gender, the star schools were attended almost exclusively by Indo-Mauritians and Sino-Mauritians. Franco-Mauritians didn't go there, mixed, working class Indo-white boys like him weren't seen there, and we knew that the very few Creoles who were there were stigmatized and generally unhappy. Star schools weren't for him.

IV.
The best star school of our constituency was the Royal College Curepipe. The school's alumni comprised many famous men, including Seewoosagur Ramgoolam, Navin Ramgoolam and Pravind Jugnauth. They also included men like Arun and Kavi.

The boys from RCC had a reserved, nervous disposition. I met them often in tuition. They hardly spoke. When I was still at my Diocese-run school I'd see them every year, on the day the laureates were announced. They'd organize a triumphant procession; they'd take a bus to different schools and scream at the gates, sing crude, vulgar songs flaunting their superiority.

I didn't question these demonstrations of barely repressed violence. All the boys' schools had their own version of a procession; students at Antoine's school, in its rare laureate years, would rampage through school premises and through town, and once partly destroyed a teacher's car. There were tuts of disapproval from the general public; the national television station covered the announcements, celebrations and 'excesses', which were declared 'in bad taste'.

One year in the late 2000s, though, the 'processions' were banned indefinitely. Students from the Royal College Curepipe had taken the bus to Loreto College Quatre Bornes; there, they'd assaulted the students, squirted bottles of their own piss on the girls' uniforms, destroyed classrooms.

Many years later, in 2023, the students of the Royal College Curepipe made the news again. Laureate celebrations were now confined to their own school. A few days before the announcement, students were given papers printed with the unofficial 'school song' to chant. I vaguely remembered the song from my adolescence, but didn't know the lyrics beyond 'off we go, shut your pussy, Royals are champions'.

The lyrics, proudly printed, describe different ethnic groups of Mauritius and what they sell: 'I go to a Hindu street, I see a Hindu, I ask what do you sell, he says "I sell bred malbar,"' 'I go to a Muslim street ... "I sell a bowl of halim!"' and so forth, with Tamils selling bol rasson, Chinese selling nian gao. But Creoles sell 'la peau fess', or the skins of their buttocks.

An infuriated parent went to the press, said they were horrified at the racism manifest in the chant. It made the news.

Online, people wrote down what they remembered of the other songs. We remembered one that attacked different female colleges: the students of the Queen Elizabeth

College sell 'their big pussies', the ones of Maurice Curé sell 'their big breasts', the students of the Diocese-run Loreto colleges sell 'their big mouths', the boys of the college St Esprit – traditionally attended by Creole boys and perceived as a Catholic-Creole institution – sell 'la peau fess'; the boys of Royal College, though, 'sell laureates'.

I wasn't surprised. These were boys who had been brought up to think that they were the inheritors of this country. The elite – if only after the whites. Markedly, so many RCC alumni I knew turned into Trump fans, entered the content tunnel that started with comedians and ended with the alt-right. So many of them, too, espoused Hindutva and its rhetoric, rebranded in new ways.

V.

Arun and Kavi wouldn't call themselves 'alt-right' or conservative, but whether they like it or not their behaviour matches, to an almost formulaic degree, the characteristics of the alt-right community worldwide. Both men are virulently transphobic – transphobia is almost their primary, defining characteristic – homophobic, misogynistic, racist. They seek the freedom to hurt, subjugate. Arun and Kavi post feminist-bashing content, sponsor the men's rights initiative, bewail civilizational decline; at the time of Trump's presidency I saw their friends writing posts that promoted rape culture, such as one photographer who said, 'every animal has a mating ritual, in our species, men are judged for those.'

Back in 2019 Arun and Kavi thought they were intellectual renegades, whipping up wit taken from the 4chan and Reddit maelstrom. They didn't want to be associated with white supremacists, but they shared pieces from *Quillette*, and their friends went a step further, sharing from Breitbart. They were products of bourgeois Indo-Mauritian strictures of power, but because they'd so wanted to differentiate themselves from the status quo – Arun had studied to be a lawyer in Britain, then dropped out, eventually working in communications; Kavi studied psychology instead of the more 'traditional' fields of medicine, business or law, and became a psychologist with some comedy gigs on the side – they didn't want to accept that their belief systems were deeply reactionary.

In 2019 Trump was President of the United States, and an incredible number of reactionary, conservative, hateful people were able to get a platform on social media and in respected news sites. Of all the men that were profiled and talked about in 2019, the man who gained the most coverage – in Mauritius at least – was unquestionably Jordan Peterson. You could even find his books here. He came to Arun and Kavi as a prophet, which was almost ludicrous, since Peterson isn't imaginative. His 'rules for life' aren't groundbreaking: young Mauritian men would have heard variations of this misogynistic discourse before. In religious doctrine in this country – and this is across religions here – the ideal woman is sacrosanct, virginal; she knows her place in the order of things and is willing to serve. Peterson was offering a doctrine based on precisely the same patriarchal values. What he was also offering, however, was a new, deeply attractive branding: a white, supposedly powerful male to look up to, who wasn't traditionally religious; a doctrine readily accessible through social media.

Take Peterson's idea of 'enforced monogamy', his solution to male violence. There is hardly any difference between that and the belief here – echoed by fathers, uncles, elder cousins, grandfathers, community and religious leaders – that a 'good wife' is there to support her husband, to calm and soothe his moods; that such a 'good woman' must be found, through an arranged marriage if necessary. Pankaj Mishra describes Peterson's diatribes as 'right-wing pieties seductively mythologized for our current lost generations', and mythology is right: Arun, especially, had essentialized his Hindu faith to a farce that year, plucking and crafting his beliefs into a fetish of vulgar Orientalism, one of mysticism and tantric sex. His followers called him 'Mahadev', another name for Shiva. It was perhaps his way of affirming that his religion too had power, was glamorous.

I wondered just how much of our postcolonial predicament might have something to do with this hero-worship, the rebranding of our old misogyny. The alt-right has gifted Mauritian men with that most elusive of dreams: a white mentor, and the possibility of white friendships. Meeting and becoming friends with other Franco-Mauritians and expatriates, in person and even online, is difficult for most non-white Mauritians, but all they need to 'meet' and converse with other white people around the world is to create an account, participate in the correct subculture, master the group's diction. An instant community is there to congratulate, welcome, nourish, endorse, add on Facebook, follow on X. And white supremacy isn't necessarily a barrier to this particular male bonding: Enrique Tarrio is a case in point. Tarrio, who is Afro-Cuban, was the chairman of the fascist Proud Boys organization from 2018–2021, and was involved in the attack on the United States Capitol on 6 January 2021. Despite his heritage, he used racist language against Black people on his social media accounts and participated in a white supremacist gathering in Charlottesville, VA. Tarrio was rewarded, effectively, for adopting views that cause severe harm to his own people; he was a symbol that the far-right could hold up: 'we're not racist! Look at who heads our organization!' but also, 'look, even the Afro-Cuban agrees with us!'. One could also argue that Tarrio was able to gain such high ground within a fascist organization because he fitted into their matrix of acceptability: he was a cis man 'of colour' who was performatively 'virile' and who pushed forward a whitewashed history of his ethnicity to gain acceptance (by claiming, for instance, that Latin Americans are 'displaced Spaniards').

I remember how quickly Trump enabled the rise to power of men like Peterson, Ben Shapiro, Joe Rogan, and later Andrew Tate. Remember the shock of seeing a man like Peterson and his 'Intellectual Dark Web' coterie profiled in the *New York Times*. These people appeared a lot less on my newsfeed once Joe Biden had taken power; they were ridiculed, in fact. Now, with another Trump presidency, I wonder who will be crowned as the next far-right celebrity, whose ideas and writings will travel around the world, and how they'll end up manifesting in Mauritius. How they'll end up hurting Mauritian women.

VI.

In Nathacha Appanah's *Blue Bay Palace*, poor, low-caste Maya falls in love with Dave, a Brahmin with sugar-estate wealth. Dave claims he loves her, uses her, endlessly talks about his feelings and himself. He doesn't tell her he is engaged; she finds out about the wedding in a newspaper announcement. Even then he uses her, spews on about how he hates all the other women in his life. Maya's story is poignant, but it is her cadaver of a mother who stays in my mind after the book is done:

My mother never talks to me in the morning. She obeys a rigid ritual: she makes tea, places my cup with the British flag – a gift from my aunt, who works as a nurse – with the handle on the right hand side of the table, places food – usually consisting of buttered toast – on the left hand side, and watches me in silence as I eat breakfast. She stays there, fiddling with her hair, and if I say something banal she nods her head and says hm, hm... As soon as I finish my tea, she hurries to clean up and, before I've even left the table, she carefully pads the crumbs up with a sponge. I get up and kiss her quickly because she's already washing up. She doesn't look at me. She says Okay and I never know if it's a question or an affirmation of something. She always speaks using the same hasty tone, it's difficult to know. She is like that, my mother, always in a hurry to make the minutes and the hours pass by as quickly as possible. She frets about, filling space and time with movement and noise.

Around me I see once youthful women reduced to filaments of their selves by their early thirties, exhausted by the effort it takes to live here.

The female friends I made during my school years are still mostly abroad. They don't want to come back if they can help it, even if they miss their families. Some are considering children and think a move back to Mauritius could make financial sense, given the costs of childcare abroad. But even more exorbitant, and intolerable, is the island's rapacious misogyny. We know of the many male star school alumni who have returned to Mauritius, and we are not stupid: the jobs they've been offered here are not something that we can aspire to, even though we're more qualified by a mile.

My friends ask me how I handle things, married with Antoine, mother to two children. I tell them that I am nourished by the island's beauty, its cultural richness, its history, the possibilities. But also that returning from university was difficult. I hardly have anyone I can talk to in person about literature, philosophy and cultural criticism, but my loneliness is staved off by books, my family, and now political commitment.

I tell them that the weight of misogyny can be staggering. I had just assumed that I'd be taken seriously when I spoke, as seriously as Antoine, and so what I am still getting used to – what I may never get used to – is that I am so readily dismissed on no other basis than my sex. It is still a surprise to people when I speak of politics, economics, current events: 'male' subjects of discussion. I am still told – sometimes gently, sometimes with disgust – that I am not 'in my place'. But I've made my place, inhabit it.

Many of my friends say they'd return if they had the capacity and power to change the country. An island in need of a deep, radical rinsing.

The star schools we attended have now been transformed into 'Academies', with both male and female students. But these rebranding exercises don't mask the fact that the quality of public education is worse than it was in my time, when it was already mediocre. The government overhauled the system in 2017 with a 'Nine-Year Continuous Basic Education programme' that, seven years on, has proven to be a disaster, with rocketing rates of exam failure. In the school year 2021–2, only 65.4 per cent of students passed the National Certificate of Education exams, which they need to pass before being able to take their O-level exams (the Mauritian equivalent of GCSEs).

The World Economic Forum's Gender Gap Report 2023 ranks Mauritius 98th out of 156 countries; we've been sliding in their ranking system ever since 2006. In terms of educational attainment we're placed 71st, and 100th in economic participation – which makes sense, since so many women leave the country. Mauritius is 97th in political empowerment. Unsurprising when the government congratulates itself on appointing five female Ministers (out of twenty-three). Unsurprising when men accused of sexual assault continue to occupy prestigious positions in the public sector. In this country, a man can be jailed for killing his second wife (then acquitted; does it matter that there are rumours he killed his first wife, too?) and continue to work as an advisor to the Prime Minister until his untimely death.

'There is no centrally consolidated data information system on domestic violence or Gender Based Violence to inform national policy,' writes the National Strategy and Action Plan of the High Level Committee on the Elimination of Gender Based Violence 2020–24. The Public Accounts Committee Report of March 2022 says that our Domestic Violence Information System 'is under-utilised and not updated. Several reported cases of

137

domestic violence were not recorded electronically but manual files were kept'. This, despite the overwhelming and continuous reports of domestic violence in Mauritius – over 8,600 cases in 2023. At least one Mauritian woman out of four suffers from gender-based violence.

In the absence of necessary statistics, a friend and I decided to set up an excel sheet documenting public cases of femicide, torture, and abuse of women of all ages. We couldn't keep up with the news stories, let alone police reports that aren't public knowledge.

Thirteen women were murdered in 2020, eleven in 2021. The eight women who were killed in 2022 – the eight women we know of – died at the hands of their husbands, partners, ex-partners, family members. In 2021, too, we learned about the so-called 'telegram leaks': screenshotted conversations revealed that over a thousand men were showing, selling and buying naked pictures of women and children – their partners, wives, exes, sisters, daughters, infants, sharing their contact and residential information.

My friends and I talk about the Minister for Gender Equality and Family Welfare, a woman who should have been able to make a difference. She studied abroad, holds a first-class degree in Biological Sciences, worked at the NHS and other 'global institutions'. She offered condolences on the murders, announced that the Domestic Violence Act would be amended 'soon'. It never was, under her tenure. She said a 'technical committee' would be set up to enquire about the telegram groups, that justice would be served, but no one has been arrested and few men have interrogated so far, despite overwhelming evidence provided in the screenshots (telephone numbers, names and surnames) and despite the fact that these groups still exist and are thriving in 2024.

What happened to her? we wonder. How did she fail so absolutely? Could this also happen to us?

We shake our heads. We say no, we wouldn't pay lip-service to the ethno-religious-patriarchy like that, the way she did. The Minister wasn't just formidably incompetent (an incompetence that harms, when one thinks of the women who counted on her to change legislation, when one thinks of the children abused in shelters under her care). She also led a massive harassment campaign against a female MP in the opposition, online violence that could have ended in bloodshed. We wouldn't betray ourselves, our convictions, our pasts.

But saying that we're the new generation changes nothing. Incredibly, around us, we began to see a small cohort of superbly educated Mauritian women flirting with the autocratic regime, attending State dinners, mingling with the Prime Minister's coterie in private cocktails.

2019; 2024

GETTING RID OF IT

As a schoolgirl I was told that abortion was illegal in Mauritius. No exceptions. And there was no reason for me to believe otherwise. At church I heard men pontificate about God's will, the sacred foetus, the mother's responsibility, the sin of murder. At secondary school in 2005 I heard women speak on the virtues of abstinence. If we were unable or unwilling to raise the baby ourselves, we should at least carry it to term, then give it up for adoption. So many parents wanted a baby so badly and couldn't conceive; if we had a baby through sin, this was a way to make things right.

No one mentioned abortion at home: my mother perhaps didn't believe she had any reason to do so. When I was six she bought me an illustrated book explaining where babies came from; when I was nine she taught me about contraception; when I was a teenager she prevented me from going out, confiscated my phone, checked my messages. She was afraid of adolescent Mauritian boys, coming into a consciousness of their power as men.

I knew nothing of the protests, the legal challenges to our colonial law, all the work that was being done by Muvman Liberasyon Fam (MLF), Mauritius' first women's rights organization to publicly stand in favour of abortion and which still remains at the forefront of abortion rights activism almost half a century later. I'd only vaguely heard of Lindsey Collen; whenever her name came up the phrase 'radical madwoman' usually followed.

It was the early 2000s and all I wanted was perfect grades, a scholarship, an exit from the island. Abroad, I hoped for kindness: the girls I knew who'd left for Europe spoke of freedom. They said no one cared about what they did, there was no surveillance; there were problems, yes, but most of the time people – at university, in the workplace – took them seriously, treated them with respect.

Kindness, care, respect. We had none of that at the Catholic school I attended. I called our despotic headmistress Folcoche, after Hervé Bazin's *Vipère au poing* (*Viper in the Fist*, 1948); Paule Rezeau, named Folcoche (folle-cochonne, or 'mad pig' in English) by her sons, is one of literature's cruellest mothers. Our Folcoche was so terrible that a group of older students planned to write a letter to the local newspapers, denouncing her sadism and the malice of some of the other teachers: the way they'd taunt, scream; the way they patrolled the gates in the early morning, ready to castigate teenage girls for talking to the boys at the school across the road, inform their parents of their bad behaviour. Parents would show up at school and publicly humiliate their daughters. *Putain. Salope. Vaux rien.* Girls beaten outside and inside their parents' cars.

One teacher seemed to have found a vocation in eviscerating her students. We were all afraid of being taught by her (and her teaching skills, like most of the staff's, were mediocre). She'd taught a Creole girl who'd taken her own life later that year. She was eleven years old; whispers were that the teacher had made this child's life intolerable. I thought she'd be merciless to my friend, Anaïs, who became pregnant at fourteen, but beyond glacial condescension she didn't say much: almost as if she expected Creole girls to end up this way. Besides, Anaïs was only following the Church's code of conduct.

Carrying the foetus to term was penance for her sin.

Anaïs drank 'ancestral remedies' of wine and spices but still the foetus grew. She'd heard of abortifacient pills but none of us knew their names or where to get them. She was terrified of her draconian parents, her violent father who clung on to the respectable middle-class position he held in society. She ended up telling them that she'd been raped by her boyfriend. They didn't know him, a sweet child who was slightly younger than us. They didn't press charges. He wasn't allowed to see the baby after he was born. I remember him crying outside the school gates, begging Anaïs to tell her parents the truth, to let him be a part of her life, her son's life.

That same year another one of my friends became pregnant. Her parents were awful, but she understood that she didn't have a choice, that attempting to get rid of it on her own wouldn't work. She went to her mother, who took her to some grotty, dark place. She didn't speak of the procedure, only that she saw the foetus dumped in a toilet afterwards. She was terrified. There was no one to comfort her.

•

The fight to decriminalize abortion in Mauritius started with Muvman Liberasyon Fam in 1976. There is an uncanny, intrinsic link between the growth of the local women's rights movement, the spread of the idea of self-governance and the birth of our nation: proof again that all bodies are political and move through politicized spaces.

Our independence was hard won. Some anti-independence politicians exacerbated conflicts caused by gangs in Port Louis, which resulted in racial riots spread over several months in 1968, leading to thousands of arrests and a hushed-up number of dead. The party that came into power in 1967 and took over the running of the country in 1968 – when we gained our Independence – established what was effectively an authoritarian state until 1976; only then were the next general elections held. In those nine years, the country witnessed multiple states of emergency, a secret police, censorship of the press, and also the creation of a new political party, the Mouvement Militant Mauricien, in 1969. Members and activists of this new socialist party were imprisoned, and a few were targeted in a series of assassination attempts. One activist was shot dead in 1971.

Even so, the country was rapidly becoming prosperous. An Export Processing Zone was set up and many women found themselves newly employed as factory workers, manufacturing products from textiles to food destined to be exported, duty-free, abroad. Their wages changed the balance of power in their homes seismically: this was still a time in which women were locked indoors by their husbands when they left for work in the morning; in which women needed special permission to leave their houses; in which it was common to be harassed and assaulted on the street. Now divorce didn't automatically mean destitution; now a woman could truly contemplate a life as a single, adult woman with an income of her own.

In February 1975, amid all the political turmoil and economic upheaval, Cyclone Gervaise – one of the most intense to have struck the island – devastated homes and infrastructure across the country. Three months later, about 20,000 students and teachers from state-owned and privately run schools marched peacefully from the centre of the island towards Port Louis, in one of the biggest protests the country has ever seen: it was the culmination of a mass nationwide student uprising, led by girls, that began in countryside high schools and then spread to towns and cities. They demanded free and equal education; they wanted schools to be allocated equal funding; they wanted Kreol introduced as a language of instruction and for the curriculum to be decolonized. As they reached Port Louis, riot police cracked down on them using tear gas and batons. A fraction of the protesters burnt buses, looted shops and the office of a politician. A hundred or so people were arrested. A year later, secondary education was declared free for all.

In the wake of the protest, thirty-two high school students (thirty girls and two boys) and teachers of the Bhujoharry College in Port Louis – including Lindsey Collen, Ragini Kistnasamy, Ashriya Somauroo, Dolly Antoine, Marie Bhagan, Danon Chelvenaigum, Mala Toussaint, Antoinette Baya and the late Salma Toorabally – set up an association of students and teachers called 'The Co-op School', an after-school-hours education co-operative. It was run as group work sessions; children would meet after school in the afternoons and on Saturdays. The children who attended the school came from all parts of the capital, which had been ripped by the violence of the racial riots that had happened less than a decade ago. The Co-op grew in size to about 150 students and was operational for around five years. Sessions were organized on any topic, depending on who'd volunteer to teach students: they had classes on everything from

Marxist economics to Einstein's Special and General Theory, Aristotle to maritime law. They didn't have a definite meeting area: sometimes they'd be at Father Henri Souchon's social centre, sometimes at the Municipality of Port Louis's small hall, places all around the capital.

The school led to the creation of key left-wing associations in Mauritius that still exist today, including Ledikasyon Pu Travayer, an association that teaches literacy to adults and which promotes Kreol and Bhojpuri; Muvman Liberasyon Fam, an association that aims for the complete and collective emancipation and liberation of women, and *Lalit de Klas*, an independent left-wing monthly magazine which grew to become the LALIT political party.

Muvman Liberasyon Fam was radical in its very name. 'Fam' was (and is still) considered a rude way of describing a woman in Mauritius; a 'fam', unlike a 'madam', is considered immoral, disreputable by conventional society's standards. The MLF reclaimed the word and the power it represented: these fam were at the helm of major protests and strikes in the 1970s and 1980s, including the general strike movement of 1979, the biggest in Mauritian history, led by sugar estate labourers, mill workers and dock workers.

'Women workers organized these huge, illegal protests, and they did so without fixed line telephones, which was all the more remarkable. And they were young women, around fifteen to nineteen years old. I was twenty-six at the time, the "granny",' Collen told me. I met her in early June 2022, at the LALIT office in Port Louis. From their office I could see part of the Grand River North West bridge, the point where riot police attacked protesting students forty-seven years ago.

Three weeks later, *Roe* v. *Wade* was overturned in the US. I hadn't set out to write a topical essay, just (hopefully) a necessary, long-overdue piece, one that I'd started researching years ago. There weren't that many people I could interview, beyond the women of the MLF. Collen herself has become an emblematic figure, indissociable from LALIT and the movements she belongs to. The fresh, intelligent newsletters she writes for LALIT are widely shared. Though I sometimes disagree with LALIT's methods, there is no questioning the party's deep commitment to socialism. They have consistently taken stances that mainstream political parties and organizations often shy away from, or won't proclaim outright, or will brandish many years later, once the issue has become somewhat palatable to the general (rather conservative, patriarchal) public. Examples include marriage law reforms; the introduction of Kreol and Bhojpuri in schools as languages of instruction; anti-imperialism and anti-militarism, in the fight against the British-American control of the Chagos archipelago; the reintroduction of village elections; social housing reparations. I could go on and on.

Collen is a warm, soft-spoken, unassuming woman. She's in her mid-seventies now and is still very much engaged in Mauritian social and political life, so much so that her own writing seems almost like an afterthought – though she is, indisputably, the greatest Mauritian writer working in the English language. She won the Commonwealth Writers' Prize for Africa twice. John Berger described her brilliant novel *Mutiny* (2001) as 'a break-out and a breakthrough. Magnificent'. *The Rape of Sita* (1993) is my favourite book of hers: it follows the story of Sita, a member of a local women's movement, as she comes to terms with her sexual assault. Collen weaves myths, folk tales, poetry and drama into Sita's reckoning with patriarchal power structures, colonial and postcolonial. The book was banned in Mauritius within days of publication, though it is doubtful that it had even been read by Mauritian censors. The title incensed Hindu fundamentalists. Supposedly speaking on behalf of the roughly 50 per cent of Mauritians of Hindu faith, they claimed that the book was an insult to the Hindu goddess Sita, a desacralization of sorts since the name of the goddess was juxtaposed with the word 'rape'. Collen had to go into hiding for a few days after publication: she was threatened by phone and through letters, messages wishing for her death and public rape. The Prime Minister at the time stated in parliament that 'a glance at the back page of the book suffices to indicate that this publication may constitute an outrage against public and religious morality' and urged police to 'take action'. He likened his decision to the local ban that was enforced on Salman Rushdie's *The Satanic Verses* in 1989. Even now, you can only find some of Collen's books in the National Library of Mauritius and the Institut Français de Maurice – they aren't sold in bookshops.

Collen told me the MLF held island-wide meetings a year after it was founded. Abortion was a topic from the very first. In another radical linguistic act, the MLF decided to call the procedure by its name. At the time, most women referred to abortion as 'getting rid of it', or 'fer li ale' in Kreol.

'We were nervous, but thought we really should speak up,' said Collen, remembering a meeting in rural Baitka, Belle Vue, in 1977. 'There were women of all ages there. We slowly tried to work our way to the topic. An elderly woman spoke up and said "yes, we all believe that hospitals must do this procedure. All women here agree, don't you worry."'

Women in their thousands supported the MLF, and as the movement grew in momentum it faced increasing hostility from the Catholic Church. The Church stood against abortion and contraception and advocated use of the temperature method – keeping a daily record of your bodily temperature for at least three to six months, so as to learn when you ovulate, a method considered risky for a number of reasons, not least being that there are many other catalysts for a rise in body temperature, including sickness, alcohol consumption, medication and travel – as 'birth control' instead. In 1982, a priest writing in *La Vie Catholique*, the Church's magazine, compared women seeking abortion to Nazis. Pressure from the Church may very well be one of the reasons why several draft bills legalizing abortion 'disappeared' from parliament.

In the decades that followed, the MLF contested the 1838 Criminal Code and its archaic, colonial diction. Though the French version of the law criminalizing abortion used the word 'enceinte' (pregnant), the English version used the term 'quick with child'. The English version, crucially, took precedence over the French. After consulting colonial-era legal tracts and papers that define 'quickening' or 'quick with child', including Bouvier's Law Dictionary (originally published in 1839), the MLF argued that the term, in medical jurisprudence, referred to the motion of the foetus in the womb – a 'quickening' that is felt around the twentieth week of pregnancy. This gave grounds to the argument that an abortion under 20 weeks of pregnancy should be legal, since no 'quickening' could be felt before then. The MLF, as part of the Common Front on Abortion, brought this to the attention of the Government and Director of Public Prosecutions in 2009. The phrase was central in the trial of Shabeela Kalla, who two years earlier had been charged with 'procuring her own miscarriage when quick with child' after having an illegal abortion when she was 8 weeks pregnant. No 'quickening' could be felt at that point; her lawyer contested her prosecution on the basis of the terminology, and won.

The movement towards decriminalization was picking up speed. The MLF had even found an effective counter to the Catholic Church's anti-abortion stance. In radio programmes and in the press, they'd question whether the Church truly intended to set the police on women and young girls who were already in a precarious position. Did they really want to see these women pulled out of their homes and put in prison?, they'd ask.

In 2009 Marie-Noelle Derby, a photographer for *L'Express*, died after a backstreet abortion gone wrong. In 2011 Sharonne Marla died on Christmas Day, after her backstreet abortion led to septicaemia; Marla feared imprisonment and didn't tell the hospital staff the exact cause of her illness. Their deaths made headlines, aroused public pity. The MLF, along with other organizations, delivered an open letter to the Minister of Justice calling on him to cease all arrests and prosecutions under the existing law. The MLF held candlelit ceremonies at their graves, accompanied by their families.

The Minister of Justice told members of the MLF that he'd prepared a Bill in view of amending the Criminal Code of 1838 with respect to abortion, though he couldn't give a schedule as to when it would be read in parliament. In early 2012, though, there was talk of a 'débat national' on abortion; public figures gave their opinion to the press, and members of parliament met religious leaders across the country. A sign that change was coming occurred when even the Bishop relented somewhat in May, stating that, though he was opposed to abortion, he understood women's distress and accepted the procedure only if the foetus was endangered.

When Parliament met to discuss the bill there were women in the galleries, protesting for their rights. Relatively few MPs stood against the bill and its amendments, which were passed in June.

At the time of writing, these amendments mean that we have more abortion rights here in Mauritius than a person does in Texas. They are still highly restrictive, however.

•

It was during my first pregnancy that I learned about the older methods of abortion. Women around me felt freer to speak about these matters. I was told that our grandmothers would eat an excessive amount of aubergine and wild pineapple; failing that, one could find an expert in these matters around the neighbourhood, who'd usually have a catheter in hand. One would go to these experts, addresses shared from mother to daughter. And if those abortions somehow failed, too, well – newborns died.

In Collen's 1997 novel *Getting Rid of It*, three Mauritian women band together to dispose of a miscarried foetus. They can't bury it, since the neighbours could be watching or a dog could dig up the grave. They can't toss it in the bin or in a river: someone may see and report them to the police, say that the foetus had been aborted. They carry the remains of the foetus in plastic bags around Port Louis, trying to find a solution that evades the patriarchal eye.

The means by which a person procures an illegal abortion are described in the span of a single conversation near the beginning of the book.

"You went to see Madam Naga? Why didn't you ask me to come with you on the day? What if you keeled over on the way back or something? Are you sure she's got it all out?"

"No. I tell you, it came down by itself. All by itself."

"You went to the chemist's and got Cytotec and took it?"

"I went to the chemist's but I didn't buy anything."

"You bought those *latizann bazar* with the wild pineapple and god knows what poisons all tied in a bundle and stewed them up, put them to draw and strained the brew and drank it?"

"No, no, no."

"You pawned god knows what and went to a doctor?"

"No. And don't you cross-question me either. I'm not a criminal, Gold. I'm just a woman. And I feel dizzy right now. Giddy woman."

Jumila was what you call "learning to talk". Talk as in talk back.

"Well, why are you acting like one then?" Meaning a criminal. "Poor thing, look at you. There's a left-over question, you slipped and fell like everyone else in the slip-and-fall ward?"

"No. I'm telling you, no. I'd tell you the truth. I didn't *do* anything. It came down by itself. I promise."

Collen writes of 'Madame Naga', the backstreet abortionist; Misoprostol, sold under the name Cytotec, a form of medication used to treat and prevent stomach ulcers which can also abort a foetus; herbal remedies sold in the bazaar for 'lateness of periods'; the 'doctor', the most expensive option of them all, and the 'slip and fall' hospital wards. Street talk suggests that women suffering from post-abortion complications are able to go to this ward and receive treatment, no questions asked.

The most recent statistics on abortion in Mauritius date from 2022. 1,130 women were treated for complications following abortion in 2020, compared to 1,850 women in 2011, the year before the amendments were passed. We don't have any information on the number of abortions that were legally performed in the years following 2012. From their work in the field, though, both the MLF and the Mauritius Family Planning and Welfare Association estimate that around 10,000 to 15,000 abortions are performed here every year. This would mean that the vast majority of abortions are still practiced illegally, despite the amendments.

Under the amendments, women are still punishable by law if they procure an abortion by themselves using medication or other devices. Power lies solely within the medical establishment: an abortion can only be carried out by a practiced gynaecologist in a prescribed institution, and only then upon conferring with a peer that one of four following conditions are met. Here are the conditions as written in the law:

1. The continued pregnancy will endanger the pregnant person's life;

2. The termination is necessary to prevent grave permanent injury to the physical or mental health of the pregnant person;

3. There is a substantial risk that the continued pregnancy will result in a severe malformation, or severe physical or mental abnormality, of the foetus which will affect its viability and compatibility with life; or

4. The pregnancy has not exceeded its fourteenth week and results from a case of rape, sexual intercourse with a female under the age of 16 or sexual intercourse with a specified person which has been reported to the police.

The amendments assume that Mauritians who need an abortion have the financial means and/or knowledge necessary to seek a gynaecologist and undertake the paperwork required by different ministries. Though public healthcare in Mauritius is free, patients face intolerable waiting times, racial and class discrimination and medical malpractice. Working-class women are sometimes turned away by public officers who claim they 'don't have time' for them. In September 2022, for instance, a Creole woman sued a hospital doctor who had 'forgotten' a swab inside her uterus after a caesarean section; he told her that her pain was due to 'panic attacks'.

The amendments do nothing for women who do not have the financial capacity to have another child. Subsection (d) is particularly vile, and ignores the fact that working-class women are often maligned when they go to the police (or any other government institution, for that matter), that police brutality and torture is widespread, that children who become pregnant don't necessarily come to their parents with this information within 14 weeks – and their parents, upon learning of the pregnancy and its circumstances, may not go to the police at all. I'm thinking here especially of children who are raped by members of their own family, who don't have the ability to go to the police and who would be unwilling to report their family to the police.

Clause 3, which follows the conditions, gives an extra incentive to women to avoid the police: if their testimony is found lacking – if, say, these women are up against men who are more powerful than they are, who are armed with lawyers – and they are charged with 'a false declaration of rape, sexual intercourse with a female under sixteen or sexual intercourse with a specified person to the police', they could be imprisoned for up to ten years.

It should be no surprise that most Mauritian women seek their salvation illegally – and are punished for it. Several newspaper articles detail 'investigations' that have occurred over the years, in which the 'investigated' parties are often poor. There's the story of Jessica, who was 'known to the police' for living in a situation of extreme domestic violence: her stepmother had stabbed her, her parents had protection orders against her. She tried to get rid of her foetus by swallowing abortifacients and inserting pills into her vagina. In January 2022, police arrested a woman who'd ingested about fifteen Cytotec pills to 'get rid of it'; she'd told the police she couldn't afford another child. She'd thrown the remains into a bin; someone must have seen her, for it was an 'anonymous call' that tipped the officers off. She already had three children and her husband was in prison.

Collen told me that these investigations are more of a form of harassment, and that actual convictions are very rare in the MLF's experience. I think of the number of times Collen was arrested for her work as an activist over the decades she's lived here; I think of the terror of the Mauritian police and prison system that she describes in her novel *Mutiny*. The protagonist Juna (who, incidentally, is pregnant) is locked up along with a young girl named Leila and an elderly woman from Chagos, Mama Gracienne. When news breaks of a mega-cyclone heading to Mauritius, Juna plots the inmates' mutiny and escape. Like many Mauritians, Juna has been imprisoned for 'allegation' – 'not for making one, oh no. An allegator, like me, is someone against whom an allegation has been made. It sometimes suffices for more than just the arrest and detention, and bleeds into judgement and sentence as well.' It is one of the most appalling aspects of the Mauritian judicial system.

It doesn't matter if women who are caught seeking an abortion are rarely imprisoned. The harassment and the threat of jail time are abhorrent enough.

Complete decriminalization of abortion in Mauritius feels epochs away. Growing global conservatism has found its way to our shores, which isn't a surprise, considering the number of supra-wealthy immigrants who

155

'fall in love' with our island and our lenient tax regime. The local anti-vaccine movement is very well-funded; a celebrity French conspiracy theorist, who is anti-vaccine and anti-abortion, has a house on the coast.

'There'll have to be a massive social movement in order for abortion to be decriminalized here, and the Catholic Church would need to stand back,' Collen said to me the last time we spoke. 'Growing conservatism, irrationality and conspiracy theories, as well as the over-turning of *Roe* v. *Wade* may worsen abortion rights across the world. And after Covid-19, people's ideas of what the state can and can't do to them has changed in ways that are not clear yet.'

I remembered a church service in 2012, before the amendments were passed. It was one of the last masses I'd ever attend. The priest ranted about the banalization of that sin, the murder of 'new life'. I was twenty years old. I took the sombre faces of the women around me seriously; now I wonder whether, like my mother, these were just masks of agreement that they removed in private.

I remembered, too, a very religious, middle-aged woman I know, who was surprised my husband was so involved in caring for me during my pregnancy. 'This is women's business. Men don't know anything. It's better that way.' She asked me if I was going to have a third baby; I said no, I'd been sick enough during my two pregnancies. 'Well!', she said, wagging her actual finger at me. 'You know the saying. "When God gives, you cannot refuse."'

Collen is right to say that we'd need a massive social

movement, and the first huge step forward would be for more women to be outspoken in public. Beyond Lindsey and LALIT, there are very few women who publicly advocate for abortion. And government schools and those run by the diocese – from what I've gathered so far – still won't teach students about abortion rights. They are shown diagrams of reproductive organs and are told how fertilization works; puberty is explained, as are sexually transmitted diseases; they are told about the importance of family, of meaningful relationships, of the sanctity of their bodies. These lessons are also mostly carried out in French. Kreol, the mother tongue, is apparently considered 'too vulgar' as a medium of instruction on sexuality.

With such 'education' in schools, it is no wonder that the general ignorance surrounding reproductive rights here is alarming. Nine out of ten Mauritian women don't know their rights, according to a study led by the Ministry of Health and the World Health Organization (WHO). The 350 women surveyed had been hospitalized for complications following an abortion, miscarriage or stillbirth. Other findings: 74 per cent of these women said abortion was morally wrong; only 14.9 per cent said that they were on contraception or some form of birth control; all women reported feeling psychological distress after the experience.

Perhaps literature could fill in some of the cognitive gaps in information. 'I wanted to very gently force people with ideas up in the air about when life begins, to come down to earth and realize what it means for all women, for the whole of society, when abortion is illegal,' Collen told me. 'As a whole, the novel is, again I only suppose this, a metaphor for women's lives, and human life, when all your long-term plans are continually challenged by short-term, often practical, matters that absolutely have to be seen to. What could be more urgent than a foetus in a plastic bag, for example?'

I'd like to know what would happen in Mauritius if we could once again have literature play a positive, central part of national conversations around political topics. When *Getting Rid of It* was published in 1997, four years after *The Rape of Sita*, it was warmly received – which gives me hope. 'People said they cried at the end, when reading it,' Collen recalled. 'Students who studied it at the University of Mauritius adored it. People loved the depiction of the women [who live in] Vallée Pitot. And young people of the intellectual elite, once they had read it, felt somewhat freed from their own blinkered lives and rosy lenses – if I can mix an eye metaphor.'

•

I wrote part of this essay under the thrall of hyperemesis gravidarum, during my second pregnancy, second battle with the condition. My bones protruded; my stomach was completely flat. I'd lost 10 kilos in three months, again. I vomited so much and so hard that I thought I'd heave an organ into the toilet, my lungs, my heart. And when I heaved my ribs felt tight as if gripped by tongs. I couldn't imagine going through this condition – repeatedly! – if this pregnancy wasn't fully and firmly my choice.

I am part of the 1 per cent and my wealth has bought me knowledge, offered to me for free. I have the contact details of the best gynaecologists in this country, a history of their practice, notable births. I know the doctors who have death on their hands, deaths that do not impede their reputation in public. The gynaecologist I chose for my second pregnancy is beloved by many. Unlike other practitioners his fees are reasonable. What really sets him apart, though, is his expertise.

I started bleeding at 16 weeks, diagnosed with a subchorionic haemorrhage. If I were to miscarry, the treatment I'd receive would be an abortion. As I bled I read about a woman who miscarried at 16 weeks in Malta, a country where abortion is illegal; she was denied proper care and had to be airlifted to Spain. Both our pregnancies were wanted, hoped for. The pain and fear I felt were depthless. There was no rest to be found in sleep, my dreams were filled with blood. I kept thinking as I read that if I were to suffer through that, miscarry and not receive basic healthcare immediately – it would be horror beyond diction.

My daughter was born at 39 weeks, in a clean blue operating room, designed to reassure mothers, designed to look cute, even – there was time for aesthetic considerations here. Before, during and after the operation, the team had informed me as to what was going on in my body; the quick flare-burn of the epidural in my back, the cutting, to prepare for tightness and discomfort as my baby was pushed through me and out. She was raised in the air, placed on my chest. She was tiny, much smaller than her brother, and she roared louder. Nursed harder. The doctors pronounced her perfect.

As I was stitched back up I thought about how this was the birth I deserved to have the first time round – the basic minimum. Informative, caring, in a clean environment.

How every Mauritian woman should expect childbirth in the same surroundings.

How every woman should be able to have a child that she wants.

2022; 2024

PANDEMIC IN NINE ACTS

I.

The waiter was nervous, jokey. 'Hey hey, my Thierry Henry,' he said to a child in a football shirt.

'I'm not a coach,' the child replied. 'And this is Mbappe's shirt.'

'Thierry Henry was a famous football player,' the waiter said, chagrined, almost to himself. He saw the colours of the French team, heard the boy's French accent, thought he could provide some camaraderie, Mauritian ease. The boy is a French expatriate; he couldn't be a tourist. Our borders hadn't reopened yet.

At dinner the previous night the waiter had implored us to please write a good review on Tripadvisor if we were satisfied with the service, and to please mention his name. 'It's really important for my CV,' he said, eyes frightened, unable to hide his feelings.

We were at a boutique hotel on 6 January 2021. I could see the hotel's small wine cellar from where I was writing all this down; the air conditioning was turned off and the bottles were dusty. Management didn't hope to sell them.

Wine shops around the island were barely able to function during the pandemic. They depended on hotels and restaurants, whose finances were about to crack. Prestigious chefs were made redundant; food budgets cut down to the absolute minimum. 'Clients don't order the same things anymore,' another waiter at a different restaurant told me. 'No more lobsters and giant shrimp.'

I read a news article that said hotel employees were

ready to sacrifice 80 per cent of their salary to change jobs and get the hell out of the hospitality industry. But it seemed like everything in Mauritius was connected to the hospitality industry. Food. Leisure. Insurance. Finance. Even copywriting. In 2020 I had lost all the contracts I had working for local and international hotels. My husband proposed to me in this hotel in 2014. It had few rooms and was decently priced despite its location: Tamarin bay, facing the slopes of La Tourelle and the vigorous, almost lilac-hued sea. Translucent pools dotted the property, framed by luxuriant flora. Now the main pool had been boarded up and the smaller ones had been filled with soil. Cost-cutting also meant there was no hot water in the room unless we rang reception; meant no one had paid pest control in months, and so we saw the occasional roach; meant that staff had been reduced by half and worked endless shifts. The hotel's personnel couldn't stop their anxiety from showing, even with their expert training and years of service, their masks of genial Mauritian warmth and care.

II.
March 2020. I thought there was a chance that Covid-19 would never susurrate in our air. We were more prepared than some of the world's richest countries. We'd been screening travellers for months. We'd sent back planes and scanned ships. Still, there were rumours of passengers ingesting paracetamol on the plane to lower their body temperature. Most of them must have known of our healthcare system's deficiencies, our limited ventilator machines, overcrowded hospitals, the fact that about a quarter of the population is diabetic.

Late at night on 18 March, the Prime Minister announced our first three cases. We'd self-isolate, as a country, from the rest of the world. Twenty-one billion Mauritian rupees were wiped from our stock market the next day; its plunging graph l'écriture du désastre, for we are tourism-dependent, import-dependent. Supermarkets and bazaars were awash with people stocking up as if we were about to face a cyclone, the only catastrophe we know how to prepare for. Tinned food was swept from the shelves, as were batteries. Newspapers published photos of trolleys filled with boxes of oil, flour, water. There's enough food for everybody, the authorities declared. Stop panic-buying. No one stopped. Essential medication was swiped from pharmacy shelves. Round-the-town queues for gas. Drugs were no longer the grand hustle on our streets; surgical masks were what everyone was after, sold at obscene prices. Hotel rooms turned into quarantine centres, housing Mauritians repatriated from abroad and anyone who had been in contact with Covid-positive patients. There was a mutiny in the Beau-Bassin prison. The deputy commissioner of police described the inmates as 'well-behaved children' the day before.

Still, in the first few days of lockdown, there were Mauritians who thought this was a prime time to go to the beach. Police ordered locals and tourists out of our lagoon. Even so, men congregated to drink on the cement floors outside neighbourhood labutik. From my apartment I'd sometimes hear men on bicycles whistle down the street, as loudly as their mouths would allow. I wondered then if part of the problem was linguistic, the way we use 'la grippe' to mean common cold and not flu. *J'ai une petite grippe.* But that complacency dissipated fast enough.

Our first Patient Zero, a superspreader, was a Mauritian man who'd immigrated to England. He returned shortly after the death of his brother; once home, he participated in pujas, visited his friends and neighbours. At the onset of his symptoms he visited Dr Bruno Cheong, a tireless, eminent physician who had devoted his life to improving healthcare on the island. Patient Zero lied when asked if he'd recently returned from abroad. He died on 22 March. Dr Bruno Cheong was the first frontliner to die of Covid-19 a month later, on 27 April. The public hospital in Flacq was renamed Dr Bruno Cheong Hospital in his honour. Though the press had withheld the identity of the patient, it took no time for WhatsApp groups to circulate his picture and address.

Schools and workplaces were closed. Educational classes for children were broadcast on national television, replete with mistakes. Unlike other countries we weren't permitted to leave the house, not even for an hour's jog. Online delivery services, slow and haphazard at best pre-pandemic – think a two-hour wait for a soggy, rain-spattered McDonalds meal – became serious business. Supermarkets and grocers began to offer online food and vegetable packs, one per household while stocks lasted, in order to streamline supply. They'd include the fundamentals of Mauritian pantries – lentils, dried milk, canned vegetables, rice, the prices of which had soared since they were all imported. I remember hoping for potatoes and onions, so scarce and overpriced that the government had to subsidize their cost; we received one or two battered varieties complete with wilted herbs, still edible, in the first and only vegetable basket I ordered. By the beginning of April, the government allowed us to go to the supermarket on specific days allotted to us through an alphabetized system. The government and non-profit organizations also distributed food packs to people in need, but it wasn't enough. People stole, robbing supermarkets and fields of produce.

There are around 100,000 stray dogs in Mauritius. A considerable number of them are fed by Mauritians, who supply them with scraps, 'ration rice', and – if they are lucky – with pellets. During lockdown barely any strays were able to be fed. NGOs operated on limited amounts of staff, and weren't able to travel outside of their premises. But at least they took care of the animals already under their charge; the government-run Mauritius Society of Animal Welfare didn't feed or water the hundreds of dogs in their care during the initial two-week lockdown. Their bodies were incinerated with great haste, but not before videos emerged.

And while our strays died en masse, our macaques were captured and exported with exceptional swiftness. They were flown to laboratories in the United States for vaccine development.

III.

Internationally, our lockdowns and protocols were described as draconian but effective. I didn't leave my apartment from March to June 2020, and March to May 2021.

Like people across the world we shared pictures of meals we'd prepared, the bread we'd baked. We dealt with conspiracist neighbours. 'I have information!' said S., who lived in the same apartment block as me. He refused hand sanitizer and defied curfew, bringing his toddlers along on his sorties, his apologetic wife trailing behind him. S. is Franco-Mauritian. I didn't know then the speed and scale at which the white community was engulfed in conspiracy theories imported from France and America, until I'd find myself at the centre of disinformation, until it struck home.

So much depended on other people's actions and choices, so much depended on trust.

It was already difficult, in the years before my son was born in 2020, to accept that so much lay beyond my control. After he was born I barely slept, frenzied and taut, my hand over his chest every other minute to make sure he was breathing. He was three months old at the onset of the first lockdown, unable to see his paediatrician, unable to get his vaccinations on time. Like many new mothers I grappled with the mundane acts of motherhood. I clutched him and walked around the apartment for hours, warding off images of his body stuck to tubes or of my parents dying alone, cremated quickly and with no ceremony.

So much depended on trusting the government.

I never missed their daily updates televised in the evenings, their Crisis Committee's rigorous graphs and statistics. Many people tuned in for the straight talk of Dr Vasantro Gujadhur, who appeared during the updates. His no-nonsense style, his branding of those who defied curfews as kokovid ('empty heads') turned him into a beloved gif. He was Director of Public Health Services in the Ministry of Health for Mauritius for years until

2021, when he suddenly disappeared from the Crisis Committee's briefings. Rumour has it that he had become too popular.

IV.

The Quarantine Act, passed in haste in May 2020, enabled police to enter homes and make arrests without a warrant. People were arrested – even during lockdown – for sharing memes mocking the Prime Minister and for propagating fake news.

Our policemen, who were emboldened enough to begin with, became social media stars during the early days of Covid, übermensch posting photos of themselves leaving their wives and children to protect the nation. They filmed themselves arresting those who broke curfew, spectacle-as-punishment complete with explosive language. In one of the videos, policemen tail an exhausted man who tried to outrun them. 'Stop, we're not going to hurt you!' they jeer. Red-blue lights hit the man's stricken face. The policemen leave their cars and run up to him. The screen darkens. You hear a body being pummelled. 'Didn't I tell you to stop?' The policeman screams. 'And you still ran? Piece of shit. Get up!'

And though people laughed at the videos of irate policemen screaming at citizens to get back inside their homes, the videos of physical abuse perpetrated by officers that quickly followed were met with outrage. The most widely spread of them all was the torture of Billy and Ricardo Samrandine, in Résidence Vallijee. Police forcefully and violently entered their homes on 23 May 2020, alleging that the Samrandines weren't respecting curfew; the men were spending time with their families, including their mother and their children. The policemen assaulted Billy and Ricardo's mother and sister; upset, the Samrandine brothers responded by damaging the police vehicle. Early the next day, policemen returned and used tear gas and batons to pummel the men; they also hit Billy's daughter, Pascaline (who was eight months pregnant at the time), another brother who suffers from epilepsy and Billy's sister-in-law who was unwell. Policemen filmed the supposed 'crackdown' in the working-class neighbourhood; they took the men to the police headquarters, where they filmed other policemen torturing the brothers with tasers and iron bars.

A day later, on the other side of the world, George Floyd was murdered by police officer Derek Chauvin in Minneapolis. Though local newspapers covered the international protests there weren't any articles decrying racism here. In fact, we had an abundance of our own stories of police brutality towards Creole men, though I don't remember any journalists explicitly stating that the cases were linked to rabid anti-Black racism in the Mauritian police force. From March to May 2020, Joselito Evenord, Michael Louise, Jean Alain Auguste, Cael Permes, Jean Maurice David Utcheegadoo and David Gaiqui were found dead. Five of the six men died in police custody.

David Gaiqui's death, in particular, caused a stir on the island, with open talk of retaliation, murder, and cover-up. In January 2018 Gaiqui was arrested for a series of petty thefts in a petrol station; a photo of him naked and chained to a chair in the Curepipe police station incensed the general public. He tried to sue the state, spoke of police brutality and became rather famous. In early May 2020, he received photos of the horrific torture of Cael Permes, a twenty-nine-year-old inmate of La Bastille, the country's high-security prison. Permes died from haemorrhagic shock. Gaiqui sent the photos to his lawyer, who shared them on social media. Later in May, Gaiqui drove to hospital and died there. The autopsy report claimed he'd died from heart failure.

V.

Lockdown officially ended on 1 June 2020. On that day, the government razed the homes of people in Riambel, claiming that they were occupying the land illegally: 'squatters', the state called these people, many of whom were Creole. They'd bulldozed the homes of 'squatters' in Pointe aux Sables two days earlier on 28 May. One woman who had her home destroyed had worked at the home of a minister's mother for years.

In July 2020, Affirmative Action – a Civil Rights Movement that campaigns for the elimination of racial discrimination in Mauritius – organized a gathering called *Mo Anvi Respire* ('I Want to Breathe'). Creole celebrities – athletes, musicians – as well as priests and social activists spoke and sang about racism in the country; the glaring lack of Creole employees in the public sector; the fact that athletes have to provide a 'morality certificate' to get their sports pension; the need for Mauritians to stop saying *ti manze, ti lakaz, ti loto, ti Kreol* (little food, little house, little car, little Creole). The gathering was generous, radical, overshadowed in the days that followed by the crash of a bulk carrier on Pointe d'Esny's reef.

VI.

In July we'd also learn of the fifty ventilators that the government had ordered from the Spanish company Pack & Blister, a contract worth MUR 77.9 million allocated without a bidding process under the Emergency Procurement clause of the Public Procurement Act. The ventilators arrived nine months later, unusable: they weren't the models originally ordered. The government is still waiting to be reimbursed.

In the months that followed we'd hear of 'emergency contracts' for medical equipment and products awarded to many small, unknown companies, who'd previously operated in advertising, hardware, transport, hospitality, import-export. Licences granted a few months before contracts were signed. Bombastic figures, haphazard dealings, all the way through the pandemic. A contract for 800,000 doses of Molnupiravir worth MUR 7,446,000 was signed on 6 December 2021; the next day, another company was awarded a contract for an additional 999,000 doses of Molnupiravir for MUR 79,842,080. And these are by no means the highest figures, the plateau of corruption. In time, too, we'd hear of how some of these small company directors were embroiled in the murder of a political agent.

On the radio and in our homes, we'd hear the constant refrain: *zot pe fer kas lor dimunn malad. Zot pe fer kas lor kadav.* They're making money over the bodies of the sick and the dead.

VII.

In March and April 2021, eighty-six patients undergoing

dialysis treatment at the Souillac Hospital caught Covid-19, though the hospital had no Covid-19 ward and the patients were being taken care of in a separate health centre.

They were taken to a quarantine centre very late at night. Once there, they were served meals that were inadequate for their health; their medical records disappeared; they were forced to clean up after themselves even as they were ailing; with the exception of three patients, they were all left completely alone. Families weren't allowed to see them. Eleven of these patients died. The circumstances surrounding their contamination, treatment and deaths will remain a government secret: authorities have refused to publish the investigative report, though journalists managed to get their hands on its conclusions, which stated that there were 'serious failures and omissions' in the way the dialysis patients were treated. The Report found four alleged cases of medical negligence and mistreatment.

Still, we were hailed as one of Africa's success stories. To this day about 80 per cent of our population is fully vaccinated, the second highest percentage of Covid-19 vaccination coverage on the continent. There was a wealth of technology and facilities engineered to make vaccination as seamless and prolific as possible, even if most of the vaccines we received seemed to be of a lesser quality than the ones distributed in Europe and America. The government's inventive lockdown measures in 2021 proved effective: instead of nation-wide lockdown periods, authorities quarantined specific neighbourhoods that recorded high levels of Covid-19.

Despite the dialysis deaths, despite the corruption and procurement scandals, despite the massive protest in Port Louis, the government seemed pleased with itself. It decided to re-open our borders in late 2021. We would welcome tourists with a new, imperative slogan: Mauritius Now. And because tourists wouldn't come if they weren't assured that the island was safe, our published statistics went awry.

VIII.

I caught Covid-19 on 15 October 2021. It was probably the Delta variant, though I will never know for sure. Authorities expected those who tested positive from lateral flow tests to get tested 'officially' at a centre; I could barely move my battered body from my home, my husband and my son were ill, and I was somehow expected to queue up for hours, form part of a crowd where social distancing and mask-wearing were no longer a priority. I tried calling the government hotline but no one picked up. The number of new infections recorded for that day, on the government website, was forty-one.

I learned two weeks later that official figures only count positive results from PCR tests and not – contrary to recommendations – rapid antigen tests. When the health minister was questioned in parliament on 7 November, he revealed that there had been 13,698 positive results from rapid antigen tests from 25 October to 7 November; a figure nearly ten times higher than the official number for the same period.

In November 2021 Mauritians were turned away from hospitals. Patients were placed on makeshift beds

172

out in the sun. Patients weren't changed or bathed, and hospital staff wouldn't give families accurate accounts of their conditions. Medical staff suffered from burnout. Covid-19 drugs were reportedly no longer available, along with many other medicines. Private clinics opened their wards but soon ran out of beds. Even in this moment of absolute crisis, the government still managed to award a controversial steel company with a contract for the supply of medical oxygen.

We still don't know how many people caught and died from Covid-19 in Mauritius. In November, at the pandemic's peak, journalists went through death announcements published by funeral homes and centres; they investigated the midnight-hour queues at crematoriums, reported the incessant traffic in graveyards. A news article estimated that about a thousand Mauritians died of the virus from September to November 2021.

IX.
The boutique hotel has been sold. Most other hospitality establishments have survived, thanks to the government's financial aid. I assume that the local conglomerates who own some of the hotels here had robust reserves, too; I think they could have done without state aid entirely in fact. Money that could have directly helped alleviate the cost-of-living crisis.

November 2022. A cascade of tourists in Arrivals, undeterred by inflation, the cost of air travel. Rumour has it that it'd be cheaper flying over here and staying for a few weeks than paying for heating in Europe during the winter.

Hotels are actively recruiting now. A spate of hotel directors and hospitality professionals are interviewed; they are dismayed by Mauritian youth who won't work at pre-pandemic rates, who choose emigration instead.

For the first time I see immigrant, contract-based workers from across the African continent in our hotels, catering to the 997,290 tourists we've welcomed this year. Nervously, quietly, the Mauritian employees still ask guests for good recommendations on Tripadvisor. Even after twenty-five, fifty years of service.

2020–2021

DEATH TAKES THE LAGOON

Grainy pictures flash on our phones on the night of 25 July 2020. A ship's crashed on the reef in Pointe d'Esny, the messages read. I pinch and splay the photos with my fingers. I can make out the ship's frame, yellow glimmers of light, but not much else.

We set out to see the ship for ourselves the next day. There's only one coastal road in Pointe d'Esny and it is clogged. People from around the island have driven to see the ship. They've parked their cars at random – there are no proper parking spaces here.

'This is what happens when you try to block public access to the beach,' I tell my husband Antoine. Pointe d'Esny is infamously exclusive. The superbly wealthy inhabitants of this stretch of coast would like the beach to be as private as possible. To get to the public beach you must cross the road and walk through a narrow path set between two grand houses, described only last year by a newspaper as a 'corridor of shame'. Once there you deal with the infuriated faces of some of the residents, who make a point of walking up and down the shore. Some of my friends have been harassed by bungalow owners and their dogs, screamed away. But no screams can turn this crowd away, nor the weather – battering winds and rain can't stop us from congregating on the beach to watch the wreck.

I thought it'd be smaller. A medium-sized vessel, not a cargo ship. I am stunned by the MV *Wakashio*'s immensity: longer than the Titanic, almost as long as the Eiffel Tower. Kitesurfers glide across the lagoon, colourful little specks against the hulking metal. My son, who has just turned seven months old, flaps his arms in the wind in delight.

None of us are sure what a cargo ship was doing so close to our shores. Hundreds of thousands of ships pass by Mauritius every year: we're a dot along a strategic, bustling shipping route.

'We have the expertise to deal with this, don't we?' I say, staring at the vessel. 'Contingency plans. Help from the United Nations or whatever. It'd be impossible not to have a plan, right?' I remember the grounding of the MV *Benita* four years ago. The vessel had crashed into a reef a few kilometres south from here, after a possible mutiny onboard. The oil was pumped out, the ship salvaged from the lagoon.

'Yeah,' Antoine answers. 'Some of the residents told me they saw officials going over to the ship in helicopters and boats, rescuing the crew, examining the hull for damage. Lights flashing all night long.'

We wait for an announcement from the government, an action plan, but the days pass by in a kind of stupor. The government had been so swift in tackling the pandemic; like the pandemic, the crash of the *Wakashio* wasn't inconceivable. There were precedents. We were prepared. Surely we were prepared.

But several high-profile corruption cases had blasted the island in July. Public trust in the government was smashed.

We aren't sure what kinds of corruption one could profit from during the grounding of a ship. We hear talk of insurance claims and foreign responsibility. But there's so much more money to be had in expediting that ship out of our waters, in preserving our coasts. We have our superlative reputation to protect, after all: some of the world's clearest lagoons, most pristine ecosystems, healthiest fish. Tourism is the heart of the economy. The majority of the island's most opulent hotels are found on the east coast. Plus, the government is heavily invested in the fishing industry. Our fish exports are a 250-million-dollar business, and parastatal fish farms dot the south-eastern lagoon. We are confident that the *Wakashio* will be removed from the reef imminently: it's in the government's self-interest. We hear talk of international assistance and are reassured.

Meanwhile, images circulate on WhatsApp and social media showing filaments of an oily substance on the shore. Then images appear showing the ship beginning to tilt. The Minister of Fisheries says the photos 'appear to be manipulated and deceptive.' 'The ship is not sinking and will not sink,' he says on 5 August 2020. All is under control.

The next day thick black streaks coat our lagoon. Oil like lacquer on the water.

•

Pointe d'Esny: a bay framed by mountains, a lagoon iridescent with shades of blue and violet, water translucent when it is still. Grapefruit-hued sunrises and plump, long beaches.

Before the oil spill, I thought that the greatest risk to our coasts was climate change.

I spent my childhood swimming in Blue Bay, the marine park that lies next to Pointe d'Esny. Twenty years ago, fish accompanied every movement you made underwater. Angelfish, butterfly fish, sleek pavillon cocher burst from coral so richly chromatic that I'd have doubted my memory of the sight, had it not been confirmed by everyone else who'd swum in Blue Bay at the time. The fish overwhelmed my vision, a fin away from my goggles, whorls around my body.

The last time I went swimming in Pointe d'Esny was February 2019, a month before I became pregnant. At the time, my main concern in the waters was encroaching jellyfish, which had smothered every other coastline around the island. Pointe d'Esny was clear.

Antoine and I snorkelled across the lagoon, prodded each other underwater when we spotted signs of health: red- and blue-tipped corals, sunflower-yellow anemones, pink planes of *Acropora cytherea*. We detected an unusual starfish, deep purple and tentacular, the largest I'd ever seen, echinate, with spikes like a sea urchin.

Later I found out that the starfish's name was crown-of-thorns, and that they were erupting in number across the lagoon. They eat hard coral; just one is able to devour ten square metres of coral a year. The creatures were of great concern when I visited Reef Conservation Mauritius later that month. They told me that the reef was sick, spoke of the necessity of a coral bleaching alert system, the necessity of planting the right coastal vegetation, mangroves, seagrass systems, rehabilitating reefs, zoning lagoons.

Reef Conservation have an educational touring bus called Bis Lamer. It teaches the public at large about our coastal and marine environments, climate change, conservation efforts. I wish the initiative had existed when I was a child. If I had attended one of the talks, maybe I would have spared the starfish I killed when I was six years old or so. My parents had rented a bungalow in Pointe d'Esny for a week. In the mornings I'd walk along the shore, throwing starfish back into the bay. One morning I thought of keeping one of the starfish for myself. I thought that if it left the ocean it'd turn into clay, just like the starfish I'd seen sold in shops. I hadn't understood that it would die. I brought it back onto the veranda, let it dry on a slice of basalt rock. By noon it had started to rot. 'That's death,' my mother told me, throwing the starfish in the bin. 'That's the smell of death. Never do that again.'

Now death smells of tar and acid. It burns eyes, throats, it makes us sick, makes us faint. Not even the crown-of-thorns could have survived its onslaught.

.

'We should have gone swimming around Pointe d'Esny more often,' I tell Antoine as the news of the spill comes in. 'We should have gone every weekend. We should have taken more pictures.' As I speak I realize that I am already memorializing the place, as if the sea were dead. Can a sea die?

No one sleeps on the night of the spill. We examine

aerial photos of the pitiful rubber booms provided by government officials. They look like a crude silhouette of a bird in flight, the kind taught to children at school – two downward curves that meet at a V, containing almost nothing of the oil. Flecks of rubber in the sea that didn't even surround the ship, that weren't even correctly positioned. We are incensed. Enraged kitesurfers and grieving fishermen describe how authorities hadn't taken their knowledge of the sea's currents into consideration when placing the booms. 'They wouldn't listen to us,' these men repeat.

A citizen-led action plan is developed and implemented before dawn. A Marxist political party and activist group sets up a base on the Mahebourg waterfront. Sometime after midnight they successfully absorb oil using a natural boom prototype they make out of nets and dried sugarcane leaves. By morning hundreds of volunteers have come to Mahebourg to help. Word spreads, and in the hours that follow boom-making stations are set up across the island. Some are helmed by private enterprises, others by students; some stations are in sugarcane factories, others right by the sea. Some experiment with different boom fillings: hair seems to work just as well as cane, inspiring Mauritians throughout the country to chop and shave for the cause.

Thousands of Mauritians stuff and knit booms over the two weeks that follow, some working all night long. We are an emblem of national unity around the world. But even this disaster won't stave off racism, the ease with which an 'operational structure' is established on the sugar estates that host boom-making activities. Franco-Mauritians ignore other volunteers of colour;

180

Franco-Mauritians work easier jobs in the shade, while non-white Mauritians are instructed to lift the booms in the sun.

But my friends shrug it off, the work now is urgent. Emcees motivate, musicians come to play for free. Some people set up makeshift food stalls, feeding the volunteers. Doctors treat those who've come into contact with the oil. Those with the necessary expertise don protective equipment and submerge their bodies in the sea, cleaning oil from the water, pouring it into large plastic buckets. A photo of Thierry Jollivet makes the rounds: the professional diver's face is matted in oil but the area around his eyes is clean. He gazes straight at the camera, his look not one of despair but of can-do courage.

Another image goes viral: a meme, a dog taking itself out for a walk, its leash in its mouth. It encapsulates the spirit of the moment. We'll have to lead ourselves, I see written time and time again on social media. The government won't help. It's up to us. Memes are never innocuous in Mauritius. If you send or post a message on the internet that the government deems an 'annoyance', you can be imprisoned for up to ten years. There's an extensive track record of citizens being arrested for 'annoyances'.

The Prime Minister hasn't shown his face in Mahebourg since the spill. There's hardly been a word from the government. It's unclear what they are doing to help. They issued a communiqué three days after the spill banning citizens from gathering in 'restricted' areas affected by oil, effectively making the citizen clean-up operations illegal.

We're breaking the law just by making booms on the coast. We grow more courageous as we knit, type, talk to each other. We feel bolstered by the international press who cover the disaster closely. They're not going to arrest us with the world watching, we think. We gather as much information as we can, we speculate. We're not told how much oil has leaked from the ship, though it's estimated at around a thousand tonnes. We wonder why the government took no action when the ship crashed onto the reef. Why no oil fingerprinting or other tests had been carried out. We wonder if the ship was carrying something suspicious. Officials say bad weather stopped them from pumping the oil out. The meteorological report says the weather was mostly fine. There are reports that the *Wakashio* could have been tugged out of the reef on the day of the crash. Anonymous sources at the port say that the disaster was the result of 'total negligence'.

We still won't have any answers three months later. But we don't know that yet. We're in the moment. We knit furiously. We're told that the ship could break apart at any moment. A news station helicopters over to the wreck and films a short video, where we hear the sharp, eerie sound of the hull slowly ripping apart.

It took the worst ecological disaster in our history to bring us all together like this, all ethnicities, all social classes side by side, knitting, cleaning. I say 'us', I write 'we', but I can't participate. It's unsafe to bring young children near the site of the spill, or to the boom-making stations. I hardly sleep, restless. I too want to help with my hands.

I start a Twitter thread, outlining essential information.

182

I read all the newspapers, the interviews with fishermen and those on the scene, translate and describe each day's events, sometimes hour by hour. I feel productive. 'She thinks she's some kind of reporter,' laugh my parents, as I go through the newspapers and radio programmes during Sunday lunch. But then I do become a reporter, for NBC. There is no time for pride. I feel desolate, stressed, mostly numb. I am interviewed on my work for the BBC, see myself on television: a thick mess of hair, big teeth, bad lighting. I hear myself on radio, a high-pitched voice like a child. No pride, just a matter-of-fact, steady, grinding conviction that everything that happens here must be reported.

My chest tightens when I speak to fishermen, wildlife directors, oceanographers who don't hide their devastation on the phone. The whole region affected by the spill is a sanctuary for our wildlife: Pointe d'Esny's wetlands are a Ramsar site, as is the Blue Bay Marine Park. Just off the coast of Pointe d'Esny is Île aux Aigrettes, an islet that's home to endemic species of birds, reptiles and plants. The oil coils around the islet like a noose. The Mauritius Wildlife Foundation races to save as many species of animals and plants as it can, but Vikash Tatayah, the foundation's director, says Île aux Aigrettes could very well die since it is made of coral, and coral drinks oil.

Tides carry the oil away from the rich beachfront homes of Pointe d'Esny and into Mahebourg. Black waves bring animals to the town's shore. Sticky corpses float on the oil-slicked surface.

•

Mahebourg: the ancient capital; traditional, relatively untouched by frenetic development. It's still the place where people sit on their flowerpot-adorned balconies drinking tea, watching and commenting on passers-by. The only place where you can eat noodles with local scallops. Its family-run restaurants are lauded in international magazines. The government had a grand, tourist-friendly refurbishment plan for the town before Covid-19.

On the waterfront crowds gather around the Rezistans ek Alternativ base. It's described as a 'people's factory', a 'mobilization zone': people come to make booms, but also create art and discuss the region's future. The base is adorned with posters expressing grief and anger at the government's inaction, hope for a people's revolution.

Residents of the town are anxious. Children can't go to school because of the smell. Oil laps the shore around Cité La Chaux, a poorer part of Mahebourg. Residents fall ill but the government doesn't evacuate the area.

Fishermen and boaters don't know how they'll survive. They gather at the waterfront base to talk about their future. Their income was already precarious before the spill. Fishermen from other parts of the coast come to join them: the oil has travelled up the east coast, coating mangroves, beaches, animals, their children's feet.

Everyone on the waterfront has an eye on the helicopters and boats circling the wreck. The ship is hanging by a sliver of metal. There's some hope that all the oil will be pumped out before it breaks in two.

.

News of the spill is covered not just by international media, but in unexpected places like *Vogue*. People from across the world donate millions, and I am relieved that the money is going to trusted, non-governmental organizations such as Eco-Sud. There are also less inspiring reactions: Lana del Rey posts a filtered, cryptic picture of the spill with no caption. Disaster aesthetics. Her fans wonder if this is the cover art for her next single.

'You've probably been put on some sort of list, so be careful,' my parents say after I appear on the BBC. I am interviewed along with other Mauritians. The BBC also shows footage of the leader of the opposition criticizing the Prime Minister in parliament. After our appearances, the Prime Minister is interviewed live by Samantha Simmonds.

'Critics and many local people are saying that the government hasn't done enough,' Simmonds says. 'They say there's a huge amount of inaction by the government, and that you owe them an apology.' She evokes the 2.3 million square kilometres of maritime space belonging to Mauritius, the necessity of an action plan. The Prime Minister appears flustered, starts talking about his government's exemplary handling of the Covid-19 pandemic, and then his connection is cut off.

In the afternoon the Prime Minister holds a press conference. He prevents two openly dissenting news stations from attending. He is asked questions about his BBC appearance, the apology owed to us. '*Ou kapav dir mwa kot monn fote?*' he asks. Can you tell me what I did wrong? 'Is the BBC a court of investigation?' he says disdainfully. 'And who are the people talking on the BBC?' He mentions members of opposing political groups, activists. 'And then there are other so-called "experts" who say we didn't do this and that. Kitesurfers have become experts now.'

On 13 August, the day after his interview, police officers prevent the leader of the opposition from holding a press conference in his office in parliament. On the coast, a volunteer is pressured by government agents to remove a sign saying, 'I love my country, I'm ashamed of my government.' The slogan goes viral. At night, the BBC interviews the former prime minister and leader of the Labour Party. After a few seconds I'm unable to watch the channel. It has been replaced by a Chinese news station. By the time connection to the BBC is re-established, the interview is out of the news cycle.

I lock the door to my home when I'm inside. I wait for the police to show up, declare that I've been charged with an annoyance, hurting my country's reputation. I sleep even less. I leave my British passport on Antoine's bedside table, along with a list of journalists and lawyers to contact if ever I'm arrested. I keep a box of formula in the pantry, so that if I'm taken away at least there's milk for our son.

On 15 August the ship breaks in two. The crowd on the waterfront isn't watching the wreck, though: policemen have descended upon the Rezistans ek Alternative base to disband their operations. They only back off when the radio starts to report their harassment.

Later in the week, an informal protest is held in front of the Mahebourg court. The Minister of Environment and the Minister of Fisheries are due to appear; an activist has lodged a case against them. The crowd, mostly comprised of Mahebourgeois, make their grievances known to the MPs as they walk by. That night, two protesters are arrested by the police without a warrant and are jailed.

.

Port Louis: our capital city. Palm trees and statues, crumbling shops and street art, tin roofs and food stalls, colonial buildings advertising the latest tech, fashion, creative venture.

On 29 August around 75,000 of us fill the city's streets. It's one of the largest protests in Mauritian history. It's citizen-led, with activists and non-parliamentary opposition parties at the helm.

We're of all ethnicities and all ages. Some march with walking sticks. Others are carried on their parents' shoulders. Mauritians abroad watch the protest online and gather in capitals around the world in solidarity. We sing Bob Marley's 'Redemption Song' and the national anthem. We wave the Mauritian flag.

There is a sign that many people carry. The Prime Minister's infamous declaration: *dir mwa kot monn fote.* Tell me where I went wrong. Protesters have turned the statement into bloody stencils.

Against all international recommendations, despite our outcry and outrage, the government sink half of the *Wakashio* in great haste on 24 August. Two days later, melon-headed whales wash up around the south-eastern coast. Dead, mutilated, glossy bodies. Authorities haul them onto the back of pickup trucks, tails hanging out, and cover them in white sheets. Videos of dying whales bobbing helpless in the ocean. A video of a mother whale trying to nudge her dying baby above the waves so that it can breathe; she watches as it dies, then dies a little while later, too. Fishermen say the ship was sunk in a whale breeding ground, that some of the corpses they found were of pregnant females.

The images choke us. We shake, we cry. We carry dolphin plush toys, plastic blow-up dolphins, dolphin art to the march. Authorities say neither the spill nor the scuttling had anything to do with the fifty-one deaths. We chant *bour li dehor*. Get them the fuck out of here. Get the government the fuck out of here.

The Prime Minister says the march showed that 'democracy was alive and working', but the government's Facebook page mocks protesters in a series of memes. On the night before the second major protest on 12 September, social media accounts of activist groups and journalists are hacked. Attempts are made to arrest a prominent activist.

·

Before the spill I thought my son's first proper meal would be fish and rice; our fish, once considered some of the finest in the world. Now when I buy fish I make sure that it's imported. Parastatal fish farms are still readily selling their produce, since officials don't believe that it is contaminated.

Hydrocarbons were found in the whales' bodies, and they also suffered some kind of barotraumatic pressure – likely the result of the scuttling of the ship, if dynamite was used. The government has never specified where the *Wakashio* was sunk, and why. The necropsy report on the whales' deaths will not be made public, either.

It is summer. Our reservoirs are almost empty. It is too hot for jeans, which stick to my skin. Too hot for make-up. Too hot to do anything but swim on the weekends.

I'd planned my son's first proper swim soon after he was born. We'd been told to wait until he was six months old, but that would be June, winter in Mauritius. It'd be too cold. We thought that the beginning of summer would be ideal. Antoine and I would drive down to Pointe d'Esny a little after dawn. We'd sit on the edge of the shore. The waves would lap around my son's sun-creamed thighs. Perhaps we'd see a starfish or two in the water. He'd splash his hands and kick and laugh.

I take my son to Pointe d'Esny late in January, just for a few minutes. The front half of the ship is still there, on the coral reef. The authorities say that oil-cleaning operations have been successfully completed. I walk timidly to the shore, my baby in my arms. The sea is luminous, coloured like a slice of blue agate. It is clear. It wets my feet and I flinch. There's no question of my son swimming here for another decade.

I remember watching two young boys in Palmar last year: they'd emerged from the sea, shaken most of the saltwater off their bodies, and were carefully reclothing themselves in stiff white shirts and black trousers.

189

Perhaps they'd briefly escaped a ceremony of some sort to find relief in the water. They'd be itchy in the hours to come: the fabric of their shirts would chafe against their skin, their hair would be crisp and stiff with salt. But they thought their discomfort was worth it for those ten minutes of joy.

2020

'Tractors, maman!' my son cries as we drive to the shopping centre. The roads from my home to the mall are littered with machines: some are ploughing the forest to make space for a new road; some are working on the tram service, rolling the earth, laying down rails; others are building yet another mall nearby. The whole island is a construction site, as was promised by the party in power during their election campaign in 2019. *Un grand chantier de développement.*

I drive past Ebene, the new business centre of the island. The would-be Wall Street of the Indian Ocean is full of defective buildings and overpriced parking spaces. Cars are parked on each side of the road throughout the town and beyond, because no one will pay the parking fees. Inside the offices there's the pervasive smell of food and rancid cooking oil. All these glassy buildings were erected haphazardly late in my childhood; I still remember when all this land was just cane. Ebene houses a multitude of offshore companies, staffed by employees who speak of 'strategic global business jurisdiction' and 'tax optimization' and the removal of the island from the Financial Action Task Force's Grey list. In 2016 the *Financial Times* stated that our offshore sector accounted for over $630 billion worth of assets, some fifty times the level of the country's GDP.

'TRACTORS, did you SEE?' he shouts, annoyed by my less than enthused responses. We wait in traffic. I am distracted by our reflection in yet another dark-glass-and-steel building. My car, the company logo emblazoned upon it diagonally, striping the entire vehicle. My face cannot be distinguished: the glass panels have transformed my vehicle and me into something murky. There is truth in this reflection. I am, after all, a real estate agent now.

·

Nothing had worked out. The copywriting and translation contracts I'd been reliant on previously had vanished during the pandemic and are yet to reappear. Local companies were happy to just use Google Translate for their communications and marketing, shrug off the Frenchisms, the strange syntax; now they conjure the words they want through Chat GPT. My corporate career beyond freelance work had been spasmodic and I hadn't accumulated much significant experience elsewhere.

I thought about the women I knew who worked as real estate agents, all of them mothers of small children. They had flexibility: they were able to schedule their lives around their kids and still earn more than most Mauritian employees – a lot more, if you proved to be good at the job. The average wage per month here is about Rs 35,000; my acquaintances, especially those who worked in the expat epicentres in the north and west, were able to make Rs 1–200,000 a month sometimes. CEO money, doctor money, lawyer money. I told myself this was the best shot I had at contributing to the household in a meaningful financial way. My husband had given up his own dreams so that I could pursue my writing. I had had hope, after graduating university, that I would make a decent amount writing essays, book reviews, whatever. Laughable in retrospect. I'd nursed dreams that I'd be teaching, too. But the only jobs available to teach English literature were at secondary school, where the pay was so low that I'd actually be costing us *more*, as a couple, given that I'd be taxed and would no longer be classified as an 'income dependent' of my husband.

We'd just bought a house; we'd wanted it for two years, weren't able to afford it at first. It had belonged to a florist, and was shaded under a centennial tree. No one had lived there for a few years – she'd moved after her divorce – and so the back garden was overrun with vine leaves, heliconias ridden with snails. We got to work. I planted jacaranda and lavender, banana trees and roses, herbs and citrus. I felt the house represented a knowledge I'd grow into. A place to rest, even though I was only thirty. But perhaps this is what I needed, given the life I'd lived so far: rest. The peace of watching sheets dry, billowing in the breeze.

Rest came with bank loans at ever-increasing interest rates.

I couldn't hope to out-earn my husband, but I thought that there was something I could do, at least, to make life just a little bit easier for him. To pay for my son's nursery, for instance. Trips to the supermarket. My books. He paid the loans, our mortgage, my car insurance, everything. Over the years he'd come back home increasingly worn out from his job, haggard, almost disoriented at times from the stress that he'd never call stress. And at night he fought against sleep to stay up late, grab some more time for his conscious self after the last of the day's emails had been sent and the last client had been called. He'd fall asleep in front of reels and TikTok.

He reassured me, said childcare was work enough already, 'I couldn't do what you do!', etc. Motherhood was exhausting and stressful, but there were also these daily highs, moments of joy that he didn't experience – no toddler to cuddle in an office. And he was the kind of parent who found perfect fulfilment in spending time with his children, who said he'd be a stay-at-home dad if he could. He didn't need a vocation, like me, or any hobbies. He relished the time he spent with our son during lockdown. Going back to work full-time (no work-from-home policies at his firm) was devastating to him.

I had been with my husband for fifteen years. Capitalism was wringing him out. He was outrunning the cost-of-living crisis, but we were spending over Rs 25,000 a month in grocery shopping, well above the national minimum wage. Even when it seemed that everything was extortionate, prices managed to rise even further. I was worried that the exhaustion would make him ill.

·

I didn't have a diploma to work as a real estate agent. In my interview my manager told me that most people in the industry here didn't have the necessary documentation and were technically called 'consultants' on paper – though everyone used the word agent anyway. All I needed to be a consultant was a clean track record of employment, a genial personality, a certain resilience in my manner and a good wardrobe. I had the record and the clothes.

I tried my hardest to present myself as outgoing and a

good fit for the job. It took her about ten minutes to see right through my posturing. A good, experienced agent is able to read people quickly upon meeting them: time is saved, time is dispensed in useful ways, ways that maximize the agent's chance of making a sale or renting out a property. I wasn't the worst she'd seen, she said, but I was reserved and quieter than her usual employees. I'd have to work on those aspects of myself. We'd spent my first day with a French expatriate who wanted to open a restaurant and invest in various properties on the west coast. My manager had looked him up: his wealth was serious, even though he treated the meeting as a date. He made slightly lewd remarks and gestures throughout the day, insisting that we walk in front of him, joking about how he'd carry me through the mud of the construction site, repeating how beautiful we both were, insisting again on getting us drinks at the end of the afternoon. We ordered coffee at a restaurant by the office. I was uncomfortable. 'Car salesgirls get it much worse,' my manager told me in the car after the day was over. 'Men literally think they're buying the girl along with the car. There's groping, stuff like that. You'll be OK.' She'd never been groped on the job, never took clients on visits in the evening, or to places that were utterly devoid of people. I would be OK. I'd just have to toughen up some more.

For all my failings, at least I had some use: computer-literate, able to use the back office without having to be taught twice, took and edited good photos. Plus, like most agent-consultants, I was working on pure commission. If things didn't work out, I would have cost the company training time but not a salary, no benefits or allowances.

•

The island's rich had invested in the north and west coasts over a decade ago. It made sense: though those regions had been underdeveloped when I was a child, they were some of the most beautiful places in the whole country. Then, as now, everyone wanted to live by the sea: the greatest impediments to doing so were wealth (land availability and cost, though the prices of coastal land twenty years ago were almost insignificant compared to today); heat (the summer months and their 34-degree temperatures on the coast made me ill); and – at the time especially – accessibility. Tamarin was little more than a picturesque village when I was a child, a strip of road with only a few homes, small corner shops and the London supermarket. My friend who lived there walked around barefoot in oversized T-shirts worn over swimming costumes, she had a freedom I envied. It used to take a good hour's drive for us to get to the West: my father had a special pass with the sugar estate company that allowed him to take a broken road that wound through mountains and sugarcane fields. Now, even with better roads, the dazzling urbanization of the West has begotten traffic jams that can last over two hours. More offices are being built, new clinics, sporting centres, international schools, smart cities and other developments that foreigners can buy; soon, there'll be little incentive for those who live in the West to leave their region at all, to take the new road that's being built from La Vigie to Beaux Songes. And with the growing move to and development of the West and North, the importance of the traditional business centres of Ebene and Port Louis is waning.

The east coast, known for its gorgeous, wild landscape and lagoons of impossible blues, has stayed relatively underdeveloped because it's a less accessible drive. Rich

196

Franco-Mauritians have second homes in Roches Noires, a coastline made deliberately inaccessible to the public – it is even more exclusive than Pointe d'Esny. Rich Mauritians 'of colour' have bungalows in neighbouring Poste Lafayette. Hotels are rare there. There are no major towns on this coast, no international schools, no clinics. Houses back from the coast and into the mainland are generally very modest. What the East does have, however, is acres of land devoted to Property Development Schemes. Until 2023, these Schemes were the only way that expatriates could buy property in Mauritius. The biggest 'Schemes' often have 'integrated resort' facilities – restaurants, boutiques, a golf course, a small marina or boathouse – and are, of course, gated. They have entire companies dedicated to the marketing and selling of homes; they barely need any outside help. Their campaigns use words like pristine, untouched, authentic, rustic.

The company needed an agent for the centre of the island, increasingly devoid of expatriates. The centre is where most Mauritians live and work, though it seemed that everyone was trying to leave for the North, the West, or for Canada.

I wasn't competing against other agencies so much as 'courtiers', or independent agents, known often just by their surnames. People in the centre favoured them over mainstream agencies, believing that they charged lesser commissions and were more effective. Though the commissions were in fact the same, they did have an incomparable knowledge of the real estate market.

But courtiers and agents alike were having trouble

with the centre.

.

We were able to buy our home in Floreal because Floreal was then out of favour.

When I was a child it was described as the boring Beverly Hills of the island. One of Mauritius' most prestigious postcodes, roads lined with the homes of company directors, lawyers, doctors, politicians. A sylvan neighbourhood with a few corner shops, a post office and one coffee place. A boutique-style shopping mall was eventually built here in 2017, but it did little to increase the region's popularity.

In the island's centre there is only one town that is considered attractive: Moka. A sugar-estate-turned-conglomerate claims the area largely for itself, since they possess immense tracts of land in the region. They've gentrified the area, turning it into a premium lifestyle-shopping-work destination. Moka even has its own logo. The wild banana trees set against electric blue houses have seemingly disappeared; if they still exist they're on the fringes of the 'smart city' Property Scheme that the conglomerate is developing using their own in-house team. Moka is a city that expatriates can buy property in.

Houses that are built on the plots of land sold by the conglomerate must be constructed according to a specific architectural style and colour palette; bland in design, marketed as tasteful. Because everything the whites do in this country is supposedly tasteful.

198

'We have a certain aesthetic that we want to uphold,' said a manager of the property development company owned by the conglomerate.

I'd come to see the manager on behalf of the agency. The development company was infamously difficult to work with: they had their own sales system and wilfully poached agents' clients, so not a cent of commission would be lost.

'Our aesthetic is why the prices are as they are. And the demand is here, let me tell you. We have a thousand-strong waitlist for this project here, and that's after we've removed the rubbish leads.'

I knew all the racist dog-whistle diction. He was echoing the belief that the non-white Mauritian has no taste, according to white and white-passing Mauritians, and others desirous of whiteness, like this manager. The non-white Mauritian cannot achieve taste, no matter his income or proximity to European culture. I'll spare the plethora of utterances revolving around this that I've heard over the years, except one that I still hear sometimes: that non-white Mauritians are nouveau riche and therefore lack a certain 'old world' grace and style. This particular phrase is as hilarious as it is disgusting: it bestows upon the wealthy Franco-Mauritian speaker a sort of grandeur based on entirely invented noble origins, and delights in the 'old world' money made from slavery. The non-white Mauritian is mocked for his always-imperfect French, his not-quite-complete grasp of culture and Western civilization. I think of Adorno and Horkheimer's phrase in *Dialectic of Enlightenment*: 'The leader acts as a representative; he portrays what is forbidden to everyone else in actual life'. When the non-white Mauritian dresses expensive, they're nouveau riche and distasteful; when they don't bother they're lower class and distasteful.

They are rubbish leads! 'Rubbish', the majority of Mauritians – those who do not have millions to buy a comparatively small home in the conglomerate's crowded developments. I wondered if he knew about the slums at the centre of the old Moka village; the families forced to rent out livestock pens to live in, the women deprived of proper latrines whose stomachs are unbearably bloated. There are slums like this all over Tamarin. A sliver of money collected from real estate developers in the region would have been enough to give all of the people there good, solid homes. If people cared even a fathom, extreme poverty would have been eradicated in Mauritius a decade ago.

Of course, 'rubbish' doesn't apply to whites and light-skinned Creoles, desperate to distance themselves from the threads of African ancestry in their DNA. The conglomerate has other plans for Franco-Mauritians who don't have the money to move to Moka: a place named Gros Bois, a newly created neighbourhood plunked in the middle of nowhere, among sugarcane fields and the ruins of a small sugar factory in the south-east of the island. In its initial stages Gros Bois was marketed almost exclusively through white word of mouth.

.

'Everyone is moving,' groaned an old Franco-Mauritian man, whose neighbours have sold their homes to move to the coast. He put his lavish Floreal home on sale, having chosen to move to Moka to be closer to his children and grandchildren. By 'everyone', he meant whites like him.

His home is still unsold, a year on from our first meeting: he wants too much for his property, refuses to accept that land prices for Floreal have actually gone down – driven down because of white emigration. I have the same problem with Franco-Mauritian clients in Curepipe, who have houses in private roads near forests and plantations. These used to be exclusive postcodes. My white clients can't imagine that Mauritians who need to work in the centre of the island would prefer to live in places like Sodnac, Quatre Bornes, Beau Bassin and Ebene. Quatre Bornes and Beau Bassin used to be home to a few wealthy Franco-Mauritian families, but both towns were abandoned generations ago. Along with Sodnac and Ebene, these towns are now heavily favoured by middle- and upper-class Mauritians of colour, particularly Indo-Mauritians. The price of land in a gated community found in Ebene, called Bout du Monde, is apparently the highest on the island (excluding the coast).

'It's just so baffling,' an agent said as we finished up a visit. The client was mine, the property hers: a grand, immaculately maintained apartment building in Floreal that I'll call Le Chateau (its true name is just as bombastic). You couldn't call the place a 'block' of flats: it had been designed to look like a sweeping colonial-style home, two apartments per floor, 300 square metres or so each. The apartments of Le Chateau had never been on sale publicly before (to my knowledge) and until recently they'd solely been owned by wealthy Franco-Mauritians. They are, to this day, the most expensive apartments in Floreal.

My client had just left. It was her second visit; she'd brought an engineer to look at potential renovations. She was the much younger wife of a rich financial director; she arrived in a brand-new Benz, donned designer clothing, possessed all the traditional accoutrements of her class. She had to be vetted by the agent before we were allowed to visit Le Chateau: potential acquirers had to be of a 'certain profile', the white agent explained, code words that meant that if my clients weren't white they had to be supra-wealthy and 'Western-presenting', i.e. English- and French-speaking, Hugo Boss-wearing, no saree, just a trace of religion – certainly no religious rituals should be held within the apartment. White agents had no problem telling me these things, as if saying 'not traditional' and 'Western-presenting' were perfectly acceptable. I've had emails from white clients saying that they'd prefer their homes to be sold to other Franco-Mauritians, but that failing this, 'elevated' non-whites of the 'same social circles' were acceptable. I've had emails from whites inquiring about my husband's surname, which I use for work. 'Are you related to this person, or this person? *De quel souche êtes-vous?*'

The agent and I both knew that this woman – or rather, her husband – could buy the apartment cash, no loan needed; they could easily acquire property at three, four times the price of Le Chateau, in fact. She said she'd get back to us with a smile that gave us some hope. And then the agent asked where she was heading back to. Home, for my client, was a Sodnac apartment that had been built by a disgraced developer who had fled the country. Cracked walls streaked with mould, an unglamorous location even though you had some nice views over Corps de Garde. When she left, the agent turned to me and vocalized her disbelief. I felt the same way, to be honest. I knew of other wealthy Indo-Mauritians who lived there, who bought their apartments a decade ago when the property had just been built – but I didn't understand anyone who would still want to live there, when they had all the wealth they needed to move.

My client never ended up buying at Le Chateau. I thought, well, she and her husband probably have friends and a solid sense of community in their block, rotting as it was. There's no beating that. I also wondered if, despite all their wealth and social status, my client and her husband felt that Floreal still wasn't for them, that they wouldn't fit in, that they'd still be on the receiving end of coruscating, condescending glances from their neighbours. That things had hardly changed since independence.

.

Though I was responsible for the centre, I occasionally represented properties in the West, especially when the company was short of staff. This is how I ended up at the launch of a major integrated resort-real-estate project: my manager was sick and the other person in charge of the West was out of the country. The project promised villas of exceptional luxury, retailing at about €2 million minimum, designed around a large golf course and a hotel.

Projects of such distinction and scope don't come up regularly, perhaps one every other year. There'd been a soft launch for potential investors: the company had poached some of the best real estate agents in the country months ago and tasked them with approaching interested expatriates and the wealthiest Mauritians. There was another launch exclusively for real estate agents, and another event a few days later where the project was announced to the general public.

All those launches took place at a five-star hotel – the resort project was close by. I sat there in the air-conditioned meeting room along with about fifty agents and directors of agencies. The racial and gender dynamics were evident, a good sample of the industry as a whole: most agents were white or light-skinned Creoles, though there were a few Indo-Mauritian women; most agents were women, most agency directors were white men. After the project was presented and the crowd had moved on to refreshments, the best agents were on their phones, sending online brochures and other sales material to their clients, posting on LinkedIn, not wasting a second to make a sale. If all the agents had something in common it was this: none of them was ashamed of the fact that they were in this for the money, that everything they did was for commission. They wouldn't talk to you to be friendly; they wouldn't cultivate good relationships in order to wring favours out of you later – they reserved that kind of behaviour for their clients, not colleagues. It was a business of sharks who were uninterested in pretending that they were genteel whales. It was refreshing. One of the agents there, a suave, slinky woman who looked like Angelina Jolie, had been accused of fraud multiple times. But she was brilliant. She could coax you into eating cat food. She was still invited to this launch and she walked in proudly, knowing the effect that she had on people, knowing that they'd forgive her actual crimes for the sake of her beauty and charisma and skills.

I'd heard, often, that this industry was replete with rich, bored housewives who thought real estate would be a fun hobby to take up, and besides, they had all the right connections to begin with. There were stories: my manager had interviewed a woman who was appalled that she wouldn't have free time – on company time – to go to the hairdresser and get a manicure and go to the gym. She articulated that being pretty and 'well-maintained' was key to the job. I'd burst out laughing as my manager told me this, and it was sad, really, the ways in which women like her so readily objectified themselves, like it was all they knew, from trophy wife to talking figurine presenting a product. But point is, she wasn't hired. Point is, there wasn't a stupid person in that hotel meeting room. There were mothers, but no ladies of leisure. These women did not have time for leisure. They were nervy, ambitious. Many of them smoked. They had the energy of a predator, the kind of energy that I'd only ever seen in Mauritian men. They were subversive in their own particular way. They were not afraid of selling, in a country where there is still a tinge of disgrace associated with on-the-ground sales work. An agent was more glamorous and had more status than a traditional salesperson in retail, but many of the agents I knew had backgrounds in sales and marketing. Some had been told by well-meaning richer relations (or absolute strangers) that sales 'wasn't their place'.

I had no luck selling the resort's would-be villas, the numbered plots of land. The Mauritian clients I had thought the prices were fantastical. Ten visits to the site in total, no sales. Ten visits in a time when the cost-of-living crisis was igniting riots across the country, a backdrop of burning tyres and tear gas. I'd drive to meetings listening to the news: protests, food trucks pillaged, Mauritians living on two or even one meal a day, mothers giving up their children to government agencies because they couldn't afford to feed them, people pushing trolleys filled with scrap metal to sell, no money left to subsidize food costs, and where had all our reserves gone, maybe it wasn't such a great idea to have given supra-wealthy conglomerates and hotel groups funds during the pandemic under the Wage Assistance Scheme. In supermarkets I was one of the many people checking their receipts in disbelief. In some months I'd see a small caddy set up next to a cashier for items that people had to return at the till.

·

The future resort's terrain was dotted with wetlands, a fact that the company tried and failed to rebrand in their favour: they said they'd protect the wetland by moving the bulk of the water to a dedicated area, touted the 'environmental thinking' behind the design of each villa-to-be. This kind of 'thinking' wasn't unique to the company: with all the mega-lux projects, you'd hear about how the epitome of 'living with nature' was in fact living on a golf course or some other highly terraformed place, 'nature' being devoid of most insects and most Mauritian people (save those who worked as staff). There was some outcry about the wetlands on social media, but it was much more restrained than the reaction to other developments across the island helmed by non-whites.

I took photos, tried to root myself in this space so I'd remember how this savannah was before it had been scrapped and shaped into a golf course. The pits of murky water, the branches onto which wasps clung. Dragonflies and butterflies and the loud hum of insects. The damp, ripe smell of water, grass, earth.

The sea level rises 5.6 mm here per year, 9 mm in Rodrigues. 17–41 per cent of our beaches suffer from coastal erosion, and within the next fifty years half of them will be lost. All the villas that'll be built here will be underwater in the next two to three decades. This is public knowledge. But coastal projects like these don't stop. There's too much money to be made. Too much lifestyle that is coveted.

◆

Real estate was obscenely different from the career I had wanted, but at least I looked good. I was polished. My nails no longer had a crescent of soil in their underbeds; now they had acrylic shells, as short as the nail technician would allow, but still long enough to feel like I risked gouging my eyes out when I removed my contact lenses. They were heavy on my fingers. They made me look presentable, less neurotic, but were otherwise completely fucking useless. I couldn't make the bed properly, couldn't care for my plants, even chopping up vegetables became a somewhat fraught exercise. Which was perhaps the point: these aren't the nails of someone who works with their hands or cares for their home in a vigorous, physical way, or who has to type a lot or change diapers and clean infant genitalia.

It was like role play. The costumes, the make-up. The eyelash extensions that took more time to be glued on than it took for me to get a c-section. I couldn't wipe my eyes with a towel, the lashes gripped the fibres and pulled and tore. The rims of my lashes felt like sandpaper sometimes, and heavy with artifice. I couldn't feel the relief of rubbing my eyes, the banal pleasure of seeing without irritation, I told myself it was perhaps worth it, since I spent less time on make-up: the lashes made my eyes appear brighter, my undereye circles were less severe. And other things began to seem worth the pain, too, once I noticed them on other people. Bleached teeth. Botox.

I thought, what happened to the girl who carried *The Society of the Spectacle* around like it was scripture? She had wanted too much. She'd never been realistic. She had a good life and still she complained.

·

Bien immobilier. Un bien. A good. Good. One word that means capital, product and virtue. Capital as virtue. A defining narrative of our lives – a whole organizational structure.

Slums run through Tamarin. When I worked for a non-profit organization I visited one of the largest, stretched out on a piece of land with a supermarket at one end and luxury villas at the other. The heat inside the tin shacks was unbearable – I have never experienced any- thing like it, heat so extreme that I could barely think or talk. The residents had no running water: they depended on sporadic water tankers managed by the government. Cables trailing across soil provide makeshift electricity. There was no hope of them owning the homes they'd constructed for themselves on this piece of land, since they'd done so illegally. A fraction of the profit from the real estate projects that bordered part of the slum would have been enough to provide decent housing for all of its residents. The developers didn't care. The rich inhabitants of Tamarin don't care, driving past the slums to go shopping in the boutique mall a few metres away.

The residents of the slum know this, and unlike all the more vapid inhabitants of the area they tend to think like a community. They net leaves and soft branches into canopies that cover whole spectrums of their homes, shielding inhabitants from some of the heat. They weave macramé plant holders out of scrap thread, hang them on their tin leaf walls.

I don't know if the government has plans to raze these homes to the mud, like they did with squatter homes in Riambel and Pointe aux Sables. I'm sure there must be a considerable number of rich people who have complained about the sight of these shanty towns in *their* neighbourhood. And I don't imagine government officials tell them – or even know themselves – that the Creole families who live in these slums are descended from people who chose a purely self-sufficient life after the abolition of slavery: fishing, vegetable planting. Some may even have had property titles to the land where villas and gated communities have been built.

I've heard some people say that they'd like to see these residents 'moved' to social housing projects, which are usually built well away from affluent towns, some quite literally in the middle of cane fields. But even those houses are a privilege – when people are able to access them, that is, given that there are still too few social housing projects to meet the demands of the country. The owners of social housing units must be able to pay a deposit of 10 per cent of the sale price of the house and must be able to adhere to strict reimbursement terms. These are impossible conditions for most people living in poverty, who barely make enough to live day-to-day. And even if you have the deposit and can fulfil the state's terms, there's a rumour that inhabitants of state homes are chosen by their ethnicity – a rumour seemingly confirmed in 2016, when the disgraced minister of social housing was caught on camera promising that 90 per cent of Hindu Indo-Mauritians would be given homes in a new project in Bassin, that no homes would be given to Muslims, and only 10 per cent would be given to 'bann melanz', 'those who are mixed', Creoles, 'and there won't be any social-project-type-Creole in these houses who will prostitute themselves.' The inhabitants of the area were no better, protesting at the construction of social housing units by saying that 'inhabitants of Bassin are not in agreement with drugs, prostitution and other social ills [that will come to Bassin] and that will face Kali Mata Mandir.' Creoles here are supposedly synonymous with 'drugs, prostitution and other social ills'. Because the Minister didn't form part of the National Housing Development Corporation, and because the Corporation is presumed to be independently run, the Minister was acquitted.

．

'You haven't tasted blood yet', my manager tells me, after my first deals fall through. 'It's easy to be discouraged. But when you get that commission, trust me, it's a rush.' Money gushing through my account. Blood rushing to my head. The adrenaline. The prowl and hunt for clients. Agents observing the Porsches and Maseratis and, yes, actual Rolls Royces rolling about Tamarin. Agents

210

always popping up at the right restaurants and bars at the right time, introducing themselves in ways that feel natural, like they're just part of the community.

Rich clients and their Olympian appetites, their absolute boredom, their propensity to accumulate capital like a disease. Rich people and their breathless ignorance, moral vapidity, immoral insouciance. It didn't matter how supposedly left-leaning they were, how much they cared about the environment: fundamentally, rich people all behaved the same.

Most if not all of my wealthy clients had enough money to stop working. They'd come to Mauritius to effectively retire – early, before their fifties. But their love of accumulating money didn't stop, the thrill of checking their ever-increasing bank accounts wouldn't cease, there was always more to be made. One of them decided to invest in and build LEED-certified buildings, an innovation he thought he'd brought to Mauritius. He professed great concern over the environment but travelled by plane every other week; he didn't think of himself as living 'as badly' as the other wealthy people he knew, the ones with private jets. He didn't think of himself as rich, in fact, though he was one of the richest men living in Mauritius at the time. In his mind, what mattered was that he wasn't in the top 500 wealthiest men in his home country – the richest country in the world, at the time – and he still flew commercial.

This is the same client who wanted to move from the north to the west coast to have a more 'authentic' feel of Mauritius, in a different gated community. He didn't want to part with his chauffeur in the north and asked me to find a new home for the man, too. He didn't think of this as uprooting the man's life: if anything he thought he was doing his chauffeur a service, that he was a Swiss-sent benediction.

'I thought real estate developers were going to hell because they're so unethical, but finance guys are worse,' said my manager to another client. She was teasing him; he was a finance bro.

'But the whole goal is to not die, right?' He replied unironically.

We all had coffee. He asked about our upcoming elections. My manager told him briefly about the political system here, the corruption. He said he didn't believe in democracy. Many of his friends had relocated to Dubai, to Saudi Arabia. He liked their systems, said the countries were so efficient. The future. 'Most people are too stupid to vote,' he said.

And what were we helping him do? Evade tax legally, in essence. Streamline. Fast-track. Optimize. There were men like him, who were on the legal side of immoral, and then there were other clients connected to drugs and horse racing who asked me for help in acquiring property. Thankfully, too, I wasn't able to sell anything to them.

•

In September 2022, a documentary by Rising Ocean went viral on social media. Rising Ocean had interviewed activists and intellectuals on the state of the Mauritian property market: in the video, they claimed that the

212

state favoured 'smart city' and expat-friendly residential schemes to the detriment of Mauritians, since the land used could have improved our agricultural autonomy, since these projects gentrified the areas and made local real estate extortionate. They said expatriates and their purchasing power were setting the property market alight and making Mauritius unliveable.

But none of these experts had consulted the statistics. Expatriates couldn't buy on the beach; expatriates only bought about 300 properties on the island every year. The clientele of these smart cities and resort developments were mainly Mauritians – and not from the diaspora either. Mauritians were getting fleeced by their own countrymen, who were on their thirtieth beachfront acquisition, making mad money on rental.

I thought I'd have better luck with middle- to lower-income clients. I thought this was where I'd find some kind of salvation in a repugnant job: I'd be able to find houses and apartments for people who genuinely needed them, who'd be satisfied with finding their perfect home.

But there was no salvation. A woman rang me up, said she was looking for someone to rent the upper floor of her home for Rs 15,000. She lived in a rather dilapidated area of Quatre Bornes. Other similar homes on her street were full of immigrant workers and though they could pay the rent, she wanted someone who was Mauritian. But she didn't want a liability. She needed to *know* who was going to rent. Women running away from their violent husbands weren't acceptable, for instance.

It seemed like such a waste of time, though at least the effort was there, the effort to improve our lives. But my son was unhappy. He'd started telling me that he was sad that I was going to visits or to the office, sad that I was speaking so much on the phone. I was on the phone all the time; I'd speak to clients in the late afternoon while in the garden with him, he'd wait for me, pick up the watering can, pour it on my feet to clear away the grass splayed on my skin. Eventually he thought that he wasn't getting his point across, that he wasn't saying the right words to make me understand. He was two years old then. '*Tu sais, maman,*' he'd repeat, circling around me. He'd put his head in my lap and cry. He stopped speaking when I picked him up from nursery, furrowing his head into my shoulder. His teachers said he had difficulties controlling his emotions: not his anger, just his immense, painful sadness at not being with me, with my husband. Before we moved house he said he'd be happy as long as we were all be together. But we were hardly together for long.

I stared at the excel sheet, updating the status of hundreds of leads I had, all the visits so far: 'not interested', 'client says it's too expensive', 'client prefers to invest elsewhere'.

'You are very unlucky,' my husband said, marvelling at my lack of income.

I thought maybe it was something in my face, the way I held myself. Perhaps I looked like someone who could be cruel. I thought I was generally nice-seeming, enthusiastic – at the very least I was knowledgeable about the properties I took my clients to visit, knew all the required information and then some. But there was an ease some of the agents had, particularly my manager, that I couldn't find within myself or develop. It was as if all her clients wanted to become her friend too, even the most reserved of them, even the snobbiest. People were comfortable with her in a way they never were with me. Clients were afraid of telling me they'd found something else, said they were relieved I wasn't angry.

I knew cold calling was tough, but I didn't expect the grind of being turned down, harshly and often stupidly, day after day. Didn't expect cold calling to transform me, too: in the space of just a few weeks I became harder, moved in the world with less feeling, my manner brisk and curt over the phone even when I wasn't speaking to clients. But even then clients wondered about my age, calling me *mademoiselle* like I was barely out of school. I was told that, despite whatever transformation I felt I had undergone, I still had the voice of a child.

By May 2022 I'd be pregnant with my second child and bed-bound with hyperemesis gravidarum; later, when the vomiting subsided, I'd develop a subchorionic hematoma which left me unable to leave the house for the rest of the year. But even before I became pregnant, the weight of this job took its toll. The manicured persona cracked. There was no hiding the horror, the repugnance.

The clients who were racist and apologized once they'd taken in my expression, clients who later backed out on a signed deal.

The proud homeowner who showed me around one of his family properties that was back on the rental market, who took me to the basement, which I had to duck to enter and where I couldn't breathe well or see properly, who announced that this was the live-in maid's quarters. Who said that the previous tenant, head of treasury at a prominent bank, had kept his maid there for five years. He didn't even bother to ring me back or ask why I hadn't contacted him again. He'd seen my face.

I cried in my car, the branded car with my phone number plastered on the back. No privacy on this island anyway, with or without the company logo.

•

On the drive back home, my son and I pass the ruins of an apartment building. The ruins lie behind the apartment block we used to live in. A homeless man lives in the ruins, watching over this heap of real estate that the owners still claim is an apartment project in the making. They pay him sometimes, but it's the caretaker of the school in the neighbourhood who watches over him, cooks him dinner.

He has repeatedly lost all his belongings during torrential rain, cyclones – all his tinned meats, bedding. In cyclones, I remember, he wouldn't leave the ruins to go to a shelter: we'd see his torch, a white glare in the darkness. He told me he couldn't apply for a job because he didn't have a morality certificate. When my husband found him something – watchman duty on a proper construction site – he didn't show up for the interview.

Shelters are sparse across the island, and we don't know how many homeless people there are in Mauritius. A 2022 study stated that no concrete solutions have been found to date due to a lack of empirical data. The study interviewed 102 people: most of them were about forty years old; a little under half had a criminal record; a little over half had some form of employment, and the wages weren't enough to give them proper shelter – they couldn't buy food *and* pay rent.

Homeless people are not this government's, or the previous government's, priority: if they were, awareness campaigns and emergency shelters would have been created decades ago. There's an abundance of state land. It'd be easy to give everyone homes.

We have more land, in fact, than most people abroad are aware of: our republic comprises the islands of Mauritius, Rodrigues, Agaléga, Tromelin, Cargados Carajos, the Chagos archipelago. And it's not just Mauritius that's a construction site.

.

The party in power has repeatedly denied that an Indian military base exists on Agaléga. They deny that the island's been sold or leased out to India, even after thorough journalistic investigations have shown images of the site, covering at least a third of the island, a slash of grey through forest; even after Agaléens have documented the destruction of their island, because yes they also have phones; even after reports that Agaléen women can no longer give birth on the island, with some claiming that Agaléga is erased from these children's citizenship upon their birth in Mauritius; even after some Agaléens travelled to Europe to protest the base; even after three hundred or so Creole Agaléens have raised the parallels between their situation and the excision of the Chagos archipelago from Mauritius in the late 1960s; even as the party in power is wresting greater control over the Chagos archipelago from the UK, claiming that doing so is 'redressing historical wrongs'.

In 2023, the party in power expressed enthusiastic and unprecedented concern over the Saint Brandon archipelago, part of the Cargados Carajos Shoals. The Raphael Fishing Company has a permanent lease on about half of the archipelago's islands. The government are seeking to 'recuperate' these islands by going to court. The company stated that never in its history has any Mauritian government interfered in or questioned their operations, and that it has protected the fragile ecosystem of the archipelago to the best of its ability.

'It's like Agaléga. Maybe Modi wants it for something. Maybe they'll dredge up the seabed and build a five-star hotel or luxury resorts, like those islands in Dubai,' says my taxi driver, who has driven me around the island since I was a month old.

'It's anyone's guess,' I reply. 'And we'll never know the details. Just like Chagos.'

We're on our way to the paediatrician. My newborn daughter sleeps in her car seat. They used to say land is bankable, land never goes anywhere, a solid investment, but by the time she'll be twenty half our beaches will be underwater, coastal properties will be unliveable in summer, the island a furnace, cyclone-ridden, drought-plagued. And amid this crisis I wonder if we will still be an independent nation, still a democracy.

2022; 2024

TEN YEARS IN POWER

On 11 December 2014 I was on a train from London to Durham. I hadn't been able to vote in the general election in Mauritius, held a day earlier. I was dazzled by the videos on my phone: an ecstatic, jubilant electorate, who couldn't believe they'd ejected the 'Lion King' from office.

Navin Ramgoolam had cultivated a God-like mythos over the decades he'd been in power. He'd been at the helm of the Labour Party since 1991. He'd been Prime Minister three times, from 1995–2000, 2005–2010 and 2010–2014. I'd spent almost my whole life, at that point, with him as leader of the country. Watched him age through state-owned television.

If you'd looked at global indices of wealth and prosperity, our country was more-or-less stable. The Labour Party in power had successfully diversified the Mauritian economy: financial services, particularly offshore, had become a key pillar alongside tourism, textiles and sugar. The unemployment rate and inflation were under control.

Mauritians, though, were growing furious at the way their country was being run. Ramgoolam became known for a life of heady excess: mistresses who became remarkably wealthy; close friends who made fortunes out of questionable 'businesses'.

A few months before the 2014 election, Ramgoolam and Paul Berenger proposed a project for a 'Second Republic'. This Republic would change the Constitution, conferring unprecedented powers on the President, who'd stay in power for seven years and wouldn't be held accountable by Parliament. If they won with a majority of seats, Ramgoolam would then become President and Berenger Prime Minister. There was concern that this Second Republic, coupled with a third straight mandate, would make Ramgoolam untouchable.

They seemed confident that they'd win. Their political rallies – we call them 'meetings' – were full of people. I remember Ramgoolam dancing on a podium to songs that glorified him: Navin our king, Navin our liberator.

Also in 2014, Anerood Jugnauth marked his return to politics at the age of eighty-four. He announced that it would be his last election, that he'd returned to clean the country of the scourge of Labour. In a meeting, dressed in plain clothes, he made a speech that was echoed throughout the electoral campaign: 'If I'm in front of you, it's not because I want to be Prime Minister. It's not for glory. I was Prime Minister for sixteen years. I've always worked in the nation's interest. Today, with my age, it is not fun for me to take the burden of this country's problems on my shoulders. But I'm doing it because I love my country.'

Jugnauth was beloved by many, called 'the father of the economic miracle'; he'd reduced the unemployment rate from 20 per cent in 1983 to 3 per cent in the early 1990s. The MSM had, and continues to nurture, strong ties to the rural-residing Hindu middle-classes (the more urban-dwelling Hindu electorate traditionally vote for Labour); in 2014, the country at large found hope in Jugnauth, who positioned himself as a virtuous Hindu paterfamilias compared to Ramgoolam. Jugnauth's son Pravind, who'd also built a strong career in politics, was named Leader of the Opposition in the run-up to the 2014 elections. Father and son led the MSM.

The Jugnauths formed a coalition together with the PMSD and some former members of the MMM called the 'Alliance Lepep' (the people's alliance). They promised to increase pensions, steady water supply ('water 24/7!'), introduce a Freedom of Information Act, new radio licences, a freer and fairer national television company. They created an ingenious viral video called *Vire Mam*, a compilation of videos of Paul Berenger and Navin Ramgoolam insulting each other over the years. We'd learn, much later, that Cambridge Analytica had been involved in our 2014 elections, but we still don't know which party got them involved, or what they provided to the party that paid for their services.

The results, as they rolled in, were incredible. The Labour Party won thirteen seats, the Lepep alliance claimed forty-seven. Videos of Ramgoolam, leaving the election centre in disgust by mid-afternoon after it became clear that he'd lose his seat, circulated widely. The ebullience of Mauritians, dressed in orange. The drums. A blow-up doll of Ramgoolam's main mistress at a rally. The former shop manager, who imported major fashion brands and opened restauration services at the airport, was known to have benefitted from major governmental contracts during the Labour Party's years in power. On the night of the results, she took the plane with twelve suitcases and Ramgoolam's illegitimate daughter, who was five years old at the time. They settled in Italy.

Three months later Ramgoolam was arrested, his home raided. Man-sized safes were dragged out of his home with about £4 million stored inside them in cash. On the way to the police headquarters in Port Louis he was shoved by the crowd. Piss was reportedly splattered on his shirt. He spent one night in police custody. It felt unbelievable.

In the years that followed, Ramgoolam faced twenty-three charges for accepting cash payments in breach of anti-money-laundering laws. The Supreme Court cleared him of all counts. He tried to rebuild his image, slowly but steadily.

The Labour Party lost the general election of 2019. The MSM had taken a marked turn towards electoral populism and had promised a significant increase in pensions along with other subsidies. They won again, with Pravind Jugnauth succeeding his father as Prime Minister of Mauritius, even though previous electoral promises hadn't seen the light: the MSM hadn't reformed colonial-era media laws, and the promised Freedom of Information Act, which would provide access to information held by public authorities, has never been drafted.

Videos of Ramgoolam at the election centre on footage from three in the morning, when he asks for a recount in disbelief, having effectively lost his seat for the second time. MSM partisans douse a tiger plush toy in alcohol and set it alight in a cage. A desacralization ceremony.

Desacralized yet undeterred, ready to present himself alongside Berenger and Duval in the 2024 elections. Though it would be difficult, there was a chance he'd return: after ten years in power, the MSM had the country on its knees.

I. *Bruneau Laurette, 'the man who came from nowhere',*
August 2020–February 2021

It was the winter of government protests, of outpourings
of grief for the state of our lagoon and our country. There
was hope that the government could be forced out, that
ministers would at least resign.

Then it was the summer of deaths pronounced as sui-
cides: the body of an agent who worked for the party in
power was found burned in a sugarcane field, intestines
splayed outside of his corpse; the body of a procurement
officer at the Ministry of Health, who had apparently
thrown himself from a cliff; a young civil servant who
worked at the Prime Minister's Office found hanged on
the doorknob of her wardrobe; another man found hanging from a tree, with amputated hands and feet.

The government's hold was cracking, we believed.
Men with outstretched hands rummaged through that
crack, claiming power for themselves, 'the power of the
people' they said. New leaders. New authority figures.
They styled themselves as superheroes seeking justice
and truth; they promised and doled out statements that
sometimes had little or no factual credence, revelations in
papers they brandished.

Laurette became a household name in 2020, during
the *Wakashio* oil spill. He was referred to as a social activist and a military and protective services professional. In
his profile picture at the time, you'd see a large, imposing,
muscular man with a rifle onboard a ship. There was no
missing the bulk of his presence, offline or online. He
promised and delivered revelations: he claimed he'd been

224

tracking the course of the *Wakashio* before the crash, and his background in maritime security gave him credibility. He wasn't afraid of the authorities, lodging cases against two ministers during the oil spill. He branded himself as a warrior – 'I was born a warrior and I will die a warrior', he'd often say. A Creole superman that Mauritians could stand behind. He'd shield them, he'd speak and fight for them.

Laurette, described as an outsider, a man who'd come from nowhere, garnered more attention than other activists and groups who'd mobilized their resources during the spill. Even though it was Rezistans ek Alternativ who had organized a makeshift base on the Mahebourg waterfront; even though it was members of the Aret Kokin Not Laplaz ('Stop Stealing our Beaches') citizen platform who cleaned up the spill where they could, who highlighted the urgency of having medical personnel on site and around the coast, and who noted that inhabitants and volunteers were experiencing breathing difficulties and allergies, still, the press and the public gravitated around Laurette, who was loud, who defied power in more obvious ways.

The protest of 29 August 2020 was not a one-man movement. Activists and environmental groups had urged Mauritians to take to the capital; politicians from major and minor opposition parties voiced their support; the Mauritian diaspora organized their own protests around the world in solidarity. But Laurette was initially responsible for the idea for the 'citizens' march', as it would come to be known. He was the one to apply for a permit to hold the event, and stood at the forefront of the protest's organization.

225

It was one of the largest marches in our history, gathering around 75,000 people of all ethnicities – though it'd be a lie to say that the march was representative of the population at large. The crowd was diverse, but observers noted that it was largely composed of a non-'Hindu belt' electorate.

Mauritians came, despite warnings sent out by major corporations saying they didn't want their staff to be associated with the protest. They came, undaunted by Hindutva posts on social media, which said that Laurette was a Creole demon, the 'enemy', and that no good Hindu should associate themselves with him. He marched, draped in the Mauritian flag, his right fist raised in an echo of the Black Lives Matter movement. Some journalists had already begun to refer to the march as *his* citizens' march, his initiative.

Laurette didn't seem awed by his celebrity status, took it as his due. He'd post photos of himself as a Masai warrior, shared artwork that portrayed him as larger than life, juxtaposed a picture of himself with one of Nelson Mandela.

An attempt was made to arrest him, later in 2020 – a bounced cheque for a small sum. Some of his attempts to organize other protests were denied. In November he wasn't permitted to hold two protests, but the police were strangely lax about an illegal 'Hindu rally' that was held in Grand Bassin on 2 December, organized by an MP's brother-in-law. During this rally, men displayed the Indian flag and brandished sabres. The police launched an investigation; some of the men identified by video said their sabres were made of plastic. None of them were ever arrested.

The ruling party and its supporters didn't bother to conceal their loathing for the man. They made memes, some of them racist, all of them ludicrous. Laurette posted on Facebook that other attempts had been made to try and arrest him by the police force and the Anti-Drug and Smuggling Unit (ADSU). The threat of jail was real: the police, by law, can arrest anyone reasonably suspected of committing or about to commit an offence which will endanger public safety or public order under a 'provisional charge', which comes *before* an official investigation.

Laurette said he wasn't afraid, that he'd talk to the officers over coffee. Over the years, even before his rise to fame, he'd scrutinized the ADSU's operations on social media, sometimes insinuating, sometimes proclaiming that the officers of the drug squad were corrupt. He said he had more revelations to make.

The ruling party galvanized Laurette as the man to watch, the man to muzzle. Many of us stood in awe as he spoke publicly of subjects considered too incendiary – topics that most mainstream politicians wouldn't touch: the rise of Hindutva, the presence of RSS organizations, the ties between the current administration and the Hindu far-right.

When Laurette revealed that Soopramanien Kistnen had personally handed his electoral notebook to him a week before he was burned to death, it felt like a benediction from one truth teller to another. Kistnen had threatened members of the party in power with revelations. He was about to go public with proof of government corruption. His notebook detailed various electoral expenses from 2019 by the party in power, accounts that surpassed the legal threshold to an extravagant degree. In the parking lot of a shopping mall, Kistnen had also told Laurette about the alleged corrupt finances and assets of the Minister of Commerce, Yogida Sawmynaden.

Laurette rallied protesters on 7 January 2021, the day the Minister was due in court. They raised their fists in defiance of the snipers on the rooftops, the heavy carapace of military vehicles that had taken over the arteries of the capital. Within a month the Minister of Commerce resigned; Nando Bodha, a long-serving minister within the MSM, left the ruling party altogether claiming that 'the situation in the country has become extremely serious.'

Another march was organized on 13 February 2021, branded the 'march of the opposition and civic organizations'. Politicians from across the spectrum rallied once more, alongside the general public. Once again, there was hope for change. The protestors burned a coffin inscribed with the name of the ruling party, as well as a papier-mâché effigy of Pinocchio – the Prime Minister's new nickname, bequeathed to him by the public.

Once more, Laurette helped amass a solid crowd. He'd launched his own civic organization, understood the weight of his presence; he said he'd participate in the march of 13 February only if certain conditions were met, claiming that the opposition had to prove the 'sincerity' of their actions in order to 'change the system'. 'We do

228

politics, but in the service of the people,' he said. I thought that it was just a matter of time before the civic organization turned into a new political party, despite Laurette's initial vow to stay apolitical. He had the momentum. He'd become an emblem.

II. *Anti-vaccine mania, January–May 2021*

The Mauritian government started its Covid-19 vaccine rollout at the end of January 2021. Within days of the vaccine's administration, local news was awash with reports of Covid vaccine after-effects. On any given day you'd hear a cornucopia of interviews of people crying on the radio, saying their relatives and friends had been paralysed by the vaccine, or had suddenly developed diabetes, or had died.

Our news industry was – is – frail. Our best journalists have either retired, been severely reprimanded by their places of work, moved onto other pursuits or have emigrated. Presses are floundering. The most successful newspapers have invested in a social media-heavy presence and have been thoroughly rewarded for it: around 80 per cent of Mauritians get their news directly from the Facebook pages of our major news outlets. Two leading outlets have about a million followers each, in a country of about 1.2 million people.

There are a good number of journalists in Mauritius who continue to provide excellent, rigorous coverage – my book wouldn't exist without their work – but the general quality of news has rotted as steadily as picked fruit left in the sun.

I read articles claiming there was an 'equal number' of deaths among the vaccinated and unvaccinated, though statistics clearly stated otherwise; I recoiled at the sheer number of anti-vaccine doctors who were interviewed, doctors who'd lost their credentials internationally, who touted ivermectin. This was what Mauritian news media considered balanced information: science 'balanced out' with conspiracy theories. There was no hope to be had in the mastheads of these papers, either: the director of one news company was accused of incest and paedophilia and still hasn't been sacked; his power within the organization has only grown. The director of another news organization is anti-vaccine.

'We must resist against the vaccine that will be imposed on us,' Laurette had written in December 2020, capitalizing on the growing vaccine disinformation. 'We have to tell them to take the vaccine and stick it deep up there in themselves. Say no to the New World Order.'* He branded the anti-vaccine movement as an act of resistance – to the government, to 'obscure forces', to the 'New World Order'.

By early 2021, Laurette seemed untouchable. At the apex of confidence. A viral video of him in May that year shows him pulling his mask down, staring straight at a news outlet's camera, and saying that the Prime Minister's place was in prison for high treason.

Laurette posed as an authority on the treatment of Covid-19 from the beginning of the pandemic. He prognosticated on how many new cases we'd have, wrote tracts

* I've had to correct his language to avoid continuous [sic]s. All his quotes have been lightly modified in this respect.

about how the virus should be handled – military-style, by warriors like himself: 'The Prime Minister was right, we are at war. But a war is prepared with people who know what war is... with people who have extensive experience in combat and not with people who don't have a scar on their body.' It is unclear if – and unlikely that – Laurette had ever participated in a war abroad. He shared reports from CNews, an ultra-conservative French broadcaster that promoted the conspiracy theories of Didier Raoult and the effectiveness of chloroquine.

Laurette's opinions were given the same credence as those of doctors in radio 'debates'. On air, he'd expostulate about the dangers of the 'experimental vaccines'. The government was 'pressurizing' Mauritians, who were 'guinea pigs'; the vaccines were an assault on freedom, 'anti-constitutional'. He wouldn't acknowledge the clear, growing correlation between the non-vaccinated and their mortality rates; he was immured in conspiracy. Instead he said that the Prime Minister, the Minister of Health and the Senior Advisor to the Ministry of Health should be imprisoned. He'd invented a series of derogatory nicknames for each of them; he had especial vitriol for this Senior Advisor, an eminent French immunologist, a woman. 'Go back to your country', he exhorted.

To his repertoire he added xenophobia towards Indian travellers to Mauritius and Bangladeshi immigrant workers, saying that they were taking up employment that should be for Mauritians and the government was 'playing with the lives of Mauritians' by allowing them to come here so freely. He wouldn't comment on travellers from European countries with high rates of Covid-19.

It wasn't as if there hadn't been any warning signs. Laurette's militarized diction, his warrior pose, his photos with guns, his ego that seemed to grow with each social media post. His sometimes illogical stances: in the early days of the *Wakashio* disaster, for instance, he gave a ludicrous statement to the police claiming that the captain of the MV *Wakashio* was guilty of 'stirring up war' by charting the bulk carrier into our territorial waters. The vulgarity of his posts was shocking, too: references to the Prime Minister's mother's genitalia, the Prime Minister's wife's genitalia. Perhaps this shouldn't be so surprising for a man whose slogan was *bour li dehor*. Initially I'd translated the phrase as the more acceptable 'get them the fuck out of here', but I'd diminished the sense of the verb. The phrase means 'fuck him out'.

III. *Creole, Catholic, anti-vaccine and anti-government, January–May 2021*

Many journalists had been all too willing to look over Laurette's dangerous posturing in order to focus on what he represented: a true threat to the government, a champion of 'free speech', a Creole hero – even though no one in the media wanted to use the word 'Creole'.

By 2021, the majority of Laurette's followers (online and offline) were Creole. And Creole Mauritians have been consistently failed by the state and its institutions. They face virulent racism in public healthcare, education, government offices. They are imprisoned, tortured and die at the hands of the police in much greater numbers than any other ethnicity. Promises to give the poorest of our community land and a home – from which they have been historically dispossessed – are continuously unmet. They had excellent reasons to be suspicious of these new government policies, of the vaccine. Successive governments had failed to care for them in the most basic way.

Laurette had a history of supporting Black rights. His first marked presence in the field, before the *Wakashio* disaster, was him showing solidarity with the Creole families who had their homes razed by the government in June 2020, mid-winter in Mauritius. He'd taken photos with his muscular right fist raised, his trademark, now printed on T-shirts and banners. The way he'd express himself on Black rights was sometimes clumsy: he'd say things like 'native African', for instance, to mean a person of African descent; he'd swap 'Black Lives Matter' for 'All Mauritian Lives Matter', adopting whatever sounded best, not identifying a difference between the two. Some of his posts on Black rights would be shared, much later, by right-wing Hindu extremists and other religious fundamentalists to portray him as a demon ('Ravaan', as described by one group). Other critics said he was exacerbating ethnic tension in the country; that expressing his views on Black rights were incompatible, somehow, with the unified Mauritian vision he'd promoted during the march of August 2020.

But those critics had nothing to say when he'd post about Jesus and vaccines and Covid-19, because, after all, he was just posting about his religion.

It is common practice here to use one's religion as a blanket term for one's ethnicity. Many Creoles in Mauritius are Catholic, so one often hears Creoles identified as 'Catholics', even if they don't practise that religion;

in fact – and unlike other ethnicities here – there is also the distinct impression that 'Creole' is a pejorative term and that it is somehow more *polite* to say 'Catholic'. In any case, Laurette used the Creole-Catholic combination for his own gain, posting things like an illustration of Jesus Christ's wounded foot pressed upon the coronavirus, with a caption saying 'God said if you believe in me you will be saved and no harm will come to you I believe in my God and I continue my fight I am only his instrument and I execute his will'. He subsumed the power and potential of the Black radical tradition in favour of a vague Catholicism that not only appealed to most Creoles, but also extended to Catholic-practising French expatriates and Franco-Mauritians, who would end up supporting him in his anti-vaccine campaigning.

Quick to join Laurette in his 'fight' was a Franco-Mauritian activist-politician who didn't 'see' race, said Mauritius had to 'evolve' and leave the past behind, and a group of obscurely well-funded white French immigrants who founded an entire anti-vaccine platform in June 2021. They were small, 'natural' business owners who also ran an 'alternative' daycare. They mainstreamed anti-vax discourse imported from the US and Europe. Their website and social media posts were a regurgitation of all the conspiracy trash I'd seen online with flavours of QAnon; the same perversion of leftist ideas and movements; the same co-opting of the language of civil rights to promote their anti-vaccine and anti-government views; the same pro-choice diction. My Body My Choice My Voice, they claimed. Entire tracts written and sometimes even translated into Kreol. Billboards were erected across the island with their slogan, brandished by a dark-skinned Creole woman.

IV. *The ICTA amendment, April–May 2021*

It worked in tandem: Laurette capitalized on his ever-ascending fame, branding himself as the true 'opposition' in every way; the government consolidated Laurette's position by descending into outright authoritarianism.

The MSM had grown its architecture of surveillance over the years. In 2017, 4,000 Huawei-made Safe City cameras were installed around the island to track citizens' faces and monitor our movements. There'd also been a steady increase in the recruitment of police officers: about 13,500 of them patrolled the country, around 1071 for every 100,000 Mauritians, one of the highest rates in the world.

In April 2021, The Information and Communication Technologies Authority (ICTA), a government agency, had created a 'proposal' for the implementation of a digital surveillance system. The general public had about a month to send their thoughts by email.

The proposal was written in cloudy, clunky English – ensuring, essentially, that great swathes of the local population wouldn't understand it, since English is used in parliament and officially in schools but is seldom spoken at home. It claimed that the system would curtail the 'abuse and misuse of social media' in response to 2,051 reported incidents of hacking, online harassment, offensive comments, online scams and sextortion in Mauritius in 2020. Because social media companies weren't able to moderate content published in Mauritian Kreol, the ICTA document suggested that the government should take monitoring into its own hands.

They'd do so by the way of a proxy server, which would fool devices and web browsers into sending secure information to the server instead of social media networks. The server would effectively create an archive of the social media information of all users in Mauritius before resending it to the social media network's servers. The ICTA would be able to decrypt, re-encrypt and archive all social media traffic in Mauritius, and its attendant information – banking details, direct messages, photos.

The consequences of the amendment were clear: it laid out a future where criticizing the government on social media would be reported as 'abuse and misuse'; where government officials would be able to block accounts, track down users via their IP addresses, possibly send them to jail. The proposal wished to reassure readers that instances of 'abuse and misuse' would be reported to the newly instated National Digital Ethics Committee, consisting of supposedly independent people 'of high calibre and good repute'. Naturally, the ICTA's board of directors was largely made up of political nominees.

The ICTA had been frightening enough without the proposal; even today, anyone in Mauritius who sends a message via the internet that causes or could cause an 'annoyance' could end up being sentenced to up to ten years in prison. Anyone can file a complaint and seek damages for a post, share, or even a like that 'is likely to cause or causes annoyance, humiliation, inconvenience, distress, or anxiety.'

At the time of the proposal about twelve people had publicly been arrested for breaching the ICTA act. Two Mauritians were arrested and jailed for sharing memes about the Prime Minister. One was the secretary of a former president. The other was a former ambassador of Mauritius to Madagascar: the seventy-four-year-old man became so ill in jail that he had to be transferred to a clinic.

When the story of the new amendment broke it was shared by only a handful of people, mostly twenty- and thirty-somethings working in tech. They broke down the implications of the proposal, deciphering the systems that would be implemented and the dangers that they posed. The public at large didn't seem concerned, initially; I thought that perhaps they didn't understand what was at stake.

Four days later and running out of ideas, I created an online petition. I didn't have much hope that emails sent to the ICTA would make a difference, if the proposal was in effect just a well-oiled mechanism in the autocratic grind, the kind of proposal that was more of a statement, that would be passed without question. I thought that a petition would help, even if, in time, it just stood as a postscript, a record of how many Mauritians truly opposed the amendment. A good, transparent gauge of public opinion.

Ten thousand Mauritians signed my petition within twenty-four hours. Aggressive statements and interviews by the ICTA and its chairman followed, claiming that the agency wouldn't concern itself with reactions on social media and in the press, and that all dissenting views had to be directly communicated to the Authority. The chairman said that the same restrictions on freedom of expression that were imposed on journalists in Mauritius should also be imposed on internet users. The same laws that could charge me with sedition or libel, even if what I reported was true and the subject of my reporting was dead. The same laws that could imprison me if someone in power took offence at a reported fact, saying that it harmed their honour or that I was 'exciting contempt' against the government.

The petition was shared widely but relatively few Mauritians were eager to sign it; the ones I spoke to were afraid. Those who worked in the private sector didn't want to be associated with any form of protest, especially those companies who were buoyed by state aid during the pandemic. Others thought it was a waste of time. Thousands of people had just marched in the capital, and for what? The revolution they were expecting hadn't materialized.

Still, I tried. I thought that international condemnation of the proposal could work. Some journalists wrote pieces for global news outlets; local tech professionals reached out to all the organizations they could. None of us would ever be as popular as Laurette – who was also busy making noise about the amendment, organizing protests, signing other letters of condemnation – but even if Mauritians were timid in their vocalizations, we believed that international support could make a difference.

I wrote, I tweeted, I was interviewed by the BBC. I hoped we'd gain momentum. It was at this time that I was introduced as an activist on air. I didn't know what to do with the term. It was certainly not how I would have chosen to describe myself. I was an ordinary, quiet writer-mother at home. Activism: 'the use of direct and

238

noticeable action to achieve a result, usually a political or social one.' Activist: 'a person who believes strongly in political or social change and takes part in activities such as public protests to try to make this happen.' Definitions given by the Cambridge Dictionary. Activism, for me: a desperate rummaging of actions that are possible in a crisis. A confrontation of these actions' limits. Of my own limits. An exploration of what one body can do, one body rallying other bodies.

By mid-May 2021 a coalition of international organizations, academics and internet companies had publicly voiced their concerns and written to the ICTA: Access Now, the Electronic Frontier Foundation, Google, Mozilla. Facebook's statement was damning: highlights include 'this proposal does not satisfy international human rights standards' and '[the proposal] would severely infringe on citizens' rights to privacy, and by extension, would facilitate increased censorship, and chill freedom of expression and access to information.'

On 20 May, Facebook posted a job opening within the company for a Mauritian Kreol market specialist. The specialist would, among other things, 'investigate and resolve issues that are reported on Facebook such as ... reports of potentially abusive content.' The next day, the ICTA issued a communiqué claiming that if the ICTA and Facebook reached a common ground, the ICTA's proposed amendment would be abandoned.

Three months later, the agency announced that they'd binned the agreement. We'd won. But by then I'd deleted my social media accounts and was too afraid to leave my apartment. I'd received death threats, rape threats, a torrent of harassment – not from the government, but from Laurette and his supporters.

V. *Harassment coalition, June 2021*

By June 2021, Laurette's following had grown to include white anti-vaccine conspiracists. Together with Laurette's clique, the French immigrants fought hard against the government's amendment of the Quarantine Act in June. Before getting into those events, though, it's worth describing Laurette's entourage.

The men and women who surrounded him came from different ethnic groups and social classes. They were united in their desire to overthrow the current administration. Some, too, were united by their murky backgrounds.

Laurette had a troupe of highly mediatized, often infamous lawyers, who'd gained fame not so much for their competence at the bar but rather for the affairs they were embroiled in. They ran in the same circles, became each other's lawyers when arrested. One of them had once been a member of the ruling party, but had to step down as Deputy Speaker in 2018 after being named in the Commission of Enquiry into Drug Trafficking. Another lawyer, close to the previous ruling party, was arrested three times for breach of the ICTA. The third lawyer was even more famous than Laurette. Rama Valayden, a former attorney general, was alleged to have fuelled the 1999 riots; he was almost disbarred following allegations of witness coercion in 2014 and he didn't get a ticket within the opposition in the 2019 general election.

Valayden would often speak about how he and his circle were victims: they were threatened for speaking the truth, there was a threat of physical violence against their person, a price on their heads; there were corrupt lawyers in the Bar Council trying to take them down, there were journalists paid by the party in power who were relaying fake news. No institution could be trusted. No death was innocent. A man with political ties, described by the press as 'known to the police', died in a motorcycle accident in February 2021: 'murder!' Valayden claimed. The man's sister was in prison for drug trafficking and died from Covid-19 a few months later. 'She was tortured and killed by police!' Valayden said.

Despite his antics, it was clear that Valayden was another man that the government was closely watching. Along with Laurette, he'd been vocal about the miasma that surrounded Kistnen's murder. On 17 May 2021, Valayden was arrested at two in the morning by the police, on the grounds of a pro-Palestine march. Many believed the arrest was actually due to a video he'd published two days previously, in which he described alleged drug trafficking in Mauritian waters, and the Indian military base in Agaléga.

Surrounding Laurette were also activists and a number of other personalities. One of them had a series of court cases on his back – harassment, illegal recruitment of immigrant workers – and had been convicted in 2012 of murdering his stepbrother. Another was a social worker reportedly accused of raping a minor. On social media these men posted about feeding and sheltering the homeless and their fight against drug trafficking (though they were staunchly pro-marijuana); they also wrote about the sin, the perversion of homosexuality and the 'gay agenda'.

A Russian tarot reader was also often by Laurette's side. In 2018 she'd been the subject of an undercover investigation by one of the main newspapers in Mauritius. During their séance, recorded on video, the tarot reader made predictions and revelations about people who didn't exist (the journalist's children, for instance). The video makes for some compelling viewing: the tarot reader has a manipulative manner, her Kreol is good, she poses as a white confidant, which would make her particularly appealing to the thousands of followers who contribute to her business. 'In your destiny, there should have been more children,' she says with a coy smile, finger on her lips. 'You had a miscarriage, or you made the baby go away?' When the investigation was published in the newspaper – the headline read 'Fortune tellers: another famous one bites the dust' – the tarot reader attempted to sue the journalist, citing false and malicious accusations based on jealousy. Two years later she'd be arrested for breach of the ICTA, for a viral video that disseminated false information during the pandemic. She won her case, then decided to sue the country, the Minister of Health, the Deputy Commissioner of Police, among others, for an astounding amount of money. Her lawyers, in both of her dealings with the court, were all men who surrounded Laurette.

Most of the people described above were engaged in a nation-wide anti-vaccine movement by June 2021, largely in response to the amended Quarantine Act. The amendment stipulated that no person would be able to access daycares, schools, universities and other educational institutions (whether publicly owned or private), hospitals or clinics and other healthcare centres unless they presented their Covid-19 vaccination card or a PCR test result slip certifying they'd tested negative over the last week. The new regulations didn't apply to students, patients or any other person who showed a medical certificate proving that they couldn't be vaccinated for medical reasons. There was understandable uproar over the fact that these PCR tests weren't free, and could represent quite a cost in the long-run to working-class Mauritians who refused the vaccine. Non-compliance to government regulations also came with heavy punishment: a person convening these regulations or who forged a vaccination pass/PCR test result would be liable to a fine of Rs 500,000 and jail time not exceeding five years.

Laurette and his troupe inundated social media with a barrage of anti-vaccination conspiracy posts and videos, turning the anti-vax campaign into a campaign against the government. The movement promised financial and legal aid to those who'd oppose the new vaccination mandates. Their popularity soared.

The political parties that made up the opposition had the power to help spread vaccine awareness, wrench back at least some of the hold the anti-vaxxers had on the population. But most members of the opposition saw a moment to capitalize on government revolt; rumour had it that the former prime minister Ramgoolam had refused to get vaccinated himself. Members of the opposition stayed relatively quiet and didn't overtly encourage vaccination.

As far as I can recall, no other popular figure encouraged vaccination either: no athlete, no artist.

No religious body. The Catholic Church, for instance, could have mitigated some of Laurette's damage. Beyond promoting ivermectin and vaccine conspiracy theories, he'd copy-pasted a post exhorting authorities to reopen churches: 'we prefer to die of hunger than remain without the Eucharist', the post read. The Church stuck to the government's sanitary protocols but wouldn't go as far as recommending the vaccine.

Anti-vaxxers were rife within the Church's benches. Some wealthy, devout Franco-Mauritians had set the tone, donating to the anti-vax movement, joining Telegram chats, sharing 'information'. And there were connections I could barely fathom, lapsed Catholic as I was who hadn't attended a service in a decade. I discovered, for instance, that a celebrity French conspiracy theorist had held quite a few seminars in the Church's Institut Jean Margeot. She was regularly interviewed in the local press, her stances backed up by once-eminent distinctions; she used to be a lauded geneticist. She lives in a stunning house on the north coast, the country's most expensive postcode. Her husband is a business magnate. Together they opened a laboratory/research institute here in 2017. The last post on the Institute's Facebook page is about embryos used in vaccines. This hardline Catholic woman is anti-abortion as well as anti-vaccine. These ideas were even present within the medical establishment. The French embassy's doctor, for example, was one of the main figures of the anti-vax campaign in the country. In an interview, the Franco-Mauritian woman promoted the use of ivermectin and claimed that we should learn to live with Covid-19 by exercising regularly and eating healthily. Death was natural, death should be accepted. 'Natural immunity' was the way forward and too bad for those whose health was fragile in the first place, too bad for those who didn't regularly see a 'garagiste du corps'.

The only people challenging Laurette and his coterie were ordinary citizens like me, and we were belittled, ridiculed, threatened. When I'd post facts that debunked content on pages such as My Body My Choice My Voice, the moderators grew aggressive: the French expatriates wrote about their emigration to Mauritius, their embrace of Mauritianism, threatened defamation. '*Des voix noires qui s'élèvent et qui y voient du noir*,' they wrote without irony.

I was sent screenshots of a conversation on Messenger. 'Do you know Ariel Saramandi personally?' A man asks an acquaintance of mine. 'She travels the world for sensational news. She hires hackers to work alongside her. She's using false identity. By military view she's dodgy.' The man appeared again in a private Telegram chat called 'freedom warriors freedom fighters'. The anti-vax platform logo was their profile picture, and the expatriates were part of the chat. 'She's working for the government,' the man said. 'People think we are spreading false information. We have to remove the stain that Ariel has put on us.'

I decided to send this man what was, in retrospect, an exceedingly stupid message on Facebook. I told him that I too believed vaccination should be an informed choice; that I realized how frightening the pandemic was. I urged him to get his information from proper news sources; I sent an actual book recommendation, Eula Biss' *On Immunity*. He told me that his account had been hacked.

I spent an enormous time on social media, in an attempt to reduce the amount of disinformation. Many Mauritians have comorbidities: we have one of the highest rates of diabetes in the world, for instance, making us especially vulnerable. And people around me had chosen not to get vaccinated because of Laurette and the My Body My Choice My Voice platform: many had fallen seriously ill, and some had died.

My mother has asthma. Her lungs work only at 50 per cent of their capacity. She barely sleeps at night; her breathing is constricted as if her ribs had grown and interlocked across her chest. She was one of the only members of her prayer group to get vaccinated. Still, she was influenced enough to take ivermectin every day, as a 'precautionary measure'. 'A doctor prescribed it to me!' she told me angrily.

One Creole woman I know worked as a secretary for a lucrative Franco-Mauritian company. Their owners were staunchly anti-vaccine. Veronique felt that accepting the Covid-19 vaccine would betray the company; she respected and admired her bosses and lived for their recognition of her work. When she caught the Delta variant at the end of 2021 she had to be treated at home: there were no beds left in the private clinics. The oxygen tanks she'd managed to buy were depleted within two weeks. She eventually found succour in a clinic's ICU and was intubated for several months. She survived. She still refuses to get vaccinated.

Laurette grew irate at my posts. 'Are PCR tests giving false positive results? Is this deliberate or under instruction of Mrs Ariel?' He had edited the post numerous times, 'Arielle' to 'Ariel', unsure of how to spell my pseudonym. Later he'd claim that he was referring to Ariel the laundry detergent, then said Ariel was his new nickname for the French immunologist he hated. Some of my friends stood up for me, suffered the deluge of comments that followed. Joanna Berenger publicly voiced her support. But I didn't feel emboldened. It was at this moment, too late, that I understood how far Laurette was willing to go for power. He wouldn't just insinuate, or lie, or transmit false information in good faith. He'd conjure shit from the ether. He'd make his followers believe whatever he wanted.

I'd told him he'd lost my respect, lost international credibility, that he shouldn't expect to be interviewed by international media anytime soon. I knew these men hated the threat of being deplatformed; hoped that, in his greed for global attention, he'd tone down his theatrics.

Reuben Pillay, one of Laurette's greatest supporters at the time, was particularly incensed by my words. We knew each other online: his drone media accompanied my words while reporting on the *Wakashio* oil spill for news outlets abroad. Soon after the oil spill though, I'd unfriended him on Facebook; I'd heard that he wasn't to be trusted, and his posts had proved the rumours right: they were homophobic, misogynistic to the extreme.

He took my comment on Laurette to mean that I was representative of international media as a whole. He harassed me on social media across multiple platforms. It was 'not my place' to tell people to get vaccinated, he said. He dug up an alt-right-produced article on me, published after 'There Is Too Much Feminism'. 'I'm not sure which word might qualify this sort of person,' he said, musing on a comment that I must be a lesbian. To him, and men like him, I was not, could not be a cis, heterosexual woman.

Monster. Virago. Shrew.
Stay-at-home mother.

In early July, a press conference was organized by Laurette, Valayden, other lawyers and activists and the anti-vaxxers. A chance for them to regurgitate conspiracy theories galore over an hour and a half. They made comparisons to Nazi Germany, to yellow stars embroidered on clothes.

'It's sad to see how last year's hero is now a menace to public health,' I posted on Twitter.

'Ms [--] is that you? It's my choice just as well as yours to lobby for who you like. You want to play, let's do it openly. I can't be bought or sold, my fight is for the people and not for lobbies or medical cartels.'

He knew what he was doing, publishing my real surname. My family is the only one in Mauritius to have it. It is one of the most obviously Jewish surnames in the world, and my father used to be one of the country's most prominent businessmen.

His followers were ecstatic. They hungered for the takedown.

Saramandi, my grandmother's maiden name. I didn't want to use my mother's original surname, a white inheritance. But Saramandi was mutable. Like my grandmother's, the name's origins were unknown: she looked

Afro-Indian, the name could be Afro-Indian. A number of Creole families I know bear iterations of it: Saramandy, Saramandine, Saramandiff. Importantly, too, my spelling of the name seems to have disappeared. I didn't want to get any other families in trouble.

Ariel, I chose after Shelley, Shakespeare, Plath. Ariel the ship, Ariel a vessel, conductor of my writing until my death.

'The Little Mermaid,' his followers mocked, which was fine.

'We have to beat her pussy'.

'Another chatwa that fucks and drinks piss with the Prime Minister'.

'That pussy shit that the government paid is back'.

'Using a fake name to mislead the population and spread your shit'.

'She wants to suck Bruneau's dick that dirty whore who speaks shit fuck her'.

'Is she a freemason? Those fucking freemasons one day I'll take a gun and shoot those devils those fuckers'.

'Bitches are barking'.

'She's looking for dick'.

'She's a Masonic Antichrist agent'.

Some of my friends tried to intervene but there was no point. I screenshotted what I could, asked them if they'd be willing to take over after the number of death and rape threats left me winded. But it didn't stop.

An anti-vax journalist posted an old interview I'd given to another paper a good decade ago. A long diatribe ensued, a fabulous mélange of alt-right theory. 'You are being called out for using so-called journalism wrapped in white supremacy, toxic femininity and "good English" as weapons to threaten and intimidate; while also glorifying self-victimisation,' she said.

There, in that sentence, I understood how so many other Mauritians must see me. In her imagination I was a white person by virtue of my white father, 'good' English, obvious wealth. For her, living in a white-minority country, there was no question of me being a light-skinned Creole woman.

I'd described myself as 'British-Mauritian', therefore, to her, a foreigner. Never mind that I was London-born out of medical necessity, flown back to Mauritius a month after birth, slept through the whole flight, slept so much my parents thought I was dead. Easy cargo. I've lived here ever since, except for the four years I spent at university. On every trip to England there'd be a file in my hand luggage with my birth certificates, proof of dual nationality, as if – and in case – my British passport wouldn't be enough. And never mind that I only use 'British-Mauritian' in my bio as a deterrent: a constant reminder to whoever was in power that I was, in theory, protected by British citizenship. Other than these documents and the theoretical human rights that accompany them, I don't know what it implies for me to say that I belong to Britain, culturally or nationally, if there are particular affinities that have somehow bestowed Britishness upon my person.

This journalist and her friend – a mutual acquaintance of Laurette – shared an article written about my father, one that describes him as 'the shylock of Bell Village', a 'shrewd' Jewish man who orchestrated 'obscure forces'. Laurette thanked them for this information.

This was a glorious day for Pillay. He shared the articles. He filmed a video late that night, revelling in the day's work. He riled against pro-vaccine 'chatwas'; the Bhojpuri word is widely used in Mauritius, derived from the verb 'chato', to lick – a bootlicker would be the most polite way of defining the term, one close to the government in power. 'One of them has been unmasked today!' he says, his eyes aglow, ecstatic. 'She attacked me, she attacked Laurette, all the while using a nom de plume, a false name, her fake identity. Now we know who she is, her real name. In a short while she'll have a defamation case against her, for spreading lies. And not one case only,' he says, beatific.

He made some enquiries and managed to call my sister.

'Your whole family is scum! Your sister is depraved!'

He wanted her to grovel, undoubtedly pleased by her natural, to him womanly, reaction – her tears, her begging him to leave our family out of this, out of what I'd done.

VI. *New politician, old legacies, July–December 2021*

Laurette launched his own political party on the first anniversary of his massive protest, in August 2021. It was something he'd been teasing for months; unlike with his anti-vaccination tirades, though, he faced criticism for the way he spoke about his party and political movement. He'd effectively blundered, by stating he was going

251

to 'conquer the electorate of the MMM and the PMSD'. Both parties had solid support within minority ethnic groups: the PMSD had strong ties to the Creole community, and the MMM had a particularly strong Creole and Muslim base. Both parties, too, were keen to show that they advocated for and represented the interests of the Mauritian population at large. What Laurette was saying, in essence, was that he'd be the one who would represent the Creole community in politics.

And there was something substantial to his claim: the MMM's leader was Franco-Mauritian, and only a third of the MMM's Bureau Politique were Creole. The PMSD's leadership was Creole, but Xavier Luc Duval embodied a certain (misguided) idea of what the Creole bourgeoisie 'looked like': light-skinned, wealthy, educated abroad. Laurette was much darker skinned, working-class, and was seen as 'of the people'. He may or may not have completed his secondary school education. His supporters counted on him to overhaul the electoral system, bring in a new constitution, make the country fairer. And the system *was* unfair. In Mauritius, a party can rule even if it only obtains the votes of half the country's constituencies. In 2019, the voting map was quite clear: the more populous town- and city-dwellers overwhelmingly voted for the opposition. The current government won the election with just 37 per cent of national votes, ascribed in popular discourse to the so-called rural 'Hindu belt'. Laurette didn't hide his disdain for the 37 per cent, though he'd never qualify them as 'Hindus' outright.

When Laurette said he'd effectively come to 'conquer' the PMSD and the MMM, I think he must have spent some time contemplating Gaetan Duval, the most infamous Creole politician that the island had known until Laurette's arrival onto the scene. He'd mention Gaetan Duval occasionally in interviews; sometimes he'd mark his distance by saying 'I am not Duval'; other times he'd say that, like Duval, he was considered a threat to established parties in power. Valayden had trained as Duval's pupil; I wonder what lessons in theatricality had been imparted from one generation to another.

Gaetan Duval – Xavier Luc's father – was leader of the PMSD from 1967 to 1996. He was Deputy Prime Minister of the country from 1983 to 1988, and, in the public eye, is most remembered for his work as Minister of Tourism during those years, where he invited French film stars to Mauritius and put the island, as it were, on the (glossy magazine) map. Born in 1930, he came from an upper-middle-class Creole family and had an excellent education in England and France. Upon his return to the island he saw an empty space in Mauritian politics that he carved for himself. There were a number of Creole intellectuals in the Labour Party, but none of note in the conservative, Franco-Mauritian-run PMSD. 'In a bigger, richer country Gaetan Duval, the Foreign Minister, might have been an actor or a pop star. He has the disquieting attractiveness...; he has the hair, the clothes; and he has the actor's needs,' wrote V.S. Naipaul in his 1972 essay 'The Overcrowded Barracoon'. He really was Hollywood-handsome.

Duval attempted to unite Creoles, Indo-Mauritian Muslims, Franco-Mauritians and other minority groups against Independence, spreading fear of a 'Hindu hegemony'. He spread his divisive, incendiary rhetoric in the full knowledge that the country was heading to

Independence anyway, since the British government couldn't afford to support the colony. 'I didn't believe for a second that we were going to win the elections. Maybe for a few seconds in certain public meetings, where 100–150,000 people came to listen to us in a kind of collective trance,' he reminisced in an interview, where he claims he had nothing to do with the racial riots of 1968. 'I've always had this kind of carnal relationship – almost sexual – with the crowd.... When you are in front of a crowd that identifies with you and repeats what you say without being able to do otherwise ... [it's] the greatest happiness of a man. An extraordinary jouissance, to speak to those who love you. When you feel the hypnotic power you have over them. When they applaud you.' There he was in rallies, dressed in head-to-toe black leather, his 'Black Panther' outfit, chanting 'Black is Beautiful', riding a horse called Black Beauty. 'King Creole', his supporters called him. There he was in his bungalow in Grand Gaube, entertaining Jean-Marie Le Pen and other members of the French Front National. Supporting trade with South Africa during apartheid. Deputy Prime Minister, Minister of Tourism. 'Mr Duval is Black Power in the daytime. In the night he white,' a local told Naipaul.

Duval hated the MMM. For him, Paul Berenger's party was taking 'his' electorate; their strikes and trade union work were a blow to his ultra-capitalist vision, his ties to the sugar conglomerates. Laurette had more ideological affinities with the MMM, if anything; the same concern for workers' rights, an articulated – if naïve – idea of socialism. But Laurette didn't want anything to do with the MMM. He was 'fed up with dinosaurs', and the oldest dinosaur leading a political party in Mauritius was Berenger.

254

Berenger, seventy-six years old in 2021, had founded the MMM in the late 1960s along with a few other university students who'd returned from abroad. They built solid links with trade unions, organized protests, strikes. They were imprisoned, found ways to survive under Ramgoolam Senior's authoritarian government, its secret police, the censorship of the press. Attempts were made to assassinate Berenger and other members of the MMM; Azor Adelaide, an MMM activist, was shot dead in 1971. Duval was widely believed to have orchestrated the attempted murders, but never charged. His agents went to prison for Adelaide's killing.

But neither Duval, nor Berenger, nor Ramgoolam, nor Laurette's new movement were able to prevent a series of new laws passed throughout 2021. Amendments to the Independent Broadcasting Authority Act, that would force journalists to reveal their sources, enforce higher penalties for supposed breaches and allow the state to suspend media licences without the possibility of appeal. The Cybersecurity and Cybercrime Act, an intelligent, subdued rehashing of the binned ICTA proposal. The Offshore Petroleum Bill.

Laurette rallied, marched, burnt masks. Couldn't stop the bills from passing. I listened to members of the MSM read and approve the bills-turned-acts on the radio, listened to radio presenters discuss the ramifications as my husband washed the dishes, suds bubbling on his hands. As my son chased the cat around the apartment singing *il était un petit navire*, pronouncing *navire* as *naverre*. I hadn't a comment to make on them online. I'd deleted my social media accounts after all the harassment.

In late 2021 Laurette promised more revelations, insider information. He had information on the Indian military base being built on Agaléga. On Kistnen's murder. On the Prime Minister's grandiose house, built on land that hadn't been paid for by the Prime Minister but by another man, who died in London a year after the scandal made the news. 'Wherever there is Pinocchio there is death, whether it be in no. 8, in Europe or the ENT Hospital. How can I put it, it's like they have a contract with corpses,' he wrote on 4 November 2021.

In November, too, there was a surge of Covid-19. Patients in trolleys lying in the sun. Wealthy businessmen unable to wrangle a bed in any clinic's ICU, bodies collapsing in public hospitals and at home. And while the dead continued to grow Laurette would say 'it's not about a virus, it's about control,' an image of a masked person controlled like a puppet from above. Would say the government had to take responsibility for vaccine-related deaths. That the Health Minister should resign because he had deaths on his conscience as a result of his incompetence. Psalm 23, *The Lord is my shepherd; I shall not want.* 'Protect yourself with efficient medicine,' he wrote, providing a list of pharmacies supplying ivermectin. His followers asking him questions like he was a doctor; Laurette doling out instructions. Later, he and his 'movement' would distribute ivermectin around the island, 'for free', he'd say, proud of his work.

Statistics showed that unvaccinated people in Mauritius were roughly ten times as likely to die from Covid-19 as vaccinated people.

Journalists from BBC Radio messaged me again, this

time for information on our local Covid-19 crisis. I directed them to other journalists whose work I trusted.

I still felt like I could make some kind of contribution to local politics, though. I wouldn't become a media personality, I wouldn't be interviewed in the local press, I'd more or less disappear from the public eye, but I'd be able to share my ideas with other people who'd be able to make a difference, who had an established voice. In late 2021, I joined the MMM and became one of the members of the party's Commission de Développement Durable. Joanna Berenger was the Commission's President.

VII. *Eating God, July 2022*

White men who were not racist, who were affable and made friends with Mauritians of different ethnicities than their own, garnered an almost religious level of adoration from non-white Mauritians. I'd seen it with my own father, who has always been a rather unassuming, quietly genial person. Because he was polite, and did basic things such as remembering his employees' names and the state of their families, because he was incapable of raising his voice or making a scene, he was beloved. And he was almost revered – I do not use the verb lightly – when people observed that not only had he married a non-white, non-wealthy Mauritian woman, he also engaged in activities that were viewed as transgressions of his class and race, such as frequenting public beaches every weekend instead of only going to hotels or owning a private bungalow by the sea.

Joanna and Paul Berenger benefited from this same

kind of adulation: class-traitors who fought for a more just country, who spoke and gave their time to everyone. But this kind of adulation turned very quickly into virulent hatred, once Hindutva figures in government were able to convince great numbers of Hindus that Joanna was in fact racist; that her warm demeanour was a lie.

In July 2022, Joanna shared a photo of the Prime Minister with his wife during a religious ceremony in the lake of Grand Bassin, the most sacred Hindu site on the island, along with the caption: '*Apel sa: Manz bondie, kaka diab*', or 'One could call this: Eat god, shit the devil', an old Creole expression. 'Do you know this proverb?' Joanna continued. 'Our Creole language has an extraordinary richness and wisdom.'

Hundreds and then thousands of comments swamped the picture. Death threats, rape threats, sometimes elaborated with precision. Demands that she be imprisoned. Most Mauritians believe that Joanna is white, and so she was also called by names that were also shot at her father, Paul Berenger, in parliament: 'kolon', colonizer. White rat. A racist.

She had no idea that the proverb would provoke such an outpouring of hatred, given that she was targeting the Prime Minister, not Grand Bassin, not the ceremony, not Hinduism. But it didn't matter: thousands of Hindus believed that their religion permeated all aspects of the sacred lake. The entrance to the lake is dominated by two huge statues of Shiva and Durga, and Hindu temples circle around the site. Travellers to Mauritius have no way of knowing that Grand Bassin was also of spiritual significance to the Creole community: Creoles believed that fairies lived in the lake, caring for maroons who made the forests surrounding the lake their home.

Ministers and partisans of the MSM successfully riled up thousands of Mauritians: they claimed that Joanna was insulting all Hindus by using '*manz bondie kaka diab*', since she was associating the devil with Grand Bassin, and doing so in a sacred month. The charge was led by – of all people – the Minister for Gender Equality, who exacerbated public outrage and sectarian abuse both for clout and in order to detract attention from the government scandal of the day. The day after the video was published, the Minister organized a press conference to further excoriate Joanna and demand her resignation from the National Assembly. Before the conference began – when the Minister believed the mics were turned off – she said 'Look at them, they're like monkeys'. She was, most likely, referring to the journalists in front of her.

It was the worst harassment a public figure – let alone politician – had faced in recent memory.

VIII. *The assembly of delegates, July 2022*

The furore had only slightly calmed down by the end of the month, when Joanna and I went to the MMM's Assembly of Delegates, a congress that reunited all members of the party. She drove me and other members of her constituency to the Assembly, drumming her fingers on the steering wheel, humming along to 'Soldat Lalit Militant', one of the MMM's anthems. I was recovering from hyperemesis gravidarum, happy to be able to leave my home without throwing up, happy to have a moth-ridden purple flag, which I brandished out of the window. I liked my flag. Proof enough that the party was honest, that financially it was making do. No brand-new party accessories, lavish biryanis or car trunks filled with cash.

The MMM is the only mainstream party largely free of corruption scandals, built on serious, labour-intensive democratic mechanisms which ensure that every member has their say. Socialist. Progressive. Concerned with climate change, feminism, anti-racism, anti-discrimination. The underdogs. The MMM was the party in power in 1982, then ruled as part of a coalition government from 1991 to 2005, surviving three general elections. A solid presence in the opposition since; the smallest of the mainstream parties. News reports said the party was in crisis, plagued by openly publicized conflicts and resignations, giving an impression that the MMM was 'done' and that the future lay elsewhere, in stronger parties or in newer ones, in younger – and more authoritarian – figureheads.

The assembly was held at the Plaza, and it was crowded. There were red plastic chairs all over the place, and even then some members and supporters had to stand at the back, sat where they could on the floor. Working class mothers brought along their children, rubber sandals slipping off and on their feet. A drone filmed all the action and relayed the images in a live Facebook feed; MMM candidates checked the feed regularly, satisfied with how many people had tuned in.

Most speeches given by prominent members of the MMM were about the cost-of-living crisis. Mauritians unable to go to the supermarket, relying instead on village grocery stores and traditional labutik sinwa where they could buy produce on credit. Mothers giving their children up to state care. Firstborns refusing meals for the sake of their siblings, their mothers. The riots in April were on everyone's mind: they erupted in working-class Creole neighbourhoods and turned violent after the arrest of yet another self-declared activist.

I'd spotted the 'activist' around before, trailing Laurette and his circle closely, walking with immense confidence around Port Louis on weekdays. He was a young, thin Creole man who preferred to go by his pseudonym; his birth name, Dominique, could be mistaken for a woman's. He had an endearing, child-like face. He'd be briefly imprisoned a few times throughout the year for 'breaching bail conditions' after his initial arrest in April, and was defended by Laurette's lawyer troupe. Whoever was advising him did not have his best interests in mind. He gave the government 'ultimatums'. In late July he said he was giving the Prime Minister twenty-four hours to resign; the next day, sans resignation, he announced he'd stop his work as a political activist. He changed his mind quickly enough. In a live video a month later, we saw him driving around Port Louis, his car blaring 'Polico Crapo', a viral song on police brutality and racism that the authorities were keen to remove from the airwaves (Laurette would later use the song as an anthem in his rallies). His expression was determined, frightened: he parked in front of the country's central police station, made 'revelations' of how drugs were planted in the home of his lawyer – in front of policemen – and was promptly arrested again.

This man was allegedly beaten, and crowds rallied in his support in front of police headquarters. The police met the crowds with tear gas and armoured vehicles, which they then deployed across the country.

Paul Berenger needed help getting onto the stage, and once there seemed absolutely untroubled by the noise from the crowd and the speakers. I had pressed my fingers to my ears throughout the assembly, convinced that I'd emerge by the end of it with ruptured eardrums. He closed his eyes sometimes while other delegates spoke, scratched his throat repeatedly; the gesture reminded me of the throat cancer that he had recovered from a few years ago. When Paul rose for his speech the crowd lit fireworks outside the Plaza. He was transformed with the microphone in his hand, endowed with an almost supernatural vigour. His voice was incredibly strong. He made jokes, his voice cracking endearingly. He talked seriously about the state of the country. The delegates and the crowd cheered him on. I saw how beloved he was, especially among the older generation who'd witnessed the rise of the MMM first hand. I saw how difficult a change of leadership would be for the party.

At the assembly, Berenger spoke of decisions that would have to be made, code for alliances that would need to be forged in view of the upcoming 2024 elections. Decisions that would be voted on by delegates in each region. There was talk of an alliance of the major oppositional parties, Labour and even the PMSD, now run by Gaetan Duval's son, a very different man from his father. It was clear that the opposition would need to be extremely strong in order to beat the MSM.

Despite its overtly autocratic ambitions, despite its handling of the *Wakashio* oil spill, despite almost unbelievable levels of inflation, the MSM was still confident that they'd win. There were rumours that they'd increase pensions, minimum wage and various allowances even more. Added to these populist measures was a distinctive, growing rise in Hindu nationalism that members of the government clearly promoted.

IX. *A telenovela of revelations, May–November 2022*

By mid-2022 Laurette had become even bolder. The country was broiling in new scandals.

He regularly posted about police brutality: people would send him media clips in which he'd sometimes appear, documenting injuries. In May 2022 he posted a series of videos shot in 2019, showing the torture of three men, two of whom are Creole, by police. The men are stripped, in chains, tasered in their genitalia, made to role-play, to sing the national anthem. The policemen are joyous; some of them sing. The videos went viral. Supposedly, in 2020, Valayden had given these videos over to the police and an inquiry was in the works, but it took public outrage two years later to expedite the 'investigation' – the policemen in the videos were all easily identifiable. One of the victims had been incarcerated for theft and murder. Laurette's lawyer troupe managed to obtain his release. The lawyers also helped other victims of torture press charges.

In June the CEO of Mauritius Telecom resigned from his job. Sherry Singh had previously enjoyed an excellent relationship with the Prime Minister and his family; in a live 'tell-all' interview, he said he'd resigned because he'd been asked to authorize a 'sniffing operation' by the Indian government. The latter's officials had allegedly extracted information from our internet submarine cables.

Some of the biggest names in local journalism didn't seem to care that Singh had stayed quiet during the proposed ICTA Amendment, that he hadn't said a word about corruption in all his years close to power: here was a new truth teller. Singh called upon Laurette's security team for his protection post-revelations. He also announced that he'd be launching his career in politics and would help to bring along a 'tidal wave of change'.

In the interview he also provided 'insider information' on the workings of local power, notably claiming that the Prime Minister's wife was the 'supreme leader' of the country, managing the Prime Minister's cabinet. He referred to Kobita Jugnauth not by name, but by two monikers: 'the kitchen' – referring to her work 'behind the scenes', as it were – and 'Lady Macbeth'.

Before the interview Kobita Jugnauth was one of the most enigmatic public figures in Mauritius. Her perfectly polished image served the MSM well: she was presented as the steadfast, elegant companion of the Prime Minister, mother of three children. Well-educated and from a prominent family, she is of both Indo-Mauritian and Creole descent but is mostly seen in sarees during public events. In essence, she was used to showcase, time and time again, an idealized image of the traditional Hindu family; an image weaponized to show the contrast between her and Veena Ramgoolam, who doesn't have children and is still married to her husband despite his well-publicized infidelities.

After the interview, journalists hunted for information that would show her as wielding tentacular power, a shadow government in her own person. But they couldn't find much evidence beyond rumours.

In the wake of the scandal the Prime Minister denied that equipment had been installed to enable such 'sniffing', stating that there was 'a security issue, and it was necessary to do this survey in Mauritius', and that he'd personally asked Narendra Modi for help. The reasons concerning the 'security issue' were deliberately kept unclear. Siddharth Varadarajan of *The Wire* news website had a good theory, which is that:

> India has very close security ties with Port Louis. India is helping to develop military infrastructure – officially described as assistance for air and sea connectivity – at the Agalega Islands about a thousand kilometres north of Mauritius proper. One measure of the closeness of ties is the fact that Mauritius's National Security Advisers ... have traditionally been retired intelligence and military officers deputed by New Delhi to the sensitive post. Thanks to the internet sniffing scandal, this arrangement has now been flagged as a concern in the National Assembly.

With Singh's aid, Laurette became even bolder. 'If the Prime Minister and his government don't resign I will trigger a worldwide diplomatic problem on Monday' he said. He shared articles on Tek Fog and Pegasus, claimed we were all being surveyed; posted a picture of himself in military gear in front of a wall with a massive insignia bearing a red star and the letters H W, said he'd been part of the security team of Huawei International since 2010, knew the Vice President of the company very well ('he personally signed his book for me and I stayed in their hotel'). 'You can get a missile from the Chinese embassy and other diplomatic problems,' he wrote. Huawei are the leading suppliers of telecommunication devices in Mauritius. In the weeks to come there were signs of discomfort between the Mauritian, Indian and Chinese governments.

Laurette, inspired by the events in Sri Lanka, perhaps thought the world was in throes of a revolutionary momentum. His posts grew more incendiary.

He claimed the Prime Minister's wife and daughter smoked marijuana. Said the ruling party's acronym stood for Men who have Sex with Men and that it was 'diseased'; he used one of the Prime Minister's verbal slip-ups in parliament – to Shakeel Mohamed, he'd allegedly said 'I will fuck you' instead of 'I will fuck you out (of the House)' – and, in a torrent of homophobia, presented it as 'evidence' that Jugnauth was gay. He said international mercenaries were on his trail. Published 'investigative videos' of men who claimed to know who killed the murdered activist. Said that it was thanks to his work and to the anti-vax platform that the government eased Covid-19 restrictions in the country. Had fights with other activists who'd made baseless accusations against him for clout. Insinuated that some MPs were doing hard drugs. Published a selfie with his new car, a black twenty-year-old BMW, 'with a V8 motor if you please.' 'Those chatwas who are stressed about where I got the money to buy my BMW Series 7, ask the question to my face.'

'Pinocchio and the Movement Synthetic Mafia your turn will come. Patience,' he wrote, sharing a photo of a man stripped of his clothes, tied to a roadside barrier, with a text explaining that this man was allegedly a Sri Lankan MP.

He organized more protests against vaccine mandates, the cost-of-living crisis, the increase in fuel prices: all of this was the government's fault.

Meanwhile, the Prime Minister – true to his awkward, unpopular style – said the opposition's criticism of the sniffing affair was pure 'India-bashing'. In a meeting in July, he claimed there was a connection between the opposition, drug barons and money launderers, all of whom were plotting to take down the government. Journalists were incensed, and shared photos of the Prime Minister alongside men accused of drug trafficking. Laurette had shared some of these photos for years.

August was a big month for Laurette and his entourage.

Laurette 'resigned' from his own political party in the middle of that month. The party had grown by then into a coalition of 'extra-parliamentary forces'. He left after refusing to solicit his party's advice before taking action and making statements. He'd broken ties with Valayden, but there was nothing to suggest that this rupture would dim his popularity. Laurette had never stopped consolidating his base, melding social work and political activism, showcasing his support, particularly to Creoles and Indo-Mauritian Muslims. He knew how to work the field. He fed the poor. He helped repair the homes of working-class Mauritians, tin shack houses damaged by torrential rain and cyclones. He was still in control of his own pre-coalition party, though, and two months later he'd rebrand it in his own name: Mouvement Bruneau Laurette. He still felt sidelined by the major oppositional parties, obviously hurt that they were banding together to form a coalition before the next general elections without including his Movement. He called some members of the opposition 'traitors', said they'd be imprisoned when he came to power.

A week later, Akil Bissessur – one of the most prominent lawyers in Laurette's clique – was arrested for drug trafficking along with his partner. His home was raided by a new unit of police called the 'Special Striking Team', headed by a man named Ashik Jagai. I didn't feel too concerned with the arrest, or with Laurette's claims that it was a conspiracy. He'd posted a 'hit list' supposedly crafted by the police, a list of names of those 'causing high disturbance to community', as per the paper. You could find Laurette's name, his troupe of lawyers, some other activists, some members of the opposition. The list said they'd all be subjected to 'scheduled raids'. It would take remarkably good faith to believe that the document was real, but that didn't stop journalists from publicizing it, interviewing Laurette for insider information.

None of the people who surrounded Laurette seemed like they had particularly clean records of conduct. It took me time to learn that I should pay attention to the terrible things that happened to those I despised. Their misfortunes weren't the result of divine, karma-laden justice; they were symptomatic of some dreadful power helmed at the top of the state, power I could barely fathom. In Bissessur's case, the police apparently had no valid warrant before entering his home; the lawyer maintains the drugs were planted, and that he and his partner were physically assaulted. They were made to hand their phones over to the police; a short while later, intimate photos and videos of the couple were leaked online.

While all this was happening, Laurette hinted online at a 'party' that would be organized by a certain 'man in black' in front of the Prime Minister's house on 29 August, to commemorate the two-year anniversary of the mega-protest. I think Laurette hoped for a Sri Lanka redux, a surge of his supporters bathing in the pool, wrecking the house. Hardly anyone turned up, but Laurette wouldn't admit defeat: he said the Prime Minister had to 'hide' in Rodrigues because of the national security risk this 'party' represented. 'War is a mindset game.... We have denuded his security system. We know what vehicles contain weapons when they are escorting him and the plans of his fortress are also available. Who says better, Pravind Jugnauth? If we didn't do anything on Sunday, it's because your children aren't responsible for your actions.' Nobody in the press wrote that this was or could have been, in effect, an attempted coup d'état.

Laurette commented on the failed 'party' in October, saying 'if I have to take a country, I will take it legally... It's not possible to have a coup d'état in Mauritius, it's not in our genes and it's not a good example for our children.' He was organizing another protest on 29 October 2022, one which would give a voice to the 'suffering and anger of the population' and 'give hope to Mauritians'. A crowd of about 10,000 people assembled in Port Louis; less than a tenth of those who came on 29 August 2020, but a sturdy number nonetheless. Laurette was exuberant, his troupe of lawyers and activists by his side, members of the Labour Party and other minor parties too.

There was plenty of material to buoy the crowd. Laurette revealed supposed links between drug trafficking and the *Wakashio*. 'I'll say it again and again, there were traces of drugs on the ship,' he said, insinuating that one of the Prime Minister's right-hand men was involved, 'controlling the cargo'. A narrative he supported by displaying transcripts between the ship and the National Coast Guard Service, as well as supposedly incriminating photos.

There was also more talk of the Kistnen murder during the protest, with fresh news to stimulate public outrage. In mid-October a prominent news organization had leaked a copy of the magistrate's report. 'I consider the conduct of the police in the present case to be abhorrent. The manner in which the enquiry was conducted fell so below what can be considered reasonable that it marks a new level of incompetence,' wrote the magistrate. In the report, Vidya Mungroo-Jugurnath describes the Safe City cameras that didn't record the murder; the policemen who decided not to verify all the CCTV footage available; accessories of the murder that disappeared, misplaced, unexamined or sent to the wrong department; tardy DNA comparisons; autopsy instructions that weren't followed; the political ties of a medical examiner who autopsied Kistnen, and whose conclusions were tenuous ('blatantly suspicious and reeks of cover-up'). Kistnen was a man of many debts, mistresses and shady deals. The strongest motive for the crime, according to the magistrate, lay in his role as a nexus between potential contractors during the pandemic and the former Minister of Commerce,

Yogida Sawmynaden. The government had responded by saying they would launch 'an enquiry' as to how the findings of the judicial inquiry were leaked to the public. The Attorney General insinuated that an officer working for the Director of Public Prosecutions could be at fault. The DPP, still an independent body, said it would 'not allow itself to be intimidated, in yet another attempt to curtail its independence and fearlessness to uphold the Rule of Law in our democratic society.'

Six days after the protest-meeting in Port Louis, Laurette and his son were arrested for drug trafficking. Police raided their home and Laurette's car, uncovering 46 kilos of cannabis worth about £4.7 million.

X. *Laurette, the man who came from somewhere, 2004–2020*

There's a limit to what you can understand by trawling through a man's presence on the internet, even in the case of prolific users like Laurette, who usually posted several times a day before his arrest. This is a tentative portrait, one inked by social media and the news.

He had three much older children from his first marriage, and his first wife died in 2021. Their children lived together with her until her death. One of them would be arrested with Laurette in early November, then released three weeks later. He seemed to have difficulties with the school system, which is particularly discriminatory towards Creole Mauritians. He wrote in Kreol and French as he pleased, which I thought was good: he wouldn't let his obvious problems with grammar shame him, stop him from voicing out his opinions. He disdained those who, he believed, waved their degrees in the population's faces without having any intelligence.

In 2013 Bruneau Laurette was interviewed for his work as a fitness instructor. By that time he'd already received military training abroad by an Israeli academy, the National Rifle Association, the Institute of Protection Specialists & Security Contractors in Michigan, among others. He worked as a bodyguard and as a securities professional in the local nightlife and events industry. By the end of 2017 he announced that he was leaving events to concentrate his efforts in security, weapons and self-defence training; he became the director of a company specializing in marine security.

From 2004 to 2019, the court seized three plots of land under Laurette's name after he'd been unable to pay his debts. From 2017 to 2018 he posted many pictures of himself with his youngest daughter from his second marriage. He shared anti-vaccine conspiracy theories and articles from untrustworthy websites on how marijuana could heal diseases. He didn't post much about marijuana publicly at the time, but his posts could indicate that he was an enthusiast like many Mauritians: it's estimated that 1–200,000 Mauritians smoke cannabis. Later, he'd advocate for the decriminalization of marijuana in his name, in the name of his civic organization and political party.

He'd write about how real men shouldn't hit women and trained local women in Krav Maga and self-defence. He posted on mental health. He loved guns. He shared a few photos from the page 'Love IDF' (Israel Defense

Forces); from military doomsday preppers; from a spiritual healing 'witch' doctor in Florida, who was later convicted of murder.

In 2017 and 2018 he worked as an agent for the Reform Party, a minor political party headed by a particularly ruthless ex-member of the MSM. Laurette believed that Roshi Bhadain was the man who'd change the country and free it of 'the dinosaurs'.

By 2019 there were photos of him across the African continent, in Europe, South Korea, Cuba and in the Seychelles, training prison staff, security forces and self-defence enthusiasts in Krav Maga and KAPAP. In 2019 he travelled with his family to Kenya and Thailand for his daughter's birthday. In a post written in June 2019, he said he was celebrating his own birthday away from his family 'as usual' and thanked his brother and wife for being there for his children when he couldn't be. He described his brother as 'more than an uncle, father that my [three eldest] children didn't have'. In an interview post-arrest, his son told the media that his father had always fought against the consumption and distribution of drugs. He revealed that Laurette's own brother had overcome drug addiction with his help. It's unclear whether this is the same brother he describes.

LALIT, in a newsletter written in September 2020, pointed out that Laurette 'must have had some strong backing of some sort for his meteoric rise'. There was his military training abroad (who paid for it?); the fact that, as a maritime security professional in charge of a security guard company, he'd financially depend on getting contracts from shipping companies (who gave them to him?); that he'd worked under the 'notoriously repressive ex-Prison Commissioner' who was now Advisor to the Prime Minister (how were they introduced?); that he'd hired a PR firm to manage and advertise the protest of 29 August 2020 (with what resources?).

In the same newsletter, LALIT described a press conference held by Laurette and his team on the night of his mega-demonstration. In the conference Laurette spoke about his work as a political agent-bodyguard for MSM candidates now turned Ministers. 'People say I'm political... [W]ho moved with [Minister of Environment] Kavy Ramano during his whole campaign? Me. I never asked for a cent.... When you have a conscience, you don't become complicit in a situation.' It was his work, he said, that that enabled Ramano to garner the Creole vote in the region.

It's not clear why he brought up his background as an MSM agent. A journalist asked if he'd been contacted by leaders of the opposition, and he said no, but he'd received plenty of congratulatory messages, some even from the MSM, from the Prime Minister's Office. He said he received information and reports from the PMO. 'I always say ... what you're able to do to me, I'm able to do to you. The information they have on me, I have on them.'

It's unclear at what point Laurette became an MSM agent – if an 'agent' is what he was in the lead up to the general election of 2019. He could have worked as a bodyguard under his company name, but then again, he said he wasn't paid for his work and didn't ask to be re-munerated either, which is strange, suffice to say, given his financial situation.

274

It's important to note, too, that Laurette had post-ed about his work as an agent-bodyguard for the MSM before he became famous, but mainstream news organizations wouldn't relay the fact; in their coverage of the conference, his past with the MSM isn't evoked at all. No one speculated that Kistnen and Laurette may very well have known each other when they worked as agents for the party in power. No one wondered what Laurette had been promised, and what had been withheld. In his dealings with Laurette in August 2020, the politician Nando Bodha – who was part of the MSM at the time – had stated that Laurette 'spoke to me of his career, of his difficulties and deceptions, notably in the political field. Following this I told him to forget about the past and to engage himself in a more constructive way in his initiatives.' To me, this indicates that Laurette was promised a career within the MSM at the time of the 2019 general election.

His post-electoral disgust for the MSM was real. In post after post I read him railing about how those MPs he'd worked for had let the Creole community of the region down, how they did nothing when tin-roofed homes were razed. There are photos of Laurette dressed as Father Christmas in a slum, distributing presents.

He never stopped posting conspiracies masked as questions, feeding the country's hysteria. 'Are there VIPSU [Very Important Person Security Unit]/RSS [members] in the squadron of death acting as a 'cleaner' for The Kitchen?' Unhinged posts on the New World Order, on freemasonry. 'Don't forget that for the father we were demons,' he wrote, referring to Sir Anerood Jugnauth's infamous retort in 1995 equating Creoles with 'demons' and 'diabolical spirits'. 'His child is making us become the slaves of freemasons with his sextant and seeks to govern like MODI. Need to say STOP to Bullshit.'

'2021 will be the year of the oppressed,' he said in December 2020. 'Pravind Jugnauth and Sawmynaden must go to jail. If the police don't have the courage to do it and if they are the tools of the MSM, we the people must do it. Are you in?'

XI. *Paranoia, November–December 2022*

Over the last few years, Mauritian journalism has been characterized by live videos unburdened with journalistic rigour; journalists who trademark their social media posts and who adopt an activist air.

About a week after Laurette's arrest, three journalists and a director of a news outlet went to the police saying they feared for their lives. They rightly pointed out that pro-government Facebook pages – there are many of these, run by supporters of the MSM – had posted false information about them. But the journalists also stated that their security was at stake after the publication of yet another hit list, broadcast on social media – a list purportedly abetted and written by the police. The list is risible upon the first read; the journalists didn't give any factual proof as to why a police statement was necessary, or of the actual threats they'd faced. Which led me to believe that they'd perhaps become paranoid, given the swamp of disinformation and threats they received, perhaps daily. I could imagine them in the newsroom, getting calls, sometimes benevolent in nature – 'Hey, as a friend, I'm asking you to tone down your criticism about this minister – you

276

never know what the repercussions could be like'. That, or they had real reasons to believe that they were in danger, and these reasons couldn't be articulated for fear of a defamation lawsuit or worse; even if the 'hit list' was ridiculous they clung on to it, since it represented proof of the unarticulated menace they were facing.

And most Mauritians, it seemed, believed that there was a climate of persecution in the country, and that the police had lost whatever little credence they'd previously had. In 2022, an Afrobarometer survey revealed that 91 per cent of Mauritians believed that the police were corrupt; only 13 per cent claimed to trust the institution 'a lot'. The Afrobarometer paper was published on 17 June 2022, following months of reports of police torture. The numbers must have risen with each passing month; in November 2022, a little after Laurette's arrest, a Creole man named Wayne Attock was arrested for heroin trafficking. A video published by Valayden, his lawyer – who'd come to Laurette's aid upon his arrest, despite their mutual grievances – showed a police officer planting a bag of drugs in the man's home.

Journalists stood by Laurette's statement that hashish had been planted in his car by police officers, notwithstanding the fact that an investigation was still under way. Their coverage was biased, with obvious incoherences swept to the side. Take for instance Laurette's son, who gave a convoluted, sometimes contradictory explanation of how the policemen planted drugs in his father's car. Take Bruneau Laurette, who claimed that the police rubbed his face with gloves to get his DNA; when the Forensic Science Laboratory stated that none of Laurette's DNA was found on the packages of marijuana, journalists didn't bring up Laurette's earlier claims at all.

The three provisional charges faced by Laurette were possession of marijuana, money laundering and possession of two (antique) firearms. Despite his work as a bodyguard and security professional, he didn't have a weapons-holder licence in Mauritius.

Loyal supporters screamed for his release at every court session, cried outside the courtroom the day Laurette was sent to prison. 'It's not his place over there!' they wail in a video. Activists shout over them, talking about political crimes, police complicity. A woman almost collapses, screams and begs Valayden – who isn't around – to intervene. She screams so hard the journalist's mic is cut.

His troupe of lawyers and activists found ways of capitalizing on his incarceration. 'Death penalty to police officers who plant drugs!', cried one such activist with over 95,000 followers – the same activist who'd accused Laurette just a few months earlier of being funded by a conglomerate. Reuben Pillay said he was being threatened by a fake profile on TikTok, 'just like Laurette before his arrest'.

Some of Laurette's followers took their distances. In late 2022, the tarot reader announced to her 72,000 Facebook followers that she'd been 'used' by protest leaders as a building block in their political careers. She then gave an interview on the astrology of 2023 to a pro-government media outlet.

New activists came onto the scene, sensing an absence,

but none had Laurette's power or charisma.

The Mauritians I talked to, even those who didn't like Laurette, felt that the drugs were planted – and that no-one should be imprisoned for marijuana anyway. 'What of the 95 kilos of cocaine?' is something I often hear, cocaine which was transported to Mauritius by ship, stowed away in a loader truck – a case in which no arrests were ever made. 'What of the heroin?', thrown overboard from cargo ships, dragged to our shores in moonlight.

I started working on this essay after I heard of Laurette's arrest. I'd wanted to write about him for a while, but when the harassment began it became impossible. When he was jailed I felt something loosen. It wasn't relief; I don't like him, and I still think he is dangerous, a man who works the country like a piece of flint, striking until it burns. But I did pity him, and I was sad at the loss of his potential, what he could have been. Because here – once again in our history – was a working-class Creole man who'd succeeded in making something of himself. Who'd tried to build a life despite the failings of this island, the active harm it sires.

XII. *Enter Franklin, January 2023*

The first days of 2023 were marked by a viral TikTok video called 'Laurette was going to expose the truth on Franklin and [Assistant Superintendent of Police] Jagai'.

The video starts with an extract of Laurette's speech, given on 29 October 2022, a week before he was arrested; Laurette is telling the crowd that Jagai chooses where he conducts his drug-raiding operations, and that there are places he doesn't touch. Then a distorted voice starts to describe Franklin, with accompanying pictures. The voice says that Jagai worked with Franklin in his drugs and weapons 'business'.

Jean Hubert Celerine, who calls himself Franklin, was so outraged by the video that he filed a complaint at the Black River police station. He said the video was causing harm to his family. He also said that he was worried that he'd be a victim of drug planting by the police. He held interviews with prominent news organizations on the evening of 14 January. 'I'm a child of poverty from Riviere Noire, but I grew up around tourists, foreigners, white people, who took care of me,' he said, believing that absolution lay in whiteness. 'I worked since I was little, I struggled, I am in the animal rearing and fast-food businesses and I have a car rental company... I don't have any drug trafficking cases... I've never seen ASP Jagai in my life.' He said that Laurette had heard of Franklin's sizeable donations and approached him. 'I helped him, gave him two trucks of groceries... then he approached me saying he has a big contact at the ADSU... that he could protect me for a fee, I said I wasn't interested... he was asking me for Rs 75–100,000 every month, I gave him some money, then stopped replying to his calls.' He produced his phone, searched for text messages that he then brandished to the journalists. 'Laurette wanted to buy a plot of land and a house at La Balise in Riviere Noire. I said the land cost Rs 75 million. He said he could buy it no problem.' The journalist asked him to read the messages on camera if possible. Franklin declined, saying that he didn't know how to read despite just having searched for the messages. Said he'd never financed political parties or met politicians. Said they called him a drug dealer because 'I'm a ti nasyon and I'm successful. I know how to run a business.'

I watched the livestreamed video in the clinic, at night, alone, after having given birth to my daughter. I watched Franklin's face mostly to try and not sleep. My baby had regurgitated breastmilk and blood, and though I knew it was probably just from my nipple I felt like I had to stay awake, stay alert, watch over her in case something happened, something that only I would see. Absolute love and absolute fear, commingling. Nauseating anxiety. I didn't understand much of what I was seeing. I thought this would just be another drug scandal that would die down by the time I was discharged. I don't think anyone could have predicted the immense ramifications that followed for over a year.

Journalists were quick. A barrage of content on Franklin followed in the loose, liquid weeks after I left the clinic. I learned that Franklin was only two years older than me. Thirty-two, with luxury vehicles, a villa by the sea, another hideous, clearly illegally funded house in La Gaulette, an animal farm, a hunting ground – but none of his properties were registered under his name. Condemned in Réunion in 2021 for trafficking zamal, the famous Reunionese strain of cannabis, wanted by French authorities and by Interpol, Franklin was nevertheless able to renew his passport in 2022 and travel freely.

People called the radio stations, incensed but also amused. 'So we're supposed to accept that if he'd never walked into the police station, he'd never have been arrested? If the Reunionese authorities had issued an extradition request for him, shouldn't he have been arrested the minute he walked into the police station anyway?' said an irate man, who ended up laughing with the presenter by the end of the call.

XIII. *Laurette's release, February–March 2023*

Bruneau Laurette was released on 27 February 2023. The DPP announced that it no longer objected to the conditional bail granted to him. He emerged from prison a much thinner man, released to public cries of victory and Kaya's 'Simé La Limière'. He gave an interview on the night of his release; he told the journalist that God was with him, that his time management skills saved his mental health, that the drugs were planted, that no fingerprints of his were found on the boot of his car or on the drug parcels. He often referred to himself in the third person. He made insinuations that we were living in a politico -narco-mafia state, giving credence to the rumours that the state enabled – even profited from – the activities of certain drug traffickers. He claimed that, before his arrest, he'd met a representative from the Government of India, responsible for intelligence gathering for the embassy, who said Laurette should work for the MSM and that they'd take care of him financially for the elections.

The journalist asked him whether he knew Franklin, who was still the infamous man of the moment. Laurette said that Franklin had congratulated him on his protest of August 2020; that Franklin had helped him in his social work during Covid by supplying chickens, but that he had never directly financed him. That the money he'd asked for was for a food bank in Riviere Noire. The journalist asked Laurette about his source of funds: he said he was a passionate football fan and made quite a bit of money through betting; that he also received donations from individuals. 'Franklin's roots are in power. Franklin's tentacles are found in the police,' he said.

Who wouldn't believe him? Laurette didn't need to convince his audience. There he was, well-built, clean-cut, well-dressed, set against Franklin, who appeared in front of the media donning a tracksuit and gold-plated teeth. More importantly still, Franklin had seemingly been protected by power. Laurette, however, had made the government furious at his release.

A day before he left prison, a Facebook page called Sun TV News – 'Sun' here being the official symbol of the MSM, though the party denied any involvement with the page in question – published a video announcing that there was a 'politio-judiciary plot' arranged by the Labour Party to free Laurette. The most extraordinary allegation in the video was that Shakeel Mohamed, a prominent Labour MP (and one of Laurette's lawyers) had paid a 'huge sum of money' to the DPP. Sun TV News brandished the face of the Director of Public Prosecutors, Rashid Ahmine, along with the words 'Narco DPP'.

The DPP filed a complaint which, when made public, brought about the disappearance of the Sun TV News page. But yet another pro-MSM page – this one called 'Power Raising Sun', posted a video whose contents matched the one that had been taken down, except that this time Power Raising Sun had removed the names of those it targeted.

On 26 February the Prime Minister had another sortie against 'the influence of the mafia on certain people in certain institutions' when questioned about Franklin. He spoke about 'people' who were helping alleged drug criminals. Any would-be ambiguity was dispelled two days later by the Commissioner of Police, who – given the Prime Minister's role as Minister of Defence – came under his rule. He said the decision of the DPP to free Laurette 'set an "evil precedent" since the lawyers of the 337 drug traffickers may now come forward to apply for bail for their clients'.

In the brief interlude between his release and his new political turn, Laurette had never been so popular. Members of the opposition were on the radio considering whether he'd join their parties, the ramifications of a new kind of alliance. Politicians called him a 'cyborg', a 'hulk'. Sometimes Laurette would use these terms to describe himself. I wondered what would happen if I rang the shows, said all those terms participated in the fetishization of Black bodies, that they were dehumanizing. The presenters would have laughed me off, said Laurette really was a superman and it was *such* a compliment, since they counted on him to save us all. And then, incredibly, Laurette decided to join Sherry Singh's new political party, One Moris.

Laurette's supporters went public with their grief. Some of his fans cried on video, voicing their incomprehension, their sense of betrayal. Singh had apparently failed in his truth-teller rebranding: few people trusted him, even after his multiple appearances on the radio. In interviews he seemed to be an exceptionally capable person, but it appeared that intelligence alone wasn't going to

284

subdue the population at large: the close association with the MSM was a permanent stain on his character. Some members of Laurette's troupe of lawyers and activists said they didn't want anything to do with him.

He kept a relatively low profile over the next few months, organizing his next move. I was still low-profile too, but for other reasons.

XIV. *Baby on one side, toddler on the other, laptop open on the bed, January–October 2023*

My infant daughter woke, slept and sucked with the radio as background noise. The radio is still the best way to learn about what's happening in the country: live reports and audience complaints provide uncensored information, and, when coupled with the investigative reporting and interview segments, the stations gave an unparalleled overview of what was happening, personal and political, since both were intertwined anyway. On and on it went, these stories of personal grief and institutional putrefaction, headlines one after the other.

The stories I remembered the most were the ones about women and children. The MSM liked to flaunt their 'care for the younger generation', especially through the new increased allowances they gave to families. All I heard, though, were stories about how we were being failed.

In March, people called radio stations to say that hospital mattresses island-wide were infected with bed bugs. 58.9 per cent of Mauritian women who give birth will have caesareans, like I did, but unlike me most will give birth and recover in maternity wards in hospitals. Those wards were already in a state, their walls streaked with blood, blooming with mould, equipped with ventilators that didn't work in high summer. I imagined these women giving birth and then being unable to move at night from the pain of their caesareans, with bed bugs biting at their necks. I felt ill with anger.

In April, the daughter of a cancer patient called in to say that one of the island's largest hospitals was overrun with rats; her mother had been bitten on her face, and she'd died the next day. Later in the year, videos filmed by a member of the opposition showed that hospitals served expired, rotten food to patients.

In May, a six-year-old child was beaten with a rod on his genitals by a 'caregiver' in a state-run shelter, called L'Oiseau du Paradis. Other caregivers then rubbed salt, chilli and pepper into his wounds. The child said that yet another caregiver in the room laughed when it happened. L'Oiseau du Paradis shelter was inaugurated in January 2021. It is still operational, even though multiple cases of child abuse and negligence have been reported year after year.

In July, another story of child abuse revolted the nation. A woman my age decided to stop using drugs, wanting to get clean for her daughter; she checked herself into a centre. Her friends told her they'd care for her two-year-old daughter while she was away; she insisted on paying them for childcare. Her daughter was then tortured for ten days. The couple wouldn't put diapers on her; she was forced to eat her faeces, forced to eat her vomit. She was beaten with a metal ruler that was heated until it burned, and burned again with cigarette stubs. They plunged her head in an aquarium. The neighbours heard her screams but didn't interfere. The couple's eldest daughter, fourteen years old, who saw it all, called a friend and went to the police. By the end of the month, the child was under the custody of the Child Development Unit. Children under the care of the Child Development Unit – there were 5,729 of them in 2023 – are sometimes placed in shelters like L'Oiseau du Paradis. Reports of rape and abuse of children have trickled out in both state-run and private shelters across the island.

In August nine babies were infected by the *Serratia marcescens* bacteria and died. They were being cared for in a hospital's neonatal intensive care unit. The Ministry of Health apparently knew of the bacteria's presence in the hospital as far back as April, but chose not to close the neonatal unit until after the babies fell ill.

We have a maternal mortality rate of about 84 deaths per 100,000 live births. An infant mortality rate of 13.7 per cent. 'Around 175 infant deaths are expected to occur in the Republic of Mauritius in 2023,' states a report from Statistics Mauritius. 'There are six to seven newborn deaths every month,' said the Minister of Health in a conference in October, quick to point out that the cases are correlated to 'mothers who aren't followed by doctors, who have multiple health problems, who are old'. Blame the poor mothers, the old mothers, old by the time they hit thirty in this country.

The Minister of Health, like all his predecessors, never spoke of Sudden Infant Death Syndrome. No government in power has ever crafted a SIDS awareness campaign. SIDS only stands for Small Island Developing State here. In that summer of 2023–4, in particular, I'd heard news story after story of babies dying at home and in nurseries from unexplained causes. Paediatricians telling newspapers that baby deaths were caused by 'pulmonary oedema', that babies should be put on their stomachs to sleep so they didn't choke on their vomit.

Some of these cases of SIDS were blamed on nurseries who operated without a permit. In October, the Minister of Gender Equality and Family Welfare promised a 'crackdown'. A number of nurseries closed. Women on the radio, saying they no longer had childcare, they'd lose their jobs. The Minister didn't seem concerned, as per her wont. She hadn't come up with a Gender Equality Bill in parliament, as had been promised, or the Protection from Domestic Violence Act. In 2023 alone, 9,519 women were assaulted.

Another epidemic: in October, a radio station published a video of a ten-year-old boy who was a drug mule, and who was given marijuana to smoke in a makeshift bong; it joined a long list of reports – some of which made international news – that pointed to an explosive, unprecedented drug usage in the country. We still don't know the extent of the problem, because families are ashamed to talk about addiction in their households. I learn about the epidemic anecdotally, tearfully, in hair salons, in living rooms. Brothers, sisters, sons, daughters. Teenagers overdosing in abandoned homes. Children selling synthetic drugs in primary school.

On 16 May 2023, an MP asked the Prime Minister in parliament about the safes seized at Navin Ramgoolam's home in 2015. It seemed that Jugnauth would seize whatever occasion he could to sully Ramgoolam's name, and there were members of parliament used almost exclusively for this role. The question had no obvious relevance to current affairs, but it proved to be an excellent, almost scheduled opportunity for the Prime Minister to remind his audience, and the country at large, of his predecessor's debaucheries.

'Money, both in local and foreign currencies, estimated at the time to amount to Rs 230 million, were secured from his premises and safes,' Jugnauth said. He then went on to describe the contents of a black Samsonite case containing, among other items, Ramgoolam's testosterone supplements and melatonin-based sleeping pills.

The MP wasn't satiated by these details alone. He asked the Prime Minister for more information on the pills. Jugnauth gladly obliged, delighted by the shouts of a shocked opposition. 'The Mega Men Health Testosterone pills contain Testofen, clinically proven to optimize testosterone levels in order to improve health and sexual performance... Mr President, after a period of sexual hyperactivity made possible by stimulating products, the beast needs a powerful sleeping aid to recuperate. I would even say that the most hardened Casanova couldn't have imagined such a cocktail.'

Over the years, the House of Parliament had turned carnivalesque. Opposition MPs were routinely expelled;

the ridiculous Speaker, who'd been a campaign manager for the MSM in the previous election, was openly biased. At the end of the year Jugnauth instigated a rigorous accounting of Ramgoolam's alcohol expenditure when he had been in power from 2010 to 2014; he also stated that there had been orgies held in the Prime Minister's official residence.

I wondered whether anyone actually cared about Ramgoolam's private life at that point. The country seemed to be rotting. By the till in supermarkets, I'd see people analysing their receipts in disbelief at the hike in prices, month after month. The grants and allowances and subsidies that the government was doling out weren't enough. The Minister of Finance said that the economy was doing well, but it was difficult to believe him, despite the statistics he offered – and hadn't the Chairperson of Statistics Mauritius resigned in July 2021? The government was awash with stories of deceit, corruption and mismanagement.

In April, Maneesh Gobin – lawyer, Attorney General and Minister of Agro-Industry – made the news. In a series of investigations, it was revealed that Gobin had partied with men with close, obvious ties to Franklin on their 'ranch' – a chassée with a building used to entertain guests – in September 2020. Bribes were allegedly involved. Those men had then applied for a lease for state land two months later; Gobin's ministry had approved the application in July 2021. In parliament, Gobin refused to give a clear answer on whether he attended the party or not, and said that he couldn't provide more information, since the matter was being investigated by the Independent Commission Against Corruption (ICAC).

This excuse would be used time and time again by ministers allegedly involved in corruption. Gobin still had the Prime Minister's 'full support', and though he was no longer Minister of Agro-Industry by August 2023 he still served as the country's Attorney General.

In May, Sherry Singh was arrested and later released. Videos were broadcast of Singh's outrageously luxurious home in Bout du Monde, a private morcellement in Ebene. The kind of house you only see on residential estates designed for expatriates, or in some select homes on the north and west coasts. A two-metre bronze statue by Singh's front door was of particular interest to the general public: people wondered at its cost, at its meaning. It was supposed to represent a gymnast performing a handstand, but on first glance it looked more like a falling man. Singh would be arrested and released many times throughout the year and into 2024 in the context of different investigations – on a charge of 'giving instructions to commit an offence', then 'conspiracy to defraud Mauritius Telecom', and 'conspiracy to commit money aundering'. Laurette was always by his side.

Another notable arrest in May: Vimen Sabapati, a Muay Thai trainer and former bodyguard of Navin Ramgoolam, previously unknown to the general public, was arrested by police after they found 10.35 kilos of heroin in his Ford Raptor. Sabapati, sensing that the police were coming for him, sent out USB sticks to all the major news and media outlets in Mauritius in November 2022. Sabapati had registered conversations with numerous policemen, who stated that they were involved in drug planting operations orchestrated by ASP Jagai. One policeman claimed that Jagai demanded payment by individuals against threat of arrest. He also said that Jagai and Franklin worked together.

I assume that the mood of the country was what made the government decide – once again – not to hold municipal elections. Instead, they passed the 'Local Government (Amendment) Bill', which allowed the mandates of the municipal city councillors and village councillors to be extended for two more years. Jean-Claude de l'Estrac, one of the country's most important journalists and former editor-in-chief of *L'Express*, said that the postponement was 'predictable' and warned that 'this government keeps using the instruments of democracy to establish its autocratic power. By granting a new mandate to existing municipal councillors, they are in effect saying that the government is choosing the councillors instead of the voters.... If they could, this government would also postpone the general elections.'

In June, the journalist Murvind Beetun scored the interview of the year, landing the now-infamous ASP Ashik Jagai on his radio show, which was also streamed live on Facebook. It was the first time I, like many Mauritians, had seen Jagai properly. He was maskless, bespectacled and suited; though his blazer fit well around his chest, the fabric was taut around his biceps. One felt that this was a man who could snap your neck with his fingers. He smiled with his mouth only; his eyes had no warmth.

Jagai seemed very concerned about establishing a timeline of his career; he said he had thirty-five years of service as a policeman, thirty-one in the anti-drug brigade. He came from a 'very modest' family in Vallée

292

Pitot, saw the influence of drugs in his neighbourhood. 'I didn't hurt poor people, little traffickers. If you look at my career, you'll see I've only gone after the big mafia types.' The interview was stressful to watch. Jagai was accompanied by two lawyers, who constantly sought to interrupt Beetun. He refused to answer many questions. His body language was mildly threatening, as if he was ready to slap Beetun down. He continuously mispronounced Beetun's name.

A month later and Beetun's interview would still be making the news. Beetun had filed a precautionary measure against Jagai: videos had emerged of Beetun being hounded, threatened and cornered in the mess room by a group of men while on a break during the interview. The men were unhappy with the questions Beetun had asked the Assistant Superintendant of Police. After the interview, Beetun was 'constructively dismissed' by his employer; the threats, however, didn't stop when he lost his job. To his immense credit, Beetun didn't stop working: he set up his own media outlet and racked up views on YouTube.

Sabapati's voice recordings and Beetun's interview were useful tools in strengthening the general belief that Laurette was innocent. Laurette had stated multiple times that Jagai was responsible for the drugs found in his car. And he was slowly trying to regain momentum. He gave Krav Maga classes. He regularly posted on Facebook about the issues of the day, issued legal documents against his would-be adversaries, fuelled conspiracy theories surrounding the firing of yet another journalist, and melded activism, social work and politics. But there was a has-been strain to his persona. He wasn't given the same kind

293

of media coverage. In September newspapers talked of a 'comeback' when Laurette supported a group of workers who'd lost their jobs after the liquidation of a building company, but his efforts and revelations didn't lead to anything. The protest he organized around the company's headquarters was sparsely attended. With the help of Singh and his wife he tried, and failed, to intervene in a constitutional complaint by the Police Commissioner against the Director of Public Prosecutions.

The biggest blow to Laurette's 'movement', in those months, wasn't political fallback. It was a survey conducted by Syntheses-Maurice on behalf of *L'Express* on 31 October 2023. The results found that 67.6 per cent of Mauritians wanted a new political leader; half of all Mauritians didn't identify with any of the political parties; that, if the elections were to be held during the survey period, 36 per cent of Mauritians would vote for the alliance of the opposition, 24.8 per cent would vote for the party in power, 4 per cent would vote for Valayden and his alliance of extra-parliamentary parties, 2.6 per cent would vote for another extra-parliamentary party led by an ex-MSM man, but no one, it seemed, said they'd vote for Laurette/Singh's party. The ruling game, the electoral choice, would always come back down to Labour, the MSM, and the MMM. Minor parties could form small support groups in potential coalitions, but weren't threats in themselves.

XVI. *Apex predator*

The MSM government tended to pass its most vicious laws at night, and at the height of the festive season.

294

December 2023 was no exception.

The Financial Crimes Commission Bill was passed on 19 December 2023. The law created a new body, the Financial Crimes Commission (FCC), which was supposed to be – in the Prime Minister's words – 'the apex agency in Mauritius' to combat financial crimes, such as corruption, money laundering, fraud, drug financing and so forth. It took over the functions and powers of the infamous, ineffectual Independent Commission Against Corruption (ICAC) and other public bodies.

There had been a lot of talk over the years of getting rid of the ICAC. It had secured a meagre thirteen convictions from 2019 to 2023, and most of them dealt in petty crimes. Over the past few years, when MPs were questioned in parliament over corruption and bribery scandals, they only needed to say that they couldn't provide more information to the house since 'investigations are ongoing'. The ongoing-ness of things was particularly convenient.

Like ICTA – like most public bodies, in fact – the ICAC was headed and managed by political nominees, allowing government figures to sleep on any files unfavourable to them with very little accountability. Navin Beekarry was the first Commissioner of the ICAC in 2002 and held the position of Director General of the same institution from July 2016 to March 2024. Beekarry was appointed as director of the new FCC. To make things even more ridiculous, the FCC took over ICAC's headquarters. But this wasn't just an old face with a new name: this new institution was formidably dangerous, with a supremacy that defied the constitution, which seemed to have been designed, in fact, to outstrip the powers of the DPP. We'd seen, over the MSM's second mandate especially, how the government had continuously tried to undermine the DPP's rulings. We'd heard of Jugnauth's irritation – and then outright anger – at Satyajit Boolell and his successor, Rashid Ahmine.

As per the Mauritian constitution, the Office of the DPP is supposed to be the apex prosecuting authority with independent powers, '[not] subject to the direction or control of any other person or authority'. This was no longer the case with the creation of the FCC: Section 4(3) of the Act provides that 'Subject to this Act, the Commission shall, in the discharge of its functions and exercise of its powers, not be under the direction or control of any person or authority'. Same wording, new instrument.

When the FCC has 'reasonable grounds' to suspect that 'it is in the public interest that customer information be provided', it can, for instance, 'request any financial institution to provide such customer information, including details of financial transactions'. The FCC can apply to a Judge in Chambers for a 'Telecommunication Order', 'ordering any public operator to intercept, withhold or disclose to the Commission any information for the purpose of an investigation'. The FCC can also 'make use, under judicial control, of Special Investigative Techniques' including 'intrusive surveillance, the conduct and use of covert intelligence human source' (a clunky term for 'undercover agent', perhaps) and 'equipment interception.' It brought to mind Opposition MP Reza Uteem's statement in parliament on 24 October 2023, where he said he had evidence that the government had bought surveillance equipment from Verint Systems, an Israeli company, for over $15 million, or about Rs 700 million. Jugnauth refused to confirm that the equipment wouldn't be used to tap phones.

If the Director-General of the FCC believes there is 'evidence which may assist it in an investigation' on 'any premises', 'he may issue a warrant to an officer authorizing him to enter and search, at all reasonable times, the said premises.' The owner or occupier of the premises, naturally, will only be there during the search 'so far as is practicable'. If the Commission seizes a company, it has the power to hire or fire the company's employees and liquidate the business if it is 'commercially advantageous to do so'.

I could go on and on about the many outrageous clauses. There would never be enough room. And there wasn't enough space in parliament or in the papers or in people's minds, preoccupied by festivities and inflation. Who could devote their headspace to a 182-page legal document while preoccupied with how much the family Christmas meal would cost this year, how much all the presents would add up to. There were other matters, too, of strong public interest: torrential rains and flooding; billions of rupees worth of contracts awarded to a company that didn't fulfil tender criteria; the Prime Minister's privy council victory, having being accused of election bribery by Suren Dayal; the frightening rates of exam failure in secondary schools and the ongoing investigation into a terrorist incident at La Citadelle in October. Approximately 1,500 people – including families and children – had gathered for a concert organized by a hotel group to celebrate their fifteenth anniversary.

About thirty armed men broke into the concert, threatening organizers, brandishing sabres. People fled down the premises barefoot. The extremists claimed they were taking a stand because the concert was pro-gay rights, anti-Palestinian and anti-Muslim. There was nothing about the event, in any convolution of the imagination, that supported their statements; Mauritius stood openly against the ongoing genocide in Gaza and for a Palestinian state. Most of the men were arrested within the month, but the incident was still in the news weeks later. A few concerts planned for the year's end were cancelled.

Most of all, there was talk about the next year – an election year – and the changes and promises it could bring.

Laurette still counted on being part of the race to power. By the end of the 2023 he was sharing songs called 'God over Government' and 'Welcome to the Revolution'. But his biggest move that December was to announce that he'd become a prophet with Joshua Generation Ministries. LALIT decried the lack of reporting on this particular piece of news in Mauritian media, 'as if this [was] not worth analysing at all', as if it wouldn't influence his politics. LALIT's research indicated that Joshua Generation Ministries, founded in America in 2003, openly rallied behind Republican candidates and stood against abortion and gay rights.

My friends and I couldn't get enough of this new move and its implications. Would he lose the support of church-going Catholics, who viewed any Christianity beyond the Catholic Church as somewhat dreaded sects? Would he lose his Muslim base? How many votes was he trying to garner, exactly, given the fringe amount of converted Christians in this country? Had we, in fact, grossly underestimated the amount of non-Catholic, Christian converts in Mauritius? We looked around us for confirmation, and it seemed true: not-so-little Christian churches had converted a consequential number of Creole and Indo-Mauritian families, especially from working-class backgrounds. If Laurette was going to be a candidate in Port Louis, then he might be up against Anabelle Savabaddy, a very popular radio show host who'd left the station to join the Labour Party earlier in 2024. Savabaddy, too, was Christian.

XVII. *'Preparedness plan', January–August 2024*

People went to work as usual in the morning of 15 January 2024. Cyclone Belal was in our environs, but the Meteorological Office had only issued a Class 1 warning, and so we thought we'd have time – a day or two – before the weather deteriorated further. Throughout the morning there was persistent torrential rain, but not much wind. The government told public sector employees that they could return home from 12.30; private sector employees had to wait for the directives of 'Business Mauritius', the representative body of the private sector. As if the country were ruled by two monoliths.

By 1 p.m. I started receiving video footage of cars swallowed by muddy water, people scrambling to get out of them, smashing their windows. The radio hadn't reported anything yet. 'Is this for real? Is this Port Louis?' I asked the members of the Commission de Developpement Durable on our group chat. Members who lived and worked in Port Louis replied in the affirmative. Joanna left us a voice message, saying she was trying to get out of the capital but even the police didn't know which roads were still open. My husband had just left the capital and had to take a foggy, meandering route through the mountains to come back home.

They were lucky; they got out in time. Whole lanes inside Port Louis and on the motorway had turned into muddy rivers by the early afternoon, their violent currents pushing people, animals, cars and detritus downwards towards the sea. Across the country, rivers burst from their banks and engulfed houses and roads. A video of a bloated body rushing past cars on a current of water in Port Louis. A video of a man on a motorcycle being submerged in Riviere Noire. Tombs in the Saint Jean cemetery of Quatre Bornes became unmoored from the soil; they floated into neighbouring homes, with residents saying the water had brought with it decomposed bodies, bones.

Port Louis had been flooded before, on 31 March 2013, killing eleven people. There'd been reports on the infrastructure works that needed to be effected in order to avoid another tragedy, and not just in the capital – the government had, in its possession, a map of the flood-prone areas of the country which it refused to make public. The party in power had had a decade to implement preventative measures to stop another national disaster. It is difficult to say whether they did anything of significance in that time. It wasn't just a question of major infrastructural reform: they couldn't even ensure that the telephone numbers of refugee centres across the country were operational.

There were power cuts across the island on the day of the flooding. There was a rush to get bottled water from supermarkets and filling stations. We didn't know what to expect; we couldn't even trust the weather reports anymore, since we'd gone from a Class 1 warning to a Class 3 in the space of a few hours.

That night we slept with the radio on, like most Mauritians across the country. We were following an old, generational tradition: listening to the voices of presenters huddled in the studio, relaying information, telling jokes, playing pop songs. A thread keeping us sane in the howling dark.

I thought of my grandmother. My mother used to say that she'd cry throughout the night during cyclones: she'd pace, gripping the metal bars of the windows and rattling them, making sure they were still fixed. Her children made fun of her, saying there was nothing to be scared of – they lived in a concrete-roofed house after all. But she'd lived through cyclones in a modest, rickety dwelling, and once, apparently, the wind had torn through her home and broke it apart while she cowered underneath a table with her parents.

The weather cleared up by mid-afternoon the next day. Joanna and I visited a few homes affected by the flooding in our constituency. Some stank of raw sewage. A river took over a whole street in La Peyrouse; inhabitants said the Municipality had started building drains in the area, but the work was never finished as the contract was given to a shady entrepreneur.

In Cité L'Oiseau, a woman had taken in her daughter, son-in-law and grandchild after the flooding. Her daughter wore a blue, blood-stained dress; her hands and leg were heavily bandaged. She'd lost her entire home in Canal Dayot, a house she and her husband had saved up to renovate. She was in shock, and couldn't talk much, so her mother told us her story.

After Canal Dayot had flooded in 2013, the authorities had said they'd raise the walls of the riverbanks and make sure that the region wouldn't suffer again. On 15 January 2024, the river poured into her home in the space of fifteen minutes. Her son, thankfully, was in a neighbouring house higher up. She and her husband tried opening the door, the windows to escape but the river current was so strong, it wouldn't allow them to leave. She'd rung her mother, thinking that she was going to die. She was able to break one of the windows with her fist, and managed to pull herself out, climb onto the roof; her husband was dragged out several metres by the current, but he too managed to latch on to a building. They were rescued a few hours later.

Her husband had just returned from their home; he'd wanted to see if there was anything he could salvage. But there was nothing: the microwave they'd bought for Christmas, their sofa, bed, wardrobe – whatever remained had been destroyed by the water and mud.

I watched footage of families in refugee centres. A Creole girl saying they only received biscuits and water, that they needed help since they'd lost everything. In the comments below the videos, an outpouring of racism. There would be more torrential rain and two smaller cyclones that summer, more reports of Creole families losing their homes, the same systematic evil in the responses.

The Director of the Mauritius Meteorological Services was suspended from his functions on 17 January. He still claims that he correctly informed the Minister of Local Government and Disaster Risk Management, Anwar Husnoo, of the risks that the cyclone presented to the country. Husnoo disagreed. He placed the responsibility for the deaths and flooding on the Director. Husnoo claimed that he'd established a rigorous 'preparedness plan' in case of natural disasters, that nothing was his fault.

The government said that the floods killed two people: the two men who'd been filmed. But the family from Canal Dayot had heard that seven people in their area had died, and I'd heard from many different people that there were a number of bereaved families who were told to stay quiet about their relatives' deaths. I thought that if the Ministry of Health had obfuscated the number of Mauritians who'd died of Covid, they could lie about those who died in the floods.

After the floods came the mosquitoes and the rats.

There was a sharp rise in cases of dengue fever in the early months of 2024. The epidemic could have been controlled in 2023, when it had been limited to a few regions in the north, but due to the Ministry of Health's usual shambolism it wasn't contained. The Ministry's obfuscating practices, too, were at work. By August – the epidemic had finally ended after a particularly cold winter – it announced that there'd been over 6,000 cases in

2024, and eight people had died 'directly' due to dengue. The Ministry had openly stated that it wouldn't count people who'd been infected with dengue but who'd died from other health complications; curiously, the Ministry also stated that most people who'd officially died from dengue had comorbidities.

I'd heard from personnel who worked in non-state-owned laboratories and medical centres, who said the government told them not to test people for dengue even though they had the right equipment; I heard from patients who said that public hospitals wouldn't test them for dengue, and that they only received a proper diagnosis once they'd been admitted to private clinics. And almost every single day that summer, I saw calls on social media to give blood. Dengue, when severe, causes a sharp drop in blood platelets. I read a few journal articles that suggested that papaya leaves and the bark of the bois de peche marron tree could help stabilize platelets, shared the information as much as I could – papaya trees are found almost everywhere here. And I thought of my grandmother again, who'd cook octopus curry with papaya leaves; recipes passed down through generations, a mark of our culture and perhaps, too, a trace of our medicinal practice.

Sixty cases of leptospirosis in 2024; a new record. Twelve dead by the end of July. The Ministry of Health, in conferences, said that poor hygiene was largely to blame. He didn't mention poor infrastructure, which meant that rotting, shoddy bazaars around the country were still in operation; didn't say that, after ten years in power, we still had no waste triage system and our land-fill was over-saturated, which meant that rubbish wasn't disposed of or collected properly; didn't say that the Ministry had failed, yet again, to control a pest that had been an island-wide menace since the early 1600s.

The government hadn't announced when it would hold the general elections: there were rumours of an early election in August, or a late one in January 2025. I figured that our climate would be the deciding factor: they couldn't risk the rainy season in mid-December, especially after what happened with Belal; couldn't hold the elections in August, in the middle of the dry season, because the water cuts would remind people again that the MSM never made good on its promise to provide water 24/7. They'd probably choose a date in October or November, I thought. And I was right.

XVIII. *A scrambling, January–April 2024*

Laurette knew that in order to gain a significant number of votes, he'd have to maintain a consistent media presence throughout the year. People's attention was increasingly turned towards the opposition coalition of the MMM, Labour Party and PMSD, though a formal arrangement still hadn't been finalized.

He started the year with a peaceful protest in front of the Indian High Commission, demanding that the Mauritian and Indian governments come clean about Agaléga, where Jugnauth was still denying the existence of a military base. It was a bold move, given the increasing show of power and 'collaboration' between both countries, the marked display of Hindu nationalism on the island. Public servants were given a special two-hour leave to pray on 22 January, upon the inauguration of the Ram Temple in Ayodhya. In the days leading to the inauguration there were rallies island-wide, large orange flags bearing the image of Hanuman fluttered out of cars. Maneesh Gobin, the infamous attorney general, stated in an interview to an Indian news outlet that 'had it not been for the Indian immigration, we would not even have Mauritius. Mauritius was built on the strength of the labour of Indian immigrants,' effectively erasing the island's history of slavery and every other non-Indian person who'd formed the nation.

The inauguration of the temple helped distract people from the catastrophe of the flooding and its aftermath; the inauguration of major infrastructural projects on the island throughout the year gave the impression that the MSM had really made good on its promise to 'rebuild' Mauritius. The most famous project was the Sir Anerood Jugnauth Bridge, the longest bridge in the country and the only one of its kind in the Indian Ocean; it was inaugurated in March, the same month in which the V-DEM announced, in its 2024 report, that Mauritius was now an electoral autocracy – the 'top "stand-alone" autocratizer', in fact.

Two events were the talk of the island in April. The first was that Franklin was extradited to Réunion island and flew business class on the plane. The second was that the tentative alliance between the three main parties of the opposition had collapsed.

An irate Xavier Luc Duval blamed Berenger for the dissolution, saying he was impossible to work with; a news report stated, however, that Duval had been questioned as to a possible rapprochement with the MSM in view of forging an alliance.

The collapse was excellent for minority parties, who said that the reign of the dinosaurs was potentially over and a new generation of politicians should take the lead. Laurette announced that One Moris was establishing regional offices across the country, recruiting candidates.

XIX. *A new coalition, April–May 2024*

Duval resigned as Leader of the Opposition in April, upon the collapse of the alliance. The next Leader should have been Arvin Boolell but he was unwell at the time, and so Shakeel Mohamed was elected Leader from April to June. The sessions of the House of Parliament, which were already tumultuous, turned even more aggressive. The first was especially remarkable.

On 16 April 2024, Mohamed questioned Jugnauth about the murder of Kistnen. Jugnauth seemed on edge. A question on Ramgoolam's safes was posed by a member of the MSM; Mohamed cited Erskine May in an attempt to move on to other matters, but the Speaker ignored his request and allowed Jugnauth to detail, in full, every cash item found in the safes in 2015. Another MP then asked about the bank cards; Jugnauth duly replied. A while later Jugnauth insulted Paul Berenger, saying he was too old to understand what 'delaying tactics' were in court; Berenger was furious, and the Speaker, enraged at Berenger, expelled him for six sittings and called him mad. Kalpana Koonjoo-Shah, the Minister of Gender Equality and Family Welfare, said she heard

Joanna Berenger say that Jugnauth had killed Kistnen; Joanna said she hadn't said anything of the kind, and that they could check parliamentary recordings for proof. The Speaker found that she hadn't, in fact, used those words, but decided to name her anyway. The Vice Prime Minister then expelled her from the house. Later, Joanna highlighted that she had been thrown out of the House at an exceptionally convenient time: she was about to ask why government funds, estimated at Rs 8 billion, had been deposited in Silver Bank.

Silver Bank had, in February 2024, been placed under conservatorship. The sinister entity was owned by Ginni Gupta, the wife of Prateek Gupta, who had been accused of 'systemic fraud' by the world's largest private metals trader. There are a number of excellent, world-standard banks operating in Mauritius today; it is damning that the government chose a shady one established in 2021. The rumours around the Mauritian financial sector suggested that some select ministers and people close to power were treating government funds as their own cash cow; a fraud so extraordinary in scale that it defied belief.

In that parliamentary session, and in the sessions that followed, unnamed MPs were reported in the Hansard to have said '*mille fois Xavier*,' in comparison to Mohamed. Joanna could hear them in the House; they were members of the party in power. She'd noted complicit looks between Duval and Jugnauth in the weeks that preceded the break-up of the alliance. I wondered, given Jugnauth's discomfort at Mohamed's questions, just how compliant Duval had been towards Jugnauth in his time as Leader of the Opposition.

Members of Duval's party had resigned in protest against a possible alliance between the MSM and the PMSD in April. They created a new political party, the Nouveau Démocrates (ND), and joined the MMM-Labour alliance in April. The three main figureheads of the new party – Veronique Leu-Govind, Khushal Lobine and Richard Duval – were promised 'tickets' in the next election, which is to say that they'd be among the sixty candidates of the alliance.

In that month, too, Rezistans ek Alternativ (REA) joined the alliance. REA's adhesion gave the coalition unparalleled freshness: it quelled any haranguing about dinosaurs or 'voting the status quo'. The party was very popular with my generation of Mauritians. They'd never actually been in the running until 2024: registering as a candidate in the elections meant that candidates had to specify what ethnic community they were part of, and REA would always leave the field blank. Over the years, this became a symbol of their rejection of the racial politics built into the electoral system. This time, though, they'd comply if it meant they might change the country. They were promised two tickets; Ashok Subron, who'd earned the wrath of the conglomerates over the years in his work as a trade unionist, brilliantly negotiated a third ticket by August.

Political parties in Mauritius traditionally hold open political meetings on 1 May. Before general elections, especially, the meetings function as a popularity contest of sorts: a strong indicator as to which parties are truly in the running. The bigger the crowd, the bigger the chance of the party winning the election. Added to this was the persistent, decades-old belief among Mauritians that the 'masse silencieuse' decided who they'd vote for at the last minute when the 'race' was particularly tight, but also tended to vote for the party that had the most momentum. The logic went that the bigger the crowd at these meetings, the bigger the party's support, the greater the momentum, the greater the chance of winning the election. This is the reason why smaller parties usually don't hold meetings. Laurette and One Moris said they'd be celebrating Labour Day the way it was supposed to be celebrated, meaning they'd spend a leisurely day with family and loved ones; the PMSD, who hadn't formally allied themselves to the MSM, didn't hold a meeting either.

That logic didn't always hold, though. In 2014, the MSM didn't hold a meeting on Labour Day, saying that the elections were near and they had to be efficient in their use of resources. The political rallies they held before the 2014 general election were small; Mauritians feared that attending meetings would cost them their jobs, or they'd suffer from other forms of retaliation. That didn't stop the MSM from winning with a majority.

The MSM and its coalition of smaller parties, called L'Alliance Lepep, assembled their supporters in Vacoas; the MMM, Labour, ND and REA – who'd formalize their alliance and call it L'Alliance de L'Espoir – held their meeting in Port Louis.

It was my first Labour Day meeting. I tagged along with members of the Commission de Developpement Durable, who tidied up and collected litter after the meeting was over. I wasn't able to join them in the clean-up operation, though, because my parents were paranoid about me being photographed, or drawing attention

310

to myself in any visible way. It was bad enough that I'd appeared in a press conference with the CDD earlier on in the year; they'd received phone calls, friends of friends of friends had told them I should 'be careful'. They implored me not to wear purple, the MMM's colour, to stay in areas where I could easily seek safety, in case the MSM sent thugs to kick up some violence. My father dropped me ten minutes away from the event in my mother's car, for fear of his number plate getting caught on the Safe City cameras. My father had been retired for seven years; he was the designated driver because – as my parents vociferated – my husband couldn't be seen in Port Louis *at all*. Private companies around the country had strongly urged their employees to not show their faces at the opposition's meeting.

Considering all of this, it was good to see that a firm crowd showed up.

We checked footage of the Alliance Lepep's meeting in Vacoas on our phones. It was packed. Some people told me that MSM activists were paying people Rs 1–2,000 to attend; I wondered whether public servants had been pressured into showing up as well. There were videos afterwards, of supposed Bangladeshi workers removing their orange shirts at bus stops after the meeting was over. I'd always hated that particular anti-immigrant rhetoric that was now being riled up again – the kind that said Bangladeshis had helped the MSM win the 2019 elections – but it occurred to me, then, that all the company managers who employed Bangladeshi workers had to go through the Ministry of Labour for their permit. One way, potentially, of showing their gratitude for the permit would be to have their employees attend the meeting, inflate the size of the crowd even if very few Bangladeshis could vote in the country. I kept this particular thought to myself though, for fear of stoking even more hatred.

The ambiance in Port Louis felt surprisingly festive. People came with their children; there was a person selling glaçon rapé in an antique cart. Young teenagers with drums. People with effigies of stags that they'd crafted themselves.

Many people knew one another. A number of attendees didn't really listen to the speeches (except for the speeches of Berenger and Ramgoolam, of course); the meeting was an opportune moment to catch up with friends. There seemed to be a particular kind of kinship, too, between elderly women of the MMM and Labour. Perhaps the friendliness was only temporary, due to the alliance, but these women had clearly known each other for decades. If, seemingly, it still wasn't 'done' for a young woman to attend a political meeting in 2024, I couldn't imagine the kind of societal pressure that these women must have suffered from in the 1960s and 1970s, and the kind of courage it must have taken for them to engage so thoroughly in political life.

I write 'not done', but there are of course exceptions within politically involved families. Joanna's campaign manager, for instance, was a single father who'd brought his daughter along to meetings when she was still a child. She is younger than I am, heavily involved in the MMM, and has the political knowledge of a veteran. Which brings me on to something else I feel is true: politics, for Mauritian women – at least within the MMM, where I experienced it – is a fundamentally radical space, even if this doesn't always translate to representation in parliament or recognition within the party. A space free of the usual constraints of patriarchy. I have attended many meetings at this point, as I write: a few massive ones, but many, many more gatherings that were small in size, in rooms that smelled of a day's hard work and cigarettes, rooms filled with men. I have never, ever, been given a look or a comment that was disrespectful. I have been stared at, catcalled and harassed on the street, in malls, on beaches, in restaurants; before I became involved in politics I had come to believe that no place was safe unless I was accompanied by male friends or my husband. But here, in these politically charged spaces where I was on my own, I had never felt so safe in public.

XX. *Image-making, June–October 2024*

On 7 June, the Minister of Finance presented the budget for 2024–5. It read more like an electoral manifesto. Highlights included increasing the minimum wage to Rs 20,000 for full-time employees and a double increase in pensions: some of the increases would occur in 2024, others by 2025. What was left unsaid – but perfectly understood – was that these measures would be effected in 2025 if the MSM won its third mandate. I felt, too, that if this Budget was treated as part of the campaign, then we could expect further faux-socialist measures to come in the weeks before the election, as well as a general cleansing of the MSM's image.

A week after the budget came the unveiling of the new Sir Anerood Jugnauth statue on the Port Louis waterfront. 'He is the idol of most of the population,' said his son, who organized a grandiose ceremony for the occasion.

My friend Marek Ahnee, PhD student at the EHESS, quickly posted a brilliant analysis of the symbolism of the statue in the capital on, of all places, Instagram. I hadn't paid attention to the fact that the three statues on the waterfront – Sir Seewoosagur Ramgoolam, Basdeo Bissoondoyal and now Jugnauth – faced the statues of Mahé de Labourdonnais and Queen Victoria around the Government House. 'They should all be considered as part of a memorial ecosystem,' Ahnee wrote:

> Labourdonnais and Victoria face the sea, symbol of imperial mercantilism, slavery and indentured labour. Ramgoolam, Bissoondoyal and now Jugnauth turn their backs on the ocean and face the old masters, as if to challenge them. But really, it's not so much of a challenge but a dialogue, an agreement. Labourdonnais and Victoria represented empire and its attendant extractive, racialised ideologies. Ramgoolam, Bissoondoyal and Jugnauth represented another kind of power (in different configurations): that of Hindu nationalism, right-wing economics and social stratification. Ramgoolam wielded state casteism, Hindu supremacy, and the maintenance of the old plutocratic order; Bissoondoyal, who stands closer to the sea, closer to his ancestral roots, heavily promoted Savarkarism under the cover of Gandhi-esque socialism. And Jugnauth represents the galvanisation of the reactionary Hindu right melded with neoliberal politics. "Navin nou lerwa" wouldn't exist without Jugnauth's "Vaish Power"; the events of February 1999 wouldn't have occurred without Anerood Jugnauth's state sanctioned anti-Black violence.

314

Jugnauth's project to cleanse the MSM's image concerned parliament, too. In July, the Speaker suddenly announced that he was ill; he was replaced by Adrien Duval, Xavier's son. While the move was initially met with an uproar – Duval was only thirty-four years old; he'd seemingly usurped the place of the Deputy Speaker, and he had a pending police case on his back after a car crash in September 2022 where he refused to take a breathalyser test – it was, after a few weeks, quietly effective: Duval wasn't prone to outrageous, obviously partisan theatrics.

Laurette was also busy polishing his image in 2024, but in doing so he seemed less incendiary, less provocative, less interesting. He still protested – after Agaléga, he went after the government's attempts to reform SIM-card acquisition, and then attacked the failures of the government to address pending land dispossession cases – but not with his usual rage. His revelations weren't doled out in the usual style on social media: gone were the days where he only had his phone. Now he spoke of scandals decked out in polo shirts and trousers, presenting information slideshow-style, in well-made videos.

Beyond his changed appearance, the trouble was that the scandal he gave the most airtime – and the one he was most interviewed about – was still the *Wakashio* disaster, whereas the general public seemed to have moved on. Despite persuasive explanations and suppositions, he also couldn't prove that the ship had been carrying drugs.

By September Jugnauth had reportedly told his ministers to organize as many inaugurations of infrastructure projects as was possible, even if they weren't completed yet. On 13 September the Minister of Labour announced that the government would be enforcing a Wage Relativity Adjustment, which effectively increased the salaries of Mauritians earning less than Rs 50,000. On 29 September Jugnauth announced he'd raise the pension to Rs 20,000 and provide free medicine to all Mauritians if elected for a third time. Given the magnitude of his promises, we expected him to announce the dissolution of assembly imminently.

There were many comings and goings in the Prime Minister's Office on 3 October. We thought today was the day they'd announce the elections. Then the news dropped like a kick in the gut: Jugnauth had successfully negotiated an agreement between Mauritius and the United Kingdom concerning the Chagos archipelago: we would have sovereignty of the islands. The timing surprised me: I'd heard rumours that an agreement would only be officialized (if reached) after the general election, so as not to skew the odds so obviously in the government's favour. The increasing hostilities between Iran and Israel, though, may have apparently helped in solidifying a quick agreement, as had the looming spectre of Trump's election. The agreement hadn't yet been ratified, but in the way Jugnauth spoke you'd be forgiven for believing that it was a done deal.

It was a bittersweet triumph for human rights: a partial victory for Chagossians, who had fought so hard for their right to return to the archipelago – though they wouldn't be able to return to Diego Garcia. The military base would still be operational, the base that sent planes to kill civilians across the Middle East. If the agreement was signed, we would become significantly wealthier, as a nation, because of that blood money. Blood rent that would end of the cost-of-living crisis. I felt sick.

Jugnauth beaming on national television, saying the agreement marked the 'complete decolonization of our republic'. Jugnauth reminding the population how the Chagossian right to return had been the MSM's fight for decades.

Pravind Jugnauth dissolved parliament on 4 October. Our general elections would be held on 10 November.

XXI. *Countdown, October–November 2024*

While Jugnauth had the dreamed-of start to his campaign, Laurette was finding that the ground was slipping under him.

On 30 September Laurette announced that he'd left One Moris in order to concentrate on 'Mouvman Bruneau Laurette'. He'd donned a suit to meet Xavier Luc Duval 'amicably' in his office, which was a huge waste of time: an alliance between the PMSD and the MSM had been on the table for months, and was officially announced on 7 October.

Laurette had 'informally' met a number of politicians, but he still hadn't secured an alliance with any other party, and time seemed to be running out. He met Roshi Bhadain: Laurette had seemingly worked for Bhadain's Reform Party in 2017–18; a newspaper announced that an alliance between both parties had been sealed on the morning of 2 October, with Laurette stating that they'd agreed to share the post of Prime Minister. Then, humiliatingly, by the afternoon of the same day, Bhadain gave a conference saying that no such agreement had been concluded, that there wouldn't be 'two captains on one ship'. Eight days later, on 10 October, Bhadain announced that his party would enter an alliance with Bodha and Valayden's Linion Moris.

I didn't have much time to feel sorry for Laurette, though. I was immersed in the Alliance du Changement's campaign. There was an incredible amount of work to be done and I was thoroughly unprepared.

Each constituency was subdivided according to their voting centres. A group of around five Labour and MMM activists 'manned' each area (my term, not theirs), depending on where they lived and the affinities they shared with their neighbourhood. This team would organize canvassing, neighbourhood meet-ups, do as much as they could to encourage people to vote (for the Alliance du Changement, naturally). My constituency, which was quite large, had twenty-three or twenty-four centres; the centre on my street, unfortunately, didn't have a lot of MMM members living nearby. The reason for this is both embarrassing and revelatory: my centre regrouped all the bourgeois upper-middle-class people who still lived in Floreal, who famously don't involve themselves publicly in politics for fear of retaliation, and there were too few working-class and middle-class activists who lived in the environs.

But there were a few heavily involved members of the Labour Party who lived on my street. We relied on them for canvassing and neighbourhood organization

318

throughout the electoral period. These men and women were extraordinary; they were middle-aged, they'd seen many elections, they knew the neighbourhood thoroughly and they were incredibly organized. I felt like an idiot most of the time, tagging along, learning.

This was my first indication that the Labour Party had a kind of mass strength that we, in the MMM, couldn't match for the moment. They were a much bigger party, of course, but they were also so well-funded. And the extent of that funding became clear within a week of Jugnauth's announcement.

In the early run-up to the general election, I thought that we'd make some impact through information. I was scared that people would get swept up in Jugnauth's promises, and so I'd compiled dossiers on inflation, monetary devaluation, budget promises not upheld, possible fraud and corruption scandals that we'd broken with the Commission de Developpement Durable. As it turned out, Mauritians were hungry to consume political content – but people weren't spending hours on their phones to view dossiers. They were watching reels posted by the Labour Party's different users across platforms, especially TikTok. And those users – including Ramgoolam's own GenNext YouTube channel – posted explosive videos that told tales of sordid corruption. There was a considerable amount of videos on the mistresses of government MPs, along with supposed 'receipts' of their behaviour. Many videos focussed on Renganaden Padayachy, the Minister of Finance. They alleged that he had many mistresses and placed them in financial companies where they earned high salaries; that he had facilitated the plundering of national banking institutions for the profit of the Jugnauth family and himself.

Some of the accounts were taken down, but the users had back-up accounts and so content survived.

Then there were the hit songs. On 4 October Labour shared a music video called 'Bour Li Dehor', a song brilliantly written by 666 Armada, which described the infernal climate of Mauritius: the drug epidemic, the cost of living crisis, police brutality, corruption. But funnily enough, this wasn't the song that became the anthem of the campaign. That honour fell to 'Ale Navin', or 'Go Navin', a thirty-second song extract which preceded the much older 'Navin nou lerwa', or 'Navin our King' sega. It was *immensely* catchy. Hundreds of Mauritians filmed themselves dancing to the beat on TikTok. I think that once the Alliance du Changement saw how popular the song was, they injected more of that joy into their communications: getting the MSM out of power was urgent, and yes the country was on its knees, but the coalition were on their way to victory, on the way to an impending national celebration. Results day, they said, would be 'Liberation Day'.

I couldn't fathom how many millions of rupees had been poured into this kind of social media organization in order to conduct such a successful campaign. Even Ramgoolam's most arrogant statements from a decade ago – such as 'you need to be classy to do what I do' had been rebranded as swag.

But there was a fear that the MSM would still amass enough votes to win a third mandate. Jugnauth was promising a new, rich era for the country after the Chagos deal; saying they'd be building hotels on the islands next, exploiting them for development. In Mauritius, 18–35-year-olds wouldn't have to pay a cent of interest for Home Loans. Children aged from 0–18 would get Rs 5,000 a month. Stay-at-home women would receive Rs 2,000 a month. And this was on top of the promised rise in pensions and minimum wage.

Everything changed for the MSM on the night of 18 October.

XXII. *Missie Moustass, October–November 2024*

On 18 October 2024, Sherry Singh announced that he'd be lending a hand to the Alliance du Changement's campaign. Singh met Ramgoolam in his house; Singh looked determined, Ramgoolam looked beatific.

That night, a series of videos were posted on Facebook by an account named 'Missie Moustass'. They were titled 'Secrets of Lakwizinn – Season 1: Spying on citizens'. 'Missie Moustass' was a reference to the Indian civil servant who was in charge of tapping the cables at Baie Jacotet in the 'sniffing operation' described by Singh in 2022. Each video opened on to a histrionic soundtrack, accompanied by an image of a grey, moustachioed mask in the foreground, with a kitchen on fire as background.

A series of audio recordings of journalists, opposition MPs, judges. The recordings were fairly innocuous in content, but they represented irrefutable proof that people's telecommunications had been spied on; conversations that seemed to have taken place around 2021–2. A number of journalists went on record saying that the audio recordings were true, despite claims already emerging by the MSM that the supposed 'Moustass recordings' were the work of artificial intelligence. Moustass' Facebook page racked up thousands of views before it was deleted by Meta, probably on behalf of the government.

That didn't stop 'Missie Moustass' from creating a TikTok account and posting, 'Season 2: Dip, Rotten Commissioner of Police', (the videos were grouped together in seasons, Netflixified). The series contained audio recordings of the Commissioner of Police, attempting to find ways to jail Adrien Duval in 2022 for driving under the influence; conniving between Dip, a minister and a close advisor to the Prime Minister, in order to get a witness of Duval's accident to lie about who was driving the car; the Minister of Health telling the Commissioner he'd beat up and sack a doctor at a private clinic who'd treated Duval and who wouldn't share his medical records with the Minister; the Commissioner telling various people they should die; the Commissioner speaking to his mistress, clearly uncomfortable on the phone, saying that she had to get ready for him, that 'I am your God, aren't I?'; the Commissioner negotiating 'biryani' with the Minister of Arts and Culture, 'biryani' a code word for bribes; the Commissioner proffering racial insults towards Creoles and Muslims in conversations, such as saying 'a nasyon is dead' to which an unnamed person replies 'good riddance'; the Commissioner saying 'tell the motherpussy Virgin Mary that when I come she'll hold my candle', candle here being a euphemism for his penis, motherpussy a literal translation of the Kreol swear word 'langetsorma'; the Commissioner ordering other policemen to not investigate his son's crimes.

A country-wide outcry. Creole Mauritians asking for the Commissioner of Police to step down; Creoles disgusted at the silence of Xavier Luc Duval and Sandra Mayotte; Creole Mauritians spreading the word not to fall into the MSM's trap, to make their voices heard through their votes only, that Jugnauth would seize the opportunity to postpone the elections even if they quietly protested. The videos were deleted from TikTok. The Commissioner of Police refused to resign.

After a few days, a Missie Moustass YouTube account was created. This one is still up at the time of writing.

Season 3: A conversation between Jagai and an unnamed man, talking about Jacquelin Juliette, a Creole man who had died on 7 January 2023 due to 'heart trouble', according to medical reports. The conversation revealed that policemen had hit his genitals and had strangled him. Another conversation, this time between Dip and Sudesh Gungadin, the Chief Police Medical Officer; Dip orders him to say that Juliette died of natural causes.

Season 4: Two close advisors to the Prime Minister discuss a plan of action following the cost-of-living riots in April 2022: they want to slow down the speed of internet, so that people can't organize effectively or share information. 'Say it's an intermittent problem, a problem with the SAFE cable'. Kobita Jugnauth's brother on the phone to one of these advisors, saying that Sherry Singh won't cooperate with the plan to slow down the internet speed.

Season 5: The Attorney General and the close advisor again, this time saying that the economy was fucked.

You must understand that these videos were all anyone could talk about for the rest of the campaign. Like me, people walked with their phones to their ears, playing and replaying the conversations, attempting to catch every word. The newspapers analysed the conversations and their implications. The Prime Minister, who continued to deny the veracity of the recordings, was thoroughly ridiculed. Our AI must be the best in the world to wield Kreol so magnificently. The MSM and all its appointees faced livid hatred from the public.

Season 6 was published on Diwali, 31 October, in a series of twenty videos. We hear Shamila Sonah-Ori, who is a lawyer and Kobita Jugnauth's cousin, talking to various people close to power: a Chief Justice, a lawyer, an Assistant Commissioner of Police. There is pressure to 'arrange' things between the Prime Minister and the Chief Technical Officer of Mauritius Telecom. We can infer, from the conversation, that this has to do with the report the CTO gave that contradicted his earlier statement on the goings-on in Baie Jacotet, denying there was a data capture operation.

We hear the Deputy Commissioner of Police telling the Chief Justice that they need to come up with a strategy in order to arrest Sherry Singh; Sonah-Ori telling the Commissioner of Police that the Prime Minister had told her to tell Dip that Singh should be arrested on departure, if he showed up at the airport; Sonah-Ori telling another member of the Prime Minister's close circle that Singh had to be arrested before he arrived at *L'Express* for his interview, and that she had to 'arrange things' imminently before the Chief Technical Officer at Mauritius Telecom gave his statement to the police; a close advisor to the Prime Minister and the Attorney General discussing Sherry Singh, agreeing that they'd tell the press that there was an international inquiry on Singh, on his money stored in Dubai, and that they'd have to bring up the warehouse of copper coils in order to fuck him over.

We hear Kobita Jugnauth talking to Sonah-Ori, saying she needed to 'take' the technician who worked at Baie Jacotet; the Prime Minister, conniving with his advisors on how to deal with the emerging sniffing scandal; the Prime Minister on the phone to the ex-Speaker of the House, attempting to change a question on sniffing. The Speaker uses 'to', the Kreol equivalent of 'tu', when speaking to the Prime Minister, saying 'until now the question is admissible... we'll do how we normally do. Read it and see, I'll wait. If you're comfortable, we'll release the question. If not, if we have to cut it up a little, we'll see.'

The next day, on 1 November, we woke up to the news that Jugnauth had restricted our access to social media. He said he'd ban social media sites until 11 November, the day after the election. There was uproar over messages, a surge in VPN acquisition, a scrambling to organize the meetings held that weekend. We sent a massive number of emails to journalists abroad, who covered the shutdown: we would have laughed more, if we weren't so sick with fear, to see the words 'Missie Moustass' written in *Le Figaro*. Even the timid business community issued a communiqué damning Jugnauth's move, saying it was destructive for all types of business, for the expatriates who'd chosen the country for its democratic ideals, for tourists who wouldn't want to vacation in an unstable country. As far as we knew, though, the streets were still, despite the eruption of anger on our phones. We were still trying to preserve our chances of an election.

Singh and a few other men were arrested that afternoon, apparently in connection with the 'Moustass Leaks'.

I was at the beach. I remember not being able to concentrate much, vaguely aware of my children playing in the sand. I was afraid that the MSM would invent a riot and justify an indefinite postponement of the elections: they could either invent a riot that didn't occur, and we would have no way of knowing for sure, or they could stage a riot and broadcast it on national television, the only form of televised, local media left.

I remember my attention focusing on a flame-hued sea urchin scuttling on the edge of the water as the sun set, its mouth opening and closing.

Within a day, Jugnauth went back on his decision. A member of Linion Reform said that the MSM was finished, and that voters would now have to choose between them and the Alliance du Changement.

That night, with YouTube restored, Missie Moustass started posting Season 7. Pravind Jugnauth trying to coax a Chief Justice to sign a document that would lead to the termination of the contract of the Mauritius Turf Club. Infamously, the contract then went to a man close to power. We hear Jugnauth shouting and swearing at the

326

Minister of Finance, again in relation to the Mauritius Turf Club affair; we hear Kobita Jugnauth talking to one of her husband's advisors on the illegal construction projects undertaken by the new management of the Champ de Mars.

Season 8, released on 2 November, the day Singh and the other 'suspects' were released from jail. We hear Pravind Jugnauth speaking to the Deputy Commissioner of Police, telling him that a policeman knew some of what had happened to Kistnen, and that this policeman may have filmed 'something' too, which is why he had to be 'approached'. We hear the Prime Minister's anger at the DPP and the Magistrate presiding over the Kistnen case; hear him saying wearily 'how much can I interfere in this?' Sonah-Ori and Ken Arian, worried, saying that Yogida Sawmynaden was proving to be quite stubborn, that if he continued they'd tell the Chief Justice to screw him, 'let him deal with his shit', and that the goal was also to 'protect other people'.

Season 9: Jugnauth intervenes in multitudinous affairs: he orders the Minister of Energy and Public Utilities to turn a blind eye to a school's electricity bill, and to send him the CV of an engineer recently employed by the Central Electricity Board, because there are suspicions that the man votes Labour; he orders the police not to search the home of the son of a 'counsellor'; he orders the police to arrest Sherry Singh's wife if she tries to leave the country, and gets impatient when the Deputy Commissioner of Police says they have nothing on Varsha Singh that would warrant a stop order; more conniving to bring down the Mauritius Turf Club; a strange act of grace to a gangster who was allegedly linked to Kistnen's

327

murder; Jugnauth on the phone again to the Speaker, trying to expel Eshan Juman from parliament; Jugnauth saying that the State Trading Corporation has no funds left, which is why the price of petrol has to be kept artificially high; the former Minister of Housing turned Ambassador to the Emirates, Showkatally Soodhun, telling Jugnauth that he has a person in Dubai willing to donate Rs 250 million to the MSM for the election.

A conversation between Jugnauth and one of the close members of his inner circle, Rakesh Gooljaury, reveals that Xavier Luc Duval sent parliamentary questions to Gooljaury and Jugnauth for their approval ahead of Parliament. In further conversations between Gooljaury and Jugnauth we can hear how Gooljaury acts as an intermediary, liaison officer and henchman. Gooljaury details, almost with glee, that the Minister of Health had assaulted an imam, but also that the Minister of Health had a tender 'made-to-measure' for the purchase of masks; Gooljaury saying, in concert with the Prime Minister, that a 'good Hindu' woman he knows should work at the DPP instead of the 'Muslim'; Gooljaury describing a sex tape made by the Minister of Arts and Culture with his mistress, as well as recordings of the couple at a hotel, asking whether the Prime Minister wanted to see them (he said he wanted a copy of the tapes); Gooljaury organizing dumplings for Jugnauth's dinner; Gooljaury adopting a different tone altogether on the phone to his ex-wife, saying that he'd make sure the Safe City cameras watched her every move.

A day after the last part of Season 9 was broadcast on YouTube, the Minister of Finance called the press for an announcement. He said that the government would pay a 'fourteenth month' to all employees working in the Small and Medium Enterprise sector, as well as to all businesses facing financial difficulties. He'd also pay a bonus to self-employed Mauritians and to Mauritians who received financial aid from the Mauritius Revenue Authority. He stated that he wouldn't negotiate with Business Mauritius, that the private sector had the means to pay the fourteenth-month bonus without financial assistance. The message was clear: if the MSM won a third mandate, almost every Mauritian would receive around two months' salary at the end of 2024.

Fearing that this would tilt votes in the MSM's favour, the Alliance du Changement vowed to implement the same measure the next day.

Season 10 was first uploaded on 6 November. It did not contain more revelations on Kistnen's murder. It didn't feature Pravind Jugnauth much at all. The thirty-three videos contained recordings of Kobita Jugnauth.

We hear her saying that the Indian High Commissioner is 'really ugly' and attention-seeking; hear her checking if a radio licence has been revoked; hear her, especially, giving instructions to advisors and members of the government, deciding who'd get a job on caste, ethnicity and party affiliation basis. It's important to note that political party kinship runs in families – I'd often heard 'my family is Labour', 'my family has always voted MMM' – and is probably the biggest identity marker among Mauritians after ethnicity, caste and religion. But there's no official register of people affiliated to different political parties, no list of political contributions given by individuals, no yearly fee to pay to help and support the party of your choice. It is still a mystery how Kobita was able to know who voted for what party: she was either excellently informed, and gathered information on each candidate from their families and social media history, or she knew, somehow, what these citizens had voted for in the last general election.

Hear her defending the gangster linked to Kistnen's murder. Hear her on the phone to the Speaker, asking for details on the Kistnen case, wondering if the widow had signed a paper in the National Assembly; her saying that Singh had to be arrested; her telling a close advisor that every week they had to find something to fuck over Satyajit Boolell, the former DPP: 'the situation has to become intolerable for him, so that he'll step down.' More recordings of her insulting people, criticizing their appearance, light-heartedly laughing on the phone to her lawyer cousin, saying she'd get someone sodomized. The most frightening recording, for me, was one where she is speaking to Showkatally Soodhun. 'I've already got a team,' says Soodhun. She asks if Soodhun has already talked to the Deputy Commissioner of Police, who is already in a particular place. 'I'm paying a few bouncers,' Soodhun says quickly, obviously stressed. 'They're bandits. They'll kill and throw away. Okay? There isn't a choice.'

In the last series of videos, Kobita insults every Mauritian ethnic community under our sun. The Maha Shivaratree pilgrims were ignorant and savage; footage of the Mauritius Broadcasting Corporation featuring the year's laureates had to be trimmed, because too many Muslims could be seen; on the phone to her cousin, she rails against an 'ugly' Chinese man who overtook her on the road while she was driving. She was incensed by

330

Creole artists and activists who protested against the government during concerts, saying that Creoles were appropriating the Mauritian flag; Creoles were 'more Mauritian than Mauritian' even though they 'fought against Independence'; the Franco-Mauritian business owners who owned the venues hosting such performances had to be investigated and their funding cut.

The last series of videos hit hard. There'd been an orchestrated campaign within MSM activists to turn the election into a communal affair; while canvassing with Joanna, I'd see posters labelling her as supposedly anti-Hindu – 'never forget that she never apologized for saying "*manze bondie kaka diab*"!' – and anti-Muslim – 'one vote for Joanna is one vote for LGBT!' I don't know if there were similar campaigns against Arvin Boolell, Hindu and Brahmin of caste, who was one of the only politicians who would later openly welcome the decriminalization of sodomy in Mauritius in October 2023.

At the same time there was a trail of Islamophobic videos on social media, showing Shakeel Mohamed and other minor Muslim members of the opposition as puppeteers, wielding Ramgoolam and Berenger marionettes. 'Are these the men you want in control over the country?' asked the images.

The last video of Missie Moustass urged Mauritians to vote for change, give all their votes to the Alliance du Changement, and vote early in the morning.

The political meetings held by the Alliance du Changement were full. People waved the Mauritian flag. The mood in the country was that the opposition would win, if our election really was free and fair. I barely slept in the days leading up to the tenth.

On 7 November, a doctor reported to the police that, at a voting centre, he heard sounds that sounded like construction work and saw cars at the centre in the early hours of the morning.

On 9 November, the day before the election, there were reports that some people had infiltrated a voting centre at one o'clock in the morning. They were spotted by agents working for the Alliance du Changement; they attempted to hide within the school. Only one security guard was in the premises, working for a company favoured by the MSM. On that same night, a man saw a fifteen-seater van and a few cars stealthily entering another centre nearby.

Social media was inundated with conspiracy theories. Hidden chambers had been built in the voting centres, to swap boxes contain ballots; the lorries carrying the ballots would have concealed chambers, so boxes could be replaced; the pens at voting centres had ink that could be rubbed away, so people should bring their own pens.

The Electoral Commissioner made a video to reassure Mauritians that all our votes would be counted, that our elections were monitored by international bodies.

About 80 per cent of Mauritians voted on 10 November. There were queues past closing time in a few centres. During the night there were fireworks and music, even if no one knew the results yet. Agents of the opposition slept inside the counting centres to 'safekeep' the boxes – the Commissioner had allowed this novelty to quell hysteria.

When the boxes were transported from voting centres to the counting centres, Mauritians accompanied the policemen. There were videos of Mauritians stopping a truck that supposedly carried a voting box; videos of Mauritians searching for boxes in abandoned plots of land; people getting angry when they saw splices of yellow tape, anything that could indicate possible tampering. Politicians of the opposition keeping people calm.

The results rolled in from mid-afternoon on the eleventh. Ramgoolam at the voting centre in Triolet, prepared to wait a while – not because he'd asked for a recount this time, but because there'd been an incredible number of candidates in his constituency. He left the centre during the day because Modi had asked to speak to him, even before the results were announced. Pravind Jugnauth, too, left his voting centre before the results were announced. He had to be escorted; his car exited a wild crowd that booed him, spat on the windows.

A win for the Alliance du Changement in every constituency. The kind of electoral thrashing that only happened three times in our history, what we call a 60-0.

No-one from Linion Reform or from Muvman Bruneau Laurette got a seat in parliament. Laurette won

4,178 votes, finishing seventh. Reuben Pillay, who also posed as a candidate, earned 541 votes.

There were a few thousand people there, in the counting centre in Vacoas. The crowd cried as Joanna gave her victory speech. She was the first elected member of her constituency, garnering 27,779 votes. She sang our national anthem. She waved our flag to the beat of the song's slow, steady rhythm. In her I saw the country's future.

2025

Notes

An Education

38 *Mo Nwar*, 'My Black', a term of endearment I've only heard Creole men over forty years old use when referring to each other (and sometimes to other younger people of different ethnicities).

38 *Nasyon*: Term that denotes both race and class, 'in that it refers to darker-skinned Creoles, who are presumed to be monolingual, and who live in social housing,' explains my friend, also cited in the essay preceding this one. 'When "nasyon" is used as a noun or an adjective to describe a particular person, it denotes a supposed racial phenotype and a negative moral stereotype associated with Blackness, such as in the phrase "*so fami milat, me li nasyon net*" – "his family is light-skinned, but he's totally Black". Nasyon comes from the early nineteenth-century distinction between "noir créole" and "noir nasyon"; the latter still followed the customs and social rules of their ancestral homeland or "nation" ("nation malgache", "nation Mozambique", and so forth). This is why, when using French or Kreol, Indo-Mauritians used "nation" to refer to Caste early on. It's why, too, that in common parlance "ti nasion" refers as much to lower-caste Indo Mauritians as it refers to Black working-class Creoles.'

Bann-la

88 *The application fee starts at $300*: These occupation permits and residency permits are delineated in the Immigration Act 2022. Lindsey Collen is challenging the Act in court, declaring that a particular amendment is dangerous as it is unconstitutional. Clause 39 (f) reads as follows: 'Notwithstanding subsections (5), (6) and (7), the Minister may, in his absolute discretion and without giving any reason, deprive any person of his citizenship of Mauritius, if he has reliable information and is satisfied that it is in the interest of defence, public safety or public order.'

There Is Too Much Feminism

129 *All the boys' schools had their own version of a procession*: And they all called it a manifest, 'manifestasyon', in Kreol, after the French verb 'manifestation'. An actual manifestation of a violence that had been restrained.

130   *'I sell bred malbar'*: A popular vine-leaf eaten in soups and as a
      side-dish.

130   *'I sell a bowl of halim!'*: An Indo-Mauritian soup of meat and lentils.

130   *bol rasson*: Another Indo-Mauritian lentil soup.

131   *the students of the Diocese-run Loreto colleges sell 'their big mouths'*: The
      'big mouths' is particularly interesting. There's the sexual reference,
      but most Mauritians would understand 'big mouths' to mean 'big
      attitudes'. The students at the RCC, in my time, mocked Loreto
      girls – who were mostly Creole – for their 'Français Lorette', which
      meant that the Loreto girls thought themselves superior to ordinary
      Mauritians and preferred to speak French, with a stupid and vain air.
      I find it fascinating,too, that the song revolves around what different
      communities *sell*, couching wealth, power, honour, status in the
      language of capitalism.

Getting Rid of It

140   *Muvman Liberasyon Fam (MLF)*: The Women's Liberation Movement,
      translated from Kreol into English. The Movement was founded in
      1976–7.

143   *it was common to be harassed and assaulted on the street*: By the mid-
      1980s, the island would see the prominent rise of women within
      the governing Militant Socialist Movement (MSM) party – Sarita
      Boodhoo, Sarojini Jugnauth, Sheila Bappoo – who transformed the
      idea of the traditional Hindu woman's place in society. The burgeoning
      tourism industry would also draw more women out from their homes
      and into the workforce. The harassment and abuse women faced at the
      time is harrowingly described in Muvman Liberasyon Fam's book, *The
      Women's Liberation Movement in Mauritius* (1988).
         Interestingly, the book also states that, by the mid-1970s, Mauritian
      women were already beginning to organize – the authors state that
      about 200 women's organizations existed in the country (most of them
      parastatal), though their 'main aim [was] grouping women together for
      things like sewing or embroidery'. The authors go on to say that these
      organizations 'cannot be written off simply because their aims [were]
      limited or ... government-controlled ... in practice their main function
      has been to raise women's consciousness about women's rights'.

144   *one of the biggest protests the country has ever seen*: The student protest
      was also a teacher protest. Lindsey tells me that many teachers were

sacked in that time: she was among thirty-one teachers in a single
school to have been fired in 1975, for setting up a Teachers' Union.

145   *Ledikasyon Pu Travayer*: 'Workers Education' [association], translated
from Kreol into English.

145   *Lalit de Klas*: 'The Class Struggle', translated from Kreol to English.
'Lalit' is the Kreol word for struggle.

148   *In 1982, a priest writing in* La Vie Catholique: Jean-Claude Alleaume,
'J'Observe', *La Vie Catholique*, 29 January 1982. The whole piece is
quoted on p. 32 of the MLF's book, *The Women's Liberation Movement
in Mauritius.*

149   *The MLF, as part of the Common Front on Abortion*: The Common Front
notably includes the Nursing Association and the Mauritius Family
Planning and Welfare Association.

152   *Collen writes of 'Madame Naga', the backstreet abortionist*: These
abortions are often performed using catheters ('lasonn' in Kreol) and
result in septicaemia. I'd like to note here, too, that I've used 'women'
throughout most of this piece because non-cis women are castigated
in Mauritius, and are advised to leave the country if they hope to
receive adequate medical care (and just care, in general).

Pandemic in Nine Acts

168   *they filmed other policemen torturing the brothers with tasers and iron
bars*: The brothers are still physically and emotionally scarred
from their ordeal. Of the nineteen policemen who took part in the
arrest and torture, only one would ever be arrested and barred from
exerting his functions.

171   *The Report found four alleged cases of medical negligence and
mistreatment*: Souillac Hospital was once again the site of death and
negligence in March–April 2024. Four patients undergoing dialysis
treatment died; the Renal Disease Patients Association suggested
that contaminated water at the hospital may be the cause, though the
Minister of Health dismissed their claims.

173   *A news article estimated that about a thousand Mauritians died of the virus
from September to November 2021*: It's worth pointing out that there
was a study published in *The Lancet* in August 2022, which aimed to
provide a more comprehensive view of the 'true burden' of Covid-19

across Africa. It suggested that 616,380 people were infected with the disease in Mauritius from 2020–21, out of which only 68,310 cases were reported. The study also estimated the number of deaths at 871, of which 786 were reported.

Real Estate

191   *some are working on the tram service*: The tram project was part of a 12.7 billion-Mauritian-rupee grant from the government of India. Other projects funded under the grant include the new Supreme Court, an imposing glass tower built over the ruins of the Royal College (founded in 1799, and one of the country's oldest buildings – one that the authorities thought unworthy of preserving); the new and improved 'state of the art' ENT hospital, described by patients and their families as 'mouroirs'; social housing projects, some of which have already flooded in torrential rain; electronic tablets for primary school students, money which should have been spent training teachers to an acceptable standard.

208   *Cables trailing across soil provide makeshift electricity*: There are no recent statistics about extreme poverty in Mauritius, but Statistics Mauritius, in its 2022 housing census, states that 99.6 per cent of households have access to electricity and 96.4 per cent of households have access to piped water within their homes. The state has identified 1.061 million households (out of an estimated population of 1.277 million people). This means that there are still about 38,000 households that are in a state of absolute poverty – and the state's definition of 'household' may not take into account tin-sheet dwellings. The average household size, as per Statistics Mauritius, is 3.3 people. We could infer that an estimated 125,400 people live in near-absolute or extreme poverty in the country.

209   *I've heard some people say that they'd like to see these residents 'moved' to social housing projects*: The party in power, for the ten years that they have ruled, have consistently fallen short of meeting their social housing targets. Out of the 10,000 homes promised in 2019, 3,100 homes were built; when the party won again they announced the construction of 12,000 homes, out of which 10,500 were estimated to have been built by 2024 – right before the general election. The NHDC estimates that 20,000 people are on the waiting list for homes, with some dossiers dating back over decades. LALIT believes that there is a housing deficit of about 100,000 homes in Mauritius, Agaléga and Rodrigues. I'd like to note here too that a number of social housing projects are sometimes developed by companies of

ill-repute, who mock safety standards out of malice, corruption or ignorance.

217   *We have more land, in fact, than most people abroad are aware of*: Over the years, different parties in power have also made sporadic attempts to reclaim sovereignty over the island of Tromelin, claimed by the French.

Ten Years in Power

229   *On any given day you'd hear a cornucopia of interviews of people crying on the radio*: It reminded me of the hysteria following the launch of the HPV vaccine. The vaccination programme was introduced here for girls in 2017 but the vaccine was available much earlier, when I was still at school, in the years 2008–10. Reports of grievous injuries and deaths abroad; reports – more importantly perhaps, for the mothers I knew – that their daughters would become promiscuous. The vaccination programme still doesn't extend to young men, as pointed out by the local NGO Young Queer Alliance.

234   *Quick to join Laurette in his 'fight' was a Franco-Mauritian activist-politician who didn't 'see' race*: This activist didn't take it well when others questioned these views, or probed her white surname, her colonist ancestry. She attempted to school an infuriated Creole woman by stating, for instance, that Africans sold their own as slaves; in degrading Kreol, the white woman told her to 'go do social work'. She'd been arrested about two decades earlier for owning and selling marijuana; she fights for the decriminalization of marijuana to this day.

240   *They ran in the same circles, became each other's lawyers when arrested*: In the wake of Kistnen's murder some of these men had joined a larger team of lawyers self-dubbed 'The Avengers', tasked with bringing 'truth' to the public and defending Kistnen's widow in court.

240   *Another lawyer, close to the previous ruling party, was arrested three times for breach of the ICTA*: Akil Bissessur: one of his arrests was for propagating fake news during the pandemic; another for defamatory statements made during a Facebook Live video about Sherry Singh in 2021, questioning his sudden riches as head of Mauritius Telecom.

240   *Rama Valayden, a former attorney general, was alleged to have fuelled the 1999 riots*: In 1999, Valayden organized a concert in support of the decriminalization of cannabis. Reginald Topize, a Creole man who

was the most celebrated Mauritian artist of his day, and went under the name Kaya, smoked a joint on stage and was arrested. He was taken to the Alcatraz prison cells. Three days after his arrest, Kaya was found dead – the third death in police custody in six weeks. His body had been violently beaten. Four days of riots around the country ensued. LALIT, in an excellent piece, states that the police technically had no grounds to torture Kaya – he had already confessed to smoking marijuana onstage. Perhaps, though, they were seeking to implicate others for the crime – maybe even Valayden himself. A number of people, including Pravind Jugnauth, have implied that Valayden was responsible for the escalating violence after Kaya's murder; he'd reportedly instigated riots in Roche Bois.

244 *The Church stuck to the government's sanitary protocols but wouldn't go as far as recommending the vaccine*: The Catholic Church's most vocal moment happened in December 2021, in Cardinal Piat's Christmas address to the population. The Cardinal had addressed the deaths caused by Covid-19, the loneliness and despair of many people in the face of the pandemic, the cost-of-living crisis and our fragile economy. State television censored his speech, to great Mauritian indignation.

258 *the lake of Grand Bassin, the most sacred Hindu site on the island*: In the late 1800s, the lake was 'rediscovered' and established as a place of ritual by a group of Hindu pilgrims; since then, the state has massively invested in making Pari Talao ('fairy lake') into Ganga Talao ('Ganges lake'). The lake is imbued with different mythologies that tie it to the river Ganges; in 1972, actual water from the Ganges was mixed into the lake in a ceremony.

260 *The MMM is the only mainstream party largely free of corruption scandals*: Largely but not entirely. The 'Illovo Deal' continues to haunt Facebook posts whenever someone seeks to throw mud on Berenger's reputation. In 2001, Illovo, a large South African sugar conglomerate, sought to sell its sugar estates and three sugar factories in Mauritius. The sale was facilitated by the Mauritian government, led by an MMM-MSM alliance at the time. The government favoured large, local Franco-Mauritian owned conglomerates as acquirers of the Illovo assets. Journalists and members of the opposition questioned why those conglomerates were so favoured.

264 *notably claiming that the Prime Minister's wife was the 'supreme leader' of the country*: Both monikers were also readily used across Mauritian media outlets, and the sexism of 'the kitchen' was of course never questioned. No-one really investigated the extent of the ties between

Sherry Singh and the Jugnauth family, either, but it's clear they were friends. When three citizens shared an innocuous photo of Kobita and Sherry on the internet in 2020 they were arrested for breach of ICTA, for *'using a telecommunication equipment to show a message which is likely to cause anxiety'*.

266 *a torrent of homophobia*: He continued with statements like 'one day Pinocchio will be deported from Anus Road and will be placed in the cell of Dr Miko. Your turn will come Pinok.' Angus Road is the street of the Prime Minister's residence; Dr. Miko was the alias of a Mauritian serial rapist. Laurette faced no repercussions for his homophobia.

277 *a police officer planting a bag of drugs in the man's home*: There were other similar cases of drug planting; in 2020, a vegetable planter known as 'John Brown' was arrested with heroin and synthetic drugs. In January 2023, his provisional charges were dropped.

292 *I assume that the mood of the country was what made the government decide – once again – not to hold municipal elections*: An AfroBarometer survey published in May 2023 confirmed the general feeling that Mauritians were dissatisfied with the state of the nation: no institution – courts of law, the police, the Prime Minister, the ruling party, the national assembly – inspires a moderate amount of trust; 72 per cent of Mauritians believe that the level of corruption has increased over the past year; a little less than 60 per cent of Mauritians believe that the Prime Minister, his officials, and members of the national assembly are somewhat corrupt; 72 per cent of Mauritians believe that they risk retaliation if they report corruption, and, on average, 81 per cent of the population feels the government is doing a bad job of keeping prices stable, narrowing gaps between rich and poor, creating jobs, reducing crime, improving the living standards of the poor, managing the economy and fighting corruption.

295 *the ICAC was headed and managed by political nominees*: The Director-General of the FCC and its commissioners are all political nominees. The Opposition had argued that the FCC's requirements for the nomination of Director-General seemed tailor-made for Navin Beekarry. Beekarry was reappointed in July 2021 to serve for four more years as Director of the ICAC, but there has been no assessment of his performance as Director since 2015 (as per the Leader of the Opposition in parliament on the 25 April 2023).

296 *Navin Beekarry was the first Commissioner of the ICAC in 2002*: In Parliament on 12 December 2023, Labour MP Mahen Gungapersad

quoted lawyer Richard Rault, and said that 'It should be understood that at the moment, ICAC is only obligated to communicate a dossier to the DPP at the end of its investigations. The DPP cannot request the file – contrary to what is done with dossiers in the hands of the police – and thus request additional investigation(s). This is the provision which allowed Beekharry [sic] to sleep on files unfavourable to the government (Angus Road, Pack & Blister, Kistnen affair etc.).' Gungapersad was then thrown out by the Speaker, along with Ehsan Juman, who told the Prime Minister 'you've killed people' while in session. It is a pity that he couldn't have finished quoting Rault: 'the worst thing is that with the FCC, there will simply be no more examination of the file by the Prosecutor's Office. There's no obligation to communicate the file to him anyway! And if the DPP decides to discontinue its prosecution of a case, [the FCC is now able] to create a procedure to challenge its decision of nolle prosequi by way of Judicial Review.'

296 *the Office of the DPP is supposed to be the apex prosecuting authority with independent powers*: For those interested in Mauritius' legal system and how the office of the Director of Public Prosecutions came to be, here's a short history of the office. It figures in the introductory statements made by the DPP in its plaint with summons against the State of Mauritius on the 20 March 2024: before 1957, there existed an Office of Procurer and Advocate General. This Office functioned as the principal legal advisor to the Government and also prosecuted criminal offences. 'Procurer and Advocate General' was restyled as 'Attorney General' in 1957. With the creation of the Mauritian Constitution in 1964, the Office of the Director of Public Prosecutions was created alongside that of the Attorney General; the new Office was now responsible for criminal prosecution and was considered to be the apex prosecuting authority with independent powers. It is able to institute and undertake criminal proceedings before any court of law; take over and continue any such criminal proceedings that may have been instituted, and discontinue, at any stage before judgement is delivered, any such criminal proceedings instituted or undertaken by the Office.

297 *the government had bought surveillance equipment from Verint Systems, an Israeli company, for over $15 million*: How Mauritius paid for this technology is another subject of great interest to me. We have no indications whatsoever of how this payment was made, given the state of the country's finances.

305 *a pest that had been an island-wide menace since the early 1600s*: 'Isle of rats', the Dutch had called Mauritius; they'd unwittingly introduced

the vermin to the island in their ships, and by the time they left in 1710, rats had made their settlement uninhabitable. Rats had threatened and killed off a number of our endemic wildlife, too.

309 *this became a symbol of their rejection of the racial politics built into the electoral system*: REA called for a complete electoral overhaul, promising the abolition of the 'Best Loser' system, initially designed to give candidates from minority ethnic groups representation in parliament, but ineffective in practice. One of the many problems of this system is that the minority ethnic groups aren't clearly defined in any way in Mauritius, and we haven't had an ethnic census here since 1972. The category 'General Population', for instance, includes Creoles, Franco-Mauritians and Sino-Mauritians.

309 *Before general elections, especially, the meetings function as a popularity contest of sorts*: The final list of candidates for the major parties was announced late, in October 2024, within a month of the general election. The delay gave parties time to amass knowledge on the candidates that would be placed in each constituency and their rapport with the public. There's a huge race axis to this exercise of candidate placing, too: in the urban areas of Port Louis, Curepipe, Rose Hill, Beau Bassin and environs, parties can confidently place non-Hindu candidates and expect them to have a good percentage of votes. But posing non-Hindu (and non-Vaish) candidates in the so-called 'rural Hindu belt' is apparently a big risk.

315 *he was replaced by Adrien Duval*: He presided over exactly five sessions before the dissolution of Parliament. Adrien Duval will enjoy his pension as former Speaker for the rest of his life.

315 *he went after the government's attempts to reform SIM-card acquisition*: Under the new regulation, passed in October 2023, telecommunication companies would have to obtain biometric data from their clients before giving them a SIM card. The MSM said that this move would hinder drug traffickers.

316 *Wage Relativity Adjustment*: The private sector, through its institutional representative, Business Mauritius, was irate at this move. It had been carried out without any consultation of companies; it represented a major, unplanned cost to private businesses, and apparently it was illegal, too (since amendments had to go through the National Remuneration Board first, which wasn't the case here).

321 *'Missie Moustass'*: Singh referred to the civil servant explicitly as a 'Missie Moustache' in his interview: 'A civil servant of the Prime

Minister's Office, accompanied by a man with a large moustache, met me in my office.... I asked Mr Moustache about what he was trying to do with the survey. He was the leader of the technical team. He explained to me that he came to analyse the set-up of the SAFE cables and their internet traffic, in order to calibrate the equipment that they were planning to install later on. I asked him why he was doing this. He said it was a piece of equipment that can capture traffic entering and exiting the cables for security reasons. In other words, he wanted to conduct a sniffing operation.' One can see the Indian civil servant and his prolific moustache in video recordings of Baie Jacotet in the time frame specified by Singh.

326 *Infamously, the contract then went to a man close to power*: A man named Jean-Michel Lee Shim, who funnily enough also funded Bruneau Laurette during the election campaign – another move that didn't serve him well. Mauritius was famous for its horse racing until 2022, when the Mauritius Turf Club's contract was terminated and Lee Shim's People's Turf Club took over the course's management. Lee Shim is one of the country's biggest gambling operators, and was one of the MSM's biggest donors. Month after month, famous stables closed down, refusing to send out their horses on the unkempt track and foul political climate.

327 *We hear Pravind Jugnauth speaking to the Deputy Commissioner of Police*: His seventeen 'yes sirs' during the two-minute conversation extract were the subject of much ridicule.

328 *Rakesh Gooljaury*: Gooljaury was one of Ramgoolam's henchmen before he lost the 2014 election; he'd worked with Ramgoolam's main mistress in opening high-end shops. He sold Ramgoolam out to Jugnauth, apparently, giving Jugnauth details about his life, and was rewarded with the same privileged henchman status in return.

330 *The Maha Shivaratree pilgrims were ignorant and savage*: This recording was met with great outrage, given that over the past two years, a few devotees died during the pilgrimage when their kanwars hit exposed electrical cables.

331 *I don't know if there were similar campaigns against Arvin Boolell*: The following extract from an article on the decriminalization is worth quoting in full (translation my own): 'The Prime Minister Pravind Jugnauth did not comment on the decision... no member of government, or the opposition has expressed themselves on the ruling, except for Arvin Boolell... from right to left, all the parliamentary parties of Mauritius are, to different degrees, aligned

on the dictates of Hindu supremacy, which has patriarchal values as its base. The right-wing party in power, the MSM, has always defended the traditional family institution as seen in its recent deeply pro-natalist positions. Between a Hindu-majority population of the island and the minority Muslims and Catholics, the political parties can't survive electorally without practising a kind of religious clientelism. Among the minority ethic-religious groups of the country, it is the Muslim community that seems to be most served by this clientelism. The Christian churches of the country (Catholic, Anglican and Presbyterian), implanted mostly among the Afro-descendant communities of Mauritius, have historically kept Indo-Mauritian state power at bay. The Catholic church is the most influential among these Christian groups, and has chosen to only politicize its opposition to abortion. The various Muslim religious bodies, on the other hand, benefit from the privilege of being of Indian descent and have chosen to play an active role as electoral intermediaries. Although Muslims are a minority in Mauritius, they are seen as a decisive "swing community" by parties during general elections – especially by the MMM, the left-wing social-democrat party, which has made the Muslim minority an exclusive support base. However, Muslim fundamentalists carried out the most violent public homo-transphobic attack in recent years [the second-most violent, at time of writing]. During the June 2018 Pride Parade in Port Louis, an Islamist militia – supported by notable public personas and elected officials – successfully stopped the parade [by staging a counter protest attended by approximately 400 people, with the slogan "homosexuality is bestiality"]. Since then, the most influential and the most conservative fringes of the Muslim electorate have made the "fight against Sodom and Gomorrah" a key axis of their negotiations with the Mauritian political class. For fear of losing this key electorate, whose decision-making force is concentrated in a particularly reactionary constituency of Port Louis, the parties avoid any position against homophobia. The parties uphold that the Muslim clergy and Muslim political appointees should have the last word when it comes to "gay matters", as it were – and so homophobia should be tolerated in order to keep "the Muslims' appeased. This entire party logic – that Muslims are homophobic and their needs must be served in order to win the elections" – is racist in itself. And it is important to note, too, that homophobia in Mauritian political parties is intertwined with Mauritian religious conservatism, and isn't limited to specific ethnic-religious groups.

Acknowledgements

This book was written with the support of the Society of Authors Foundation.

Thank you to my husband and partner of seventeen years. To my children. To the women who care for my children so that I can write.

To Natasha Soobramanien, for her friendship and guidance, and for introducing my work to Fitzcarraldo. To Joely at Fitzcarraldo, for her excellent editing.

To Marek Ahnee, whose friendship and immense wells of knowledge have steered and built this collection.

To Vijaya Teelock, for her friendship throughout the years and her extraordinary scholarship.

To Jeffrey Zuckerman, friend and translator extraordinaire. The title of this collection, in fact, comes from a *Kirkus* review of Carl de Souza's *Kaya Days*, which Jeffrey translated. The review said the book was 'an electrifying portrait of a tiny island nation on fire.' I thought that it made sense: my book, hopefully, showed a certain confluence in our island's agonies, the anti-Black racism that has sired immense harm here since the very beginnings of Mauritius' colonization.

To all the wonderful people who read, edited and guided my work. To my friends. To Lisa Baker at Aitken Alexander Associates, who took a chance on me eight years ago.

Fitzcarraldo Editions
133 Rye Lane
London, SE15 4ST
Great Britain

ISBN 978-1-80427-161-2

Design by Ray O'Meara
Typeset in Fitzcarraldo
Printed and bound by Pureprint

fitzcarraldoeditions.com

Fitzcarraldo Editions